THE BURNOUT
EPIDEMIC

THE RISE OF CHRONIC STRESS AND
HOW WE CAN FIX IT

THE BURNOUT
EPIDEMIC

JENNIFER MOSS

Harvard Business Review Press
Boston, Massachusetts

The web addresses referenced in this book were live and correct at the time of the book's publication but may be subject to change.

Cataloging-in-Publication data is forthcoming.

ISBN: 978-1-64782-036-7
eISBN: 978-1-64782-037-4

The paper used in this publication meets the requirements of the American National Standard for Permanence of Paper for Publications and Documents in Libraries and Archives Z39.48-1992.

For my tiny island and my entire world,
Jim, Wyatt, Olivia, and Lyla

Contents

THE BURNOUT
EPIDEMIC

Introduction

The Burnout Epidemic

Let's quickly try a simple reverse Rorschach test. I'll write the word. You come up with an image.

Burnout.

When you see that word, do you envision one of those gray-washed stock images of a guy resting his head in his hand as he gloomily stares at his blank computer monitor—stacks of paper piled up on either side?

Perhaps you imagine a single match with its flame recently snuffed out—smoke snarling upward, then dissipating into the black?

Do you picture a harried mom carrying three bags of jam-packed groceries while multiple kids tumble out of the van—each one sporting a different uniform?

Maybe for you, burnout looks like some Seth Rogan–type character who's parked on the couch at two in the afternoon, lighting up a bong while awaiting his next zany adventure.

I assume there are others I missed.

Sadly, for over a millennium, we've turned the concept of burnout into tragically biased memes. And, in response to the stock photo way we see this serious illness, we'll lose nearly $1 trillion in productivity globally each year, spend $190 billion in health-care outlays, and 120,000 people will die from burnout in the United States alone.

When Japan was forced to create a Karoshi hotline (*karoshi* can be translated literally as "overwork death") to help stem the increase of suicide from overwork in Japan, shouldn't that have given us a bigger sense of urgency? And, when the suicide rate is 130 percent higher for female physicians than the national suicide average in the United States, then shouldn't we consider this a crisis?

And what about the pandemic, which made an existing problem exponentially worse? I've studied burnout and worked with organizations to address it for years, but nothing would inform my understanding of the topic more than living through 2020. For some time, I'd been sounding the alarm: "Burnout is getting worse. People are sick!" Then we were all suddenly thrust into unknown territory: by April, 2.6 billion people had gone into lockdown, and places of employment for 81 percent of the global workforce were fully or partially closed.[1] A huge percentage of knowledge workers began doing their jobs from home—many collaborating on Zoom, whose daily active users skyrocketed from 10 million to 200 million.[2] This sudden shift did what little else had been able to accomplish before: expose how thinly stretched and worn down we all were—and had been for a while. And it also made our burnout much, much worse.

Although I know I'm not the only one who considers burnout a massive and emergent threat to our mental health, our small yet mighty group is just not enough.

We need to get out ahead of this. Not only does ignoring this pervasive and rapidly evolving problem claim too many financial costs, but the human costs are simply unacceptable. Instead, we need to create the conditions in our workplaces that lead to a healthy, happy, and high-performing workforce—one that is flourishing, not just surviving.

Though it may seem that combating burnout is an overwhelming and Herculean task, it can be easier than you might think—as long as we have the right tools. And ready or not, we can't ignore the urgency; we are in a burnout epidemic.

I say it's time, as we witness this illness overcoming workplaces around the globe, to rethink burnout.

Rethinking Burnout

Although the concept of occupational burnout originated in the 1970s, the medical community has long argued about how to define it. In 2019, the World Health Organization (WHO) finally included burnout in its International Classification of Diseases (ICD-10), describing it as "a syndrome conceptualized as resulting from chronic workplace stress that has not been successfully managed."[3] It is characterized by three dimensions:

- Feelings of energy depletion or exhaustion

- Increased mental distance from one's job, or feelings of negativism or cynicism related to one's job

- Reduced professional efficacy

The WHO definition is important because it acknowledges that burnout is more than just an employee problem; it's an *organizational* problem that requires an *organizational* solution.

In my experience, good leaders know that burnout is an issue, and companies do their best to offer services and perks to help employees lower their stress and improve their well-being. But let's be honest: these attempts, however well intentioned, aren't working. Self-care has been the prevention strategy du jour for decades. And yet burnout is on the rise. Why? Because we're ignoring the systemic and institutional factors that are the real causes of burnout.

If you want to address the burnout problem, the first step is repeating and internalizing this mantra: burnout is about your organization, not your people. Yoga, vacation time, wellness tech, and meditation apps can help people feel optimized, healthier. But when it comes to preventing burnout, suggesting that these tools are the *cure* is dangerous. What does this mean? It means that, for starters, we can no longer suggest wellness strategies that place ownership on individuals for preventing and managing their own burnout. Instead, we need to look at ourselves as leaders, at the role our organizations play.

According to Christina Maslach and her coauthors, Susan Jackson and Michael Leiter, the leading experts on burnout, there are six main causes of burnout. Although similar, here is the list on which most academic research has been based:[4]

1. Workload

2. Perceived lack of control

3. Lack of reward or recognition

4. Poor relationships

5. Lack of fairness

6. Values mismatch

The list clearly demonstrates that the root causes of burnout do not really lie with the individual and that they can be averted, if only leadership starts its prevention strategies much further upstream.

When I spoke with Maslach, she asked me to picture canaries in a coal mine. They are healthy birds, singing away as they make their way into the mine. But if the canaries come out, exposed to carbon monoxide and no longer singing, can you imagine asking why the canaries made themselves sick? No, because the answer would be obvious: the *coal mine* is making the birds sick.

This visual struck me. Although developing emotional intelligence skills—like optimism, gratitude, and hope—can give people the rocket fuel they need to be successful, if an employee is dealing with burnout, we have to stop and ask ourselves why. We should never suggest that if they'd just practiced more grit or joined another yoga class or taken a mindfulness course, they would have avoided burnout. I have long been a proponent of empathy and optimism in leadership. I believe in practicing gratitude skills for a happier, higher-performing work and life experience. I endorse the idea of building resilience to better handle stress when it arises. But these tools are not the cure for burnout, nor are they the vaccine.

Let's imagine that good culture is like a well-executed recipe. You should have the right ingredients (people), the right directives (policy), and someone who can work with these ingredients to create the right outcome (leadership). It's also a template for others to draw from so we keep enjoying the fruits of our labor.

When you have bad culture, it's a result of these components not combining properly. I use this analogy to drive home the point that when it comes to burnout, culture plays a massive role. It's why burnout has become an epidemic and why we must rethink the way we prevent it.

Yes, we need to help our people develop the skills that support their mental health and happiness. But, to battle burnout, we're talking a different game. Though employees are ultimately responsible for their own happiness, it is our responsibility to provide the conditions that support, and not detract, from their happiness. Burnout occurs when those conditions fail.

Clearly burnout is not quarantined to just one field. Millions of employees in thousands of industries and sectors globally also experience extreme burnout. I've heard so many of their stories over the years. They never cease to surprise, enrage, and break my heart. I would say the most interesting learning, and why I wanted to write this book, was the consistency of burnout's origin story. It almost always ties back to preventable causes. And despite nearly every book on burnout suggesting that self-care is the cure, it surprises most people to know that self-care can't actually solve burnout.

To produce better outcomes, we need to do a better job of identifying the upstream impacts that lead to happiness and, conversely, well-being detractors.

How Burnout Happens

Gallup data claims that only 15 percent of the global workforce is engaged at work. That data is roughly 30 percent in the United States, markedly better but still a depressing stat since we spend so much time at work.[5] Actually, it's 90,000 hours or 50 percent of our waking hours, according to some who've done the math.[6]

Work, when it feels great and we're engaged and energized, can bring us significant joy. It is part of what increases our satisfaction by giving our lives meaning and a sense of accomplishment. But, with so many people claiming to be disengaged and unhappy in their jobs, work has taken on a reductionist reputation, much to the benefit of TV sitcoms and humorists.

If you were an alien watching the television show *The Office*, you'd wonder if you were watching a tragedy or a comedy. At least you'd learn from the wisest of wise men, Michael Scott: "Nobody should have to go to work thinking, 'Oh, this is the place that I might die today.' That's what a hospital is for . . . [A]n office is a place where dreams come true."[7] At least work has that going for it, right?

The workplace clichés won't go away because as clichés go, they tend to mirror real life, like the meetings that go consistently overtime. Their time theft is as frustrating as someone stealing your lunch from the communal fridge despite your name on it. It shows up in the broken copiers, the rainbow wheels, and the loading ellipses. We find it in the passive-aggressive notes stuck above the sink and the sloppy dishes lazily left in the sink—the reason why someone felt compelled to write a passive-aggressive note in the first place.

These are the tiny pebbles. If work is still satisfying and we feel valued and engaged in our work, these annoyances are manageable. We trust they will be remedied, and in good cultures they are. If our organizations consistently emphasize a human-centered approach to leadership, we let these tiny problems live in the background and give them nothing more than an eye roll.

But, if our systems are failing and we feel overworked, undervalued, and micromanaged, we've lost faith in leadership; these tiny pebbles turn into boulders, impossible to ignore.

Burnout tends to start with exhaustion, but soon comes to shame or doubt, or both, about our capabilities. Our self-efficacy deteriorates; we start to feel cynical and then helpless. And the stories of burnout are vast. Most originate from the simple wear and tear resulting from chronic stress.

For organizational psychologist and executive coach and trainer Eyal Ronen, the day he noticed the company where he was working in sales had changed his laptop screen saver, he realized he was burning out. The screen saver rotated pictures of vacations employees could "win" if they'd reached certain sales targets. This isn't atypical for sales-focused teams, but for Ronen, it was a values mismatch: "I felt like they were trying to motivate me like a monkey in a very primitive way. I loved the company and the products they were selling, but this isn't how I am motivated. I wanted to feel connected to a purpose."

Ronen shared that he'd seen the signs for a while, the long hours and the misalignment with his values and the organization's goals; it was already in progress when he walked in and saw that screen saver. That was just the push he needed to leave the company.

This is how burnout happens. We see similar examples of pebbles becoming boulders in thousands of instances across our workforces. Perhaps it's months of perpetual arguing with coworkers, or maybe someone has been thrust into a new role where they had little to no training and are struggling to keep up. It pops up in the innocuous and the seemingly boring stuff, but the final straws are what breaks us.

Marie Åsberg, a psychiatrist and professor at Karolinska Institute in Stockholm, refers to it as "hitting the wall." This is when some additional burden is placed on the employee and they experience a mental break. She described this lack of ability to take on anything else as "living without margins." Because we are so stretched and have experienced chronic stress for so long, we have zero margin for error. Unfortunately, that isn't how life works. There are always stressors coming at us, so it would be unrealistic to expect that our margins won't be tested.

For Ronen, this was the screen saver. It was the final blow. It symbolized a transactional relationship between him and his work. He'd wanted purpose and to feel valued; instead, he felt disconnected and disengaged. Ronen had hit the wall.

In our interview, Åsberg shared that in Sweden, burnout is defined differently. In the ICD-10, burnout contains a medical condition category that is in the same group as adjustment disorder and post-traumatic stress disorder, other conditions caused by excessive stress that continue once the stressors have been removed. Swedish sufferers of severe burn-out are treated as having this medical condition.

Åsberg says the conditions start at work and then spill over across all areas of life. It is chronic stress-induced exhaustion disorder. She developed the concept of an "exhaustion funnel" to illustrate how work can take over our lives and our space for other interests disappears, leading us to total exhaustion.

According to Åsberg, most people will take months to recover. Some, she said, can take upward of two years and still experience the lasting effects of their trauma for years afterward. She said, "In my experience, time is the only real tool that works for a patient to recover from severe exhaustion disorder. This is why it is so critical that we prevent this catastrophic event from happening in the first place."

Ronen left the company and the industry. After his recovery, he kicked off his startup, now a successful multinational company. This was a loss of talent for the organization he left but a win for the new company he's leading. This good news offers hope. Despite the trauma of burning out, many can get back what they lost, but that may require leaving behind some things they once cared about.

Despite suffering from burnout, Ronen has been able to reframe his time at the company in a healthy way. He said the perks didn't really stop his burnout. This has been a giant "aha!" for me in recent years and has massively influenced my research and writing. Ronen said that he thinks it was a "good company" to work for, but in the same discussion, he showed how out of tune the leadership was in preventing burnout.

Well-Being in a Crisis

I started writing this book in early 2020. For years, as a journalist and consultant helping leaders combat chronic stress, I'd witnessed the pernicious effects of burnout, but the pandemic took the problem to epidemic levels. We're beyond burned out.

In late 2020 and into early 2021, I teamed up with Leiter, Maslach, and David Whiteside, director of insights and research at YMCA Work-Well, to better understand the impact of the pandemic on well-being and burnout. Our survey combined several evidence-based scales, including the Maslach Burnout Inventory General Survey (MBI-GS), a psychological assessment of occupational burnout; and the Areas of Worklife Survey, which assesses employees' perceptions of work-setting qualities that affect whether they experience engagement or burnout.

With support from *Harvard Business Review*, we gathered feedback from more than 1,500 respondents in 46 countries, in various sectors, roles, and seniority levels, in the fall of 2020. Sixty-seven percent of respondents worked at or above a supervisor level.

What did we learn, in a nutshell? Burnout is a global problem. Some stats:

- Eighty-nine percent of respondents said their work life was getting worse.

- Eighty-five percent said their well-being had declined.

- Fifty-six percent said their job demands had increased.

- Sixty-two percent of the people who were struggling to manage their workloads had experienced burnout "often" or "extremely often" in the previous three months.

- Fifty-seven percent of employees felt that the pandemic had a "large effect on" or "completely dominated" their work.

- Fifty-five percent of all respondents didn't feel that they had been able to balance their home and work life—with 53 percent specifically citing homeschooling as the reason.

- Twenty-five percent felt unable to maintain a strong connection with family, thirty-nine percent with colleagues, and fifty percent with friends.

- Only twenty-one percent rated their well-being as "good," and a mere two percent rated it as "excellent."

Not only did the 1,500 people in our survey much more squarely fit the burnout profile than did the nearly 50,000 respondents who had taken the MBI-GS before the pandemic, but they also scored very high on exhaustion and cynicism—two predictors of burnout, according to the MBI-GS.

"These survey responses make it clear that a lot of people are having serious disruptions in their relationship with work," Leiter noted. "It's not surprising that people are more exhausted—people are working hard to keep their work and personal lives afloat. But the rise in cynicism is even more troubling. Cynicism reflects a lack of trust in the world. So many people feel let down by their government's poor preparation for the pandemic, as well as by the injustices in work and well-being that the pandemic has highlighted."

Millennials have the highest levels of burnout, we found. Much of this is due to having less autonomy at work, lower seniority, and greater financial stressors and feelings of loneliness. The last was the biggest factor leading to burnout, according to our research. As one millennial put it: "The pandemic has had a tremendous impact on my well-being—I've had mental health challenges, and I've hit major roadblocks with that. My physical health has changed because I can't exercise like I used to. It's affected me economically. I feel as though my career has been set back yet again."

As our team read through the 3,300 qualitative responses, we were heartsick. There were so many stories of stress and anxiety seeping in through any available crack and coming up through their psychological floorboards. I could feel their fear in my bones. Worse, their degrading mental health was left unchecked. Many respondents didn't feel they could speak about mental health in the workplace, and as a result, 67 percent in that group were at risk of burnout.

The data demonstrates that the pandemic weighed heavily on workers. Yet, during this time, employers still asked their people to engage in well-being practices that felt like "just one more thing" for many.

One executive at a global accounting firm shared with me that her company recently offered everyone access to a meditation app. After a series of emails from corporate, reminding her about all the cool features and benefits the app could offer, she still couldn't find the time to log on. The executive says that if she has time left in the day, it goes to jamming a granola bar in her mouth and getting to the bathroom. She laughs, "It's just so ironic. Shouldn't they make this place less stressful so I don't need an app to calm down? It all feels a bit tone-deaf."

Yet, there's good news: some people I spoke to were grateful for their employers' interest in helping them work through their stress. Despite the cornucopia of wellness offerings, it was "the thought that counts" that reminded me why some companies do alright in these moments of crisis and some don't.

From our research, I learned that a big predictor for well-being at work during times of stress was trust and communication. If you trust that your employer is doing the best it can despite the circumstances, it gets a ton of latitude. So what if your boss asked you to do Zoom yoga and you hated it—at least they tried. Who cares if the pet parades and the "family happy hour" didn't stick? The company was just figuring it out.

I learned that this trust would have been built up long before the crisis hit. But it could be developed with frequent and humble communication. Some companies made it less about what they knew and more about how the leaders as a team were going to try to figure it out. And, it was how everyone worked together as unified team that would define success.

When something is as new as a global pandemic, humility and empathy in leadership go a long way, which is why it's important to build up those capabilities in advance.

Toward Empathic Leadership

In my communication with leaders, I encourage them to rethink the definition of empathetic leadership, particularly as it pertains to preventing burnout. We tend to connect empathy to the Golden Rule, "Do unto others as you would have them do unto you." But I don't believe that goes far enough. If you authentically want to demonstrate empathy, you have to "do unto others as they would have done unto themselves." That requires stepping outside of our own needs, assessing and removing bias and privilege, actively listening to our people, and then taking action.

We also need to take care of ourselves, too. We need to acknowledge that our work can be an essential and healthy part of our lives, particularly when it fulfills and uplifts us. Research by the Mayo Clinic suggests that doctors who take a more integrated approach to their work and life are significantly less likely to experience burnout.[8]

Still, purpose-driven people—and leaders like you—are not immune to burnout. Actually, they can be at risk. We go deeper later in the book where we highlight how the old saying, "Love what you do and you'll never work a day in your life," is a nice idea but a total myth.

Cool fact: in 1599, William Shakespeare wrote the seventh poem of *The Passionate Pilgrim*. Here the phrase 'burn'd out' appeared for the first time. It would form the context for passion as a process of energy exhaustion in relation to love.[9] Needless to say, plenty of people love their jobs. Lots of them burn out. We can be fueled by purpose-driven work, but for people like me, who are driven by a mission, it's tough to follow our own advice. And, in truth, my own burnout took me from expert to casualty.

We can have all the knowledge and all the tools, but we have blind spots. Yet, it's all preventable with simple solutions. Therefore, it shouldn't take hitting a wall to make these changes in our lives or our people hitting the wall before we react. We hold our accountability to others and to ourselves on every level.

· · ·

One last note: This is not just a leadership book so I can give you tips on how to prevent burnout in your organization. This is also a book about how to rethink burnout entirely. We are at epic levels of burnout across the entire global industry, and you could easily be one of those people who has burned out. You are probably acting as I did, telling people to take time off and ensuring they're well but not taking care of yourself at all.

We can't have that. We need to go through the process of understanding what burnout really is and what it truly means to live in a world with a burnout epidemic happening around us, then reeducate ourselves about what role we can play to stop the spread.

Throughout this book, I'm going to ask you to question everything you currently know about the topic of burnout and then rebuild new skills to take it on. Through real-world storytelling that pulls us into the best and the worst of our workplaces, combined with fascinating case studies, research, and rare insights, we can develop a shared approach to solving a completely solvable problem.

PART ONE

Insights

1

The Six Causes of Burnout

Burnout isn't something that just happens overnight. It's a slow erosion of coping skills and one's ability to adapt to the daily chronic stress that finally overwhelms. So, perhaps this is a good time to remind those of us in leadership positions what preventing burnout isn't.

One of my least favorite suggestions for reducing burnout is telling people, "Just say no." It's not as if most employees have the luxury of telling their boss or their clients, "Sorry. No can do." It's chalk full of bias, privilege, and worse, victim blaming. Unfortunately, we still see this as the standard advice for reducing overwork.

It may also be a good time to remind leaders that burnout can't be stretched out of people in yoga class or sweated out of them at the gym. Burnout doesn't care if they breathe better or deeper. And it most certainly isn't prevented by suggesting that maybe they should just listen to the sound of rainfall for thirty seconds instead of fifteen. This is the psychology of leaders in denial.

Yes, self-care is good. It can boost moods when we need it, and it's part of a fulsome well-being strategy. But it's a tactic, not a strategy. And it's too far downstream to truly prevent burnout.

Rather, burnout is a complex constellation of poor workplace practices and policies, antiquated institutional legacies, roles and personalities at higher risk, and systemic, societal issues that have been left
unchanged, plaguing us for far too long.

Now that we've brushed off the denial, let's start by digging deeper
into what is actually at the root of burnout. The good news is that the
causes *can* be prevented, if only we get to know where they live and interact with them further upstream.

The Maslach Burnout Inventory (MBI) and decades of research
by Christina Maslach, Susan Jackson, and Michael Leiter suggest that
burnout is most often triggered by the following:

1. Workload

2. Perceived lack of control

3. Lack of reward or recognition

4. Poor relationships

5. Lack of fairness

6. Values mismatch

When I cite the six root causes of burnout in my work, some people
ask, Does a person need to experience all of these to be burned out?
And the answer is emphatically no. Each one is equally damaging, but
some crop up more than others.

I'll devote a good deal of attention to each root cause, but first let's
examine the major force behind these six causes—poor corporate
hygiene—and how it conflicts with the needs and wants of employees.

Motivation-Hygiene Theory

The roots of burnout are often associated with poor corporate hygiene.
What does that mean? An oversimplified definition can be found in
examples of what most of us know to be good hygiene. Brushing your

teeth, showering, brushing your hair—the table-stakes stuff to maintain physical health that is so routine we forget we're even doing it. But, if we stopped, we'd feel it almost immediately and, eventually, so would the people around us.

In the workplace, these types of basic needs must be met. Organizational hygiene should be so deeply embedded that no one knows they're even missing. Examples of good hygiene include paying people what they're worth and on time; they feel physically and mentally safe; everyone knows what they're doing or can get access to tools and resources if they don't; people get along—you know, the basics. But sadly, the old saying, "common sense isn't all that common," often rings true.

As leaders, we can have blind spots to basic hygiene requirements not being met inside our organizations. Is someone feeling bullied and we haven't noticed it? Do people feel psychologically safe? Have we been rewarding and recognizing the wrong people? Does everyone on my team know what they are supposed to be doing right now?

Frederick Herzberg is responsible for coming up with hygiene theory in the early sixties, which has now become known as dual-factor, motivation-hygiene theory, essentially, what motivates us versus what basic needs must be met in order to maintain job satisfaction.[1] Herzberg found that satisfaction and dissatisfaction are not on a continuum, with one increasing as the other diminishes, but instead are independent of each other.

Essentially, hygiene factors are needed to ensure an employee is not dissatisfied, whereas motivation factors are needed to encourage an employee to higher performance. Herzberg also further classified our actions and how and why we do them. For example, if you perform a work-related action because you have to, that is defined as *movement*, but if you perform a work-related action because you want to, that is defined as *motivation*.

Think of an employee who says, "I have to clean the hospital room floors because it's my job" versus "I love making the floors shine for my patients because I feel like it helps them heal faster." We need to ensure the latter statement is a more accurate reflection of how people feel about their work.

In order to apply this theory, employers are encouraged to design jobs that enhance and motivate employees' basic objectives for their role. Herzberg's theory emphasizes the value of recognition and rewards systems as a key ingredient to both meeting needs and enhancing motivation. We'll cover these later. Herzberg also argues that both motivation and hygiene are equally important. By preventing dissatisfaction, we reduce opportunities for burnout. However, that doesn't mean it will generate a positive attitude or motivation to work. We must ensure good hygiene—this is a given—but to increase motivation, the work should feel purposeful, passion-driven, and engaging.

The Hierarchy of Needs at Work

There is an interesting intersection between Herzberg's theory and the work of Abraham Maslow, one of the most prolific academics of the twentieth century who is widely recognized for creating the hierarchy of needs. Maslow's theory suggests an individual's most basic needs must be met before the person becomes motivated to achieve higher-level needs. The most fundamental and basic four layers of his now-famous pyramid contain what Maslow called "deficiency needs," which are esteem, friendship and love, security, and physical needs. If these deficiency needs are not met—with the exception of the most fundamental physiological needs: air, water, food—then the individual will feel anxiety and stress.[2]

Cool fact: Maslow would mentor Herzberg and deeply influence his work in the overrun New York City drug clinics. There Herzberg discovered and defined burnout for the first time. Maslow's hierarchy of needs—our human thirst for compassion, love, security, and physical safety—powered the scientific research. It contextualized Herzberg's analyses by helping him to see that when our fundamental needs are being stripped away in the workplace, we will struggle to endure.

This also reinforces why it's important to differentiate between hygiene and motivation—basic fundamental needs and the extras that motivate us to be more engaged, more productive, and optimized. In Maslow's version, this is the difference between deficiency needs versus growth needs. Maslow believed that these needs are similar to instincts and play a major role in motivating behavior. In one example, physiological, security, social, and esteem needs are deficiency needs, which surface when we are deprived. They need to be satisfied to reduce sadness, depression, anxiety, stress—otherwise unpleasant feelings.[3]

Self-actualization needs, the highest level in Maslow's hierarchy, refer to the realization of a person's potential, self-fulfillment, and the search for personal growth and peak experiences. At the top of the pyramid, "need for self-actualization" occurs when individuals reach a state of harmony and understanding because they are engaged in achieving their full potential.[4] We see this same pattern show up in Herzberg's theories.

Motivators are different from hygiene factors. Motivation factors include challenging work, recognition for one's achievements, responsibility, the opportunity to do something meaningful, involvement in decision making, and a sense of importance to the organization. On the other hand, hygiene factors include salary, work conditions, company policy and administration, supervision, working relationships, and status and security.

Often, employees don't recognize when an organization has good hygiene, but bad hygiene can cause a major distraction. People feel it. Burnout happens when these expected features in our day-to-day work lives are missing or taken away.

Now, let's dive into the six root causes of burnout, starting with the most consistently problematic: overwork.

ROOT CAUSE 1

Workload

According to Gallup's report on the biggest burnout myths, "Employees who strongly agree that they always have too much to do are 2.2 times more likely to say they experience burnout very often or always at work. Even high-performing employees can quickly shift from optimistic to hopeless when they're struggling with unmanageable performance goals and expectations."[5]

The legacy of overwork has been a problem for millennia. According to Zahi Hawass, an Egyptian archaeologist, evidence shows that those who dragged and laid the 2.5-ton granite blocks making up the pyramids were condemned to an early grave, and they died with deformed bones and broken limbs. Workers died, on average, between the ages of thirty and thirty-five, compared to between fifty and sixty for members of the nobility. Hawass said, in a *New Scientist* article, "They literally worked themselves to death."[6]

Today, according to Joel Goh, Jeffrey Pfeffer, and Stefanos Zenios, work is the fifth leading cause of death in the United States, a statistic made famous in Pfeffer's book *Dying for a Paycheck*.[7] The International Labour Organization reports that excessively long working hours contribute to the deaths of 2.8 million workers every year.[8] And work-related pressure has increased over the past five years, with more than one-third of respondents citing excessive workloads and tight deadlines as their biggest concerns.[9] Then a crisis hits and reveals how quickly an already massive problem can explode.

Burnout and the Pandemic

In 2020, workloads increased sharply and seemingly overnight. The accelerant to an already-overworked society made for an alarming increase in burnout that year. According to data from NordVPN, which tracks when users connect and disconnect from its service, the United States added three more hours to its workday, while France, Spain, and the UK stretched theirs by an additional two hours.[10]

As I mentioned in the introduction, our survey data provided an extraordinary amount of qualitative data—essentially thousands of people's stories about how burnout was impacting them. I consistently felt moved by their words. It was the added fuel I needed to keep going, to keep writing. I had to share their stories.

One person said, "It seems like everyone in my company and team is working more intensely and for longer each day. It's a period of very concentrated effort, which does not feel sustainable. Working remotely is adding more stress, by necessitating more calls to align/check in/work together. In addition to that, the workload seems to be increasing, and as we are absorbing/delivering more, it seems we are also getting asked to do increasingly more."

While workdays lengthened and meetings increased, most of us were still feeling mentally foggy, stressed about countless outside factors, including our physical health and safety. Yet, a global study of more than twelve thousand employees, managers, HR leaders, and C-suite executives across eleven countries discovered that during the stress of 2020, 42 percent of respondents still felt pressure to meet performance standards, 41 percent said they were expected to handle more routine and tedious tasks, and 41 percent said they were juggling unmanageable workloads.[11]

When we are in the middle of significant change, business as usual is a myth. It's bizarre that acknowledgment was lacking during this time frame. I repeatedly told leaders to cut themselves and everyone else some slack. The expectations leaders were placing on themselves and others were completely unsustainable and the reason burnout spread so quickly.

The pandemic just put a giant spotlight on the problem. But there were strong examples of how leaders, despite being in totally unknown territory themselves, prioritized solutions.

Fridays "Off"

I interviewed Todd McKinnon, CEO of Okta, an identity and access management company based in San Francisco that boomed during the pandemic. The company had received solid investments for years, but after being ten years in the red, it was the pandemic that would value it at a billion dollars. The company helps employees work from anywhere with the same identity protection they would get if they were within the firewalls of a physical office. McKinnon discussed how he was re-defining paid time off, as employees were handling working conditions during both a pandemic and a rapid growth phase.

As a company where remote employees are at the core of the business, the virtual experience is an ever-present consideration. McKinnon says he's always strived to empower his employees to make their own decisions about flexible hours and time off. But he realized during the pandemic that his people weren't taking the time off they needed to recuperate.

McKinnon said, "The data shows that, at home, our staff were kind of working 24/7. So, the next reaction from us was to mandate holidays. The company then gave Fridays off, but that didn't work either. Why? Because the workload was the same, but the working week was shorter. So, people were working Saturdays to catch up. What works is actually changing the deliverables—that is what it takes. If you really want to take the pressure off the team, you have to adjust the workload."

This is exactly the right approach when we're attempting to prevent burnout. And not just in a crisis. McKinnon is a good example of someone who takes data and acts on it, which is helpful when we have no historical framework to lean on.

The Impact of Overwork

Chronic overwork not only has a severe impact on our mental and physical health, it can prove fatal if unmanaged.

Research on hospital sanitary workers in India found that the biggest risk factors included the number of working hours. Weight loss, generalized body pain, physical exhaustion, and chronic joint pain were the main impacts of heavy workload on employee health.[12]

One study of two hundred women in Sweden revealed that increased cortisol showed up in the saliva of women when they overworked. An overabundance of cortisol can cause hypertension, immune deficiency, and unsustainable weight gain. The researchers found significant positive correlations between the amount of overtime at work and increase in cortisol. In addition, participants with excessive overtime (more than ten hours per week) had on average cortisol levels about twice as high as women with moderate overtime (less than ten hours per week).[13]

Another study by University College London of over 600,000 workers found that those who worked more than 55 hours per week had a 13 percent greater risk of a heart attack and were 33 percent more likely to suffer a stroke, compared with those who worked 35 to 40 hours per week.[14]

According to Gonzalo Shoobridge, director of strategic partnerships and client solutions at Great Place to Work UK, "When employees feel overwhelmed at work, they lose confidence and may become angry, irritable, or withdrawn. Other signs and symptoms of excessive stress at work include anxiety, depression, apathy, loss of interest in work, noticeable fatigue, trouble concentrating, muscle tension or headaches, stomach problems, social withdrawal—some employees may even use alcohol or drugs to cope."[15]

In addition to flexible goal setting, other strategies decrease the potential for overwork:

- Ensure people know exactly what is expected of them. Create a safe communication channel between you and your team so they feel comfortable asking questions. Make sure everyone is aware of their number one priority. Don't allow employees to put false urgencies on low-priority goals, which only increases inefficiencies. Be clear about changing needs by resetting goals weekly—even daily if necessary.

- Focus on strengths. Ensure employees are optimally leveraging their assets and skills. For example, physicians are burning out at record rates; a big reason is the added time spent updating electronic health records (EHRs). Physicians are experts in medicine, not data administration. Issues like this are costly. Wasting talent on tasks that are not their skill set is bad for business and burns people out.

- If people are having a hard time mastering certain parts of their role, then increase training. In 2020, a year where people had to pivot quickly and learn new skills on the fly, most were left to fend for themselves. When times are more stable, robust trainings should occur.

- In the initial stages of a project, campaign, or product launch—whatever it is that will require heavier-than-normal resources—ensure enough support, tools, budget, and people to adequately complete the job. We can't say yes to our boss and then just pass that expectation down to our team. If we don't have what we need, we should communicate it further up the leadership chain.

- Give everyone a voice at the table to share concerns or ideas. This helps to prevent errors and increase speed.

- Recognize hard work. Employees can work for periods when there is increased workload, but there can't be a pervasive culture of overwork. However, when there are acute increases in workload, make sure that everyone feels as if their time was respected.

- Check in frequently but don't micromanage. Make sure employees aren't getting bogged down in the minutiae like overreporting and constantly updating; trust has to be the foundation for a good manager–employee relationship. Plus, micromanaging is annoying, exhausting, and what I define as lazy leadership. There are other more effective ways to manage productivity and output.

- Ask questions and provide ways for people to share how they are doing through anonymous data gathering. Leading blind in times of change and stress is, at best, ineffective and at worst, unsafe.

We're witnessing a growing "always on" experience of work that is making tired employees even more exhausted. According to the National Bureau of Economic Research, the number of meetings has increased by 12.9 percent; data from North America, Europe, and the Middle East shows the workday added exactly 48.5 minutes, nearly a 9 percent increase between 2019 and 2020.[16]

NordVPN data also showed employees are logging in later and later. Spikes in usage showed up between midnight and 3 a.m., which were not present before 2020.[17]

To help employees stop feeling the need to be always on, ensure they are digitally detoxing. Here are some suggestions:

- *Encourage daily walks.* Have staff block off twenty-minute chunks in their calendar; celebrate when those times occur in order to show support and model the same behavior. Leaders need to demonstrate that there is *always* time for self-care.

- *Try a fake commute.* Most people who work from home find that separating their work and home life can be challenging. During the pandemic, it was even worse. I recommended a fake commute as a way to create a divider between work and home. Start the morning with twenty minutes of walking around the block or jump in the car to get a coffee and come home—and listen to music or a podcast on the way. Then repeat when you finish work. This action primes our brains to feel like one part of our day is ending and the other is beginning.

- *Stop the desk lunches.* Don't have meetings over lunch. I even strongly suggest the end of virtual "lunch and learns." They are work-related, so make them part of the workday. Everyone should have time to eat mindfully and get a break from being "on."

- *Create guidelines.* France now has a law giving employees the "right to disconnect" from email, smartphones, and other electronic devices.

- *Consider a four-day workweek.* It's not that radical. A large-scale study at the University of Reading in the United Kingdom showed improved staff productivity; three-quarters of staff reported they were happier, less stressed, and took fewer days off. Sixty-seven percent of Gen Zers said a four-day week would help them determine a place to work.[18]

What happens when employees are overwhelmed and stretched? Our upstream interventions are initiated, but people are still suffering. How can we help?

Signs of Chronic Stress and Mental Illness

According to the WHO, one in four people in the world will be affected by mental or neurological disorders at some point in their lives. Around 450 million people currently suffer from such conditions, placing mental disorders among the leading causes of ill health and disability worldwide.[19]

Therefore, it's a high statistical probability that we will deal with mental health issues in our workplaces at some point in our careers. I'm constantly surprised at how challenging it is for organizations to properly address this problem.

In our survey data, we found that discussions about mental health were still stigmatized in far too many companies worldwide. Despite data that shows 65 percent of people who couldn't discuss their mental health at work experienced burnout often or always, nearly 50 percent of respondents didn't believe they could openly discuss their mental health at work.

This is a problem. We need to make our workplaces safe for discussions related to mental health and mental illness. We can start off by first recognizing some signs of someone struggling with mental health issues.

- *Changes in work habits.* It's easy to confuse poor work behaviors with performance problems, but in more cases than we realize, mental illness is the real issue. Examples can include lack of motivation, increased errors, difficulty concentrating, or lower-than-normal productivity.

- *Behavior changes.* Look for signs of personality changes like more volatility in their moods (up and down), increased restlessness, anxiety or worry, or irritability; perhaps they are quick to anger or have trouble coping with regular work stuff that shouldn't trigger a stress response.

- *Frequent absences from work.* When someone is normally punctual and suddenly is constantly late or calling in sick, it is important to check in.

- *Recurring complaints of physical symptoms.* Often, someone struggling with mental illness will develop physical symptoms like fatigue or insomnia, headache, abdominal distress (nausea, pain, etc.), and change in weight.

Now, if you've recognized a combination of these changes in your employees' behavior and want to address it with them, here's where to start.

I've observed that managers shy away from discussions related to mental health simply because they didn't feel equipped to handle the conversation. I remind them that they are not expected to be mental health experts. Rather, they need to know where the experts live in the organization and what support tools, programs, and applications are available. Leaders are a conduit to the mental health professionals—they are not expected to be one.

It is critical, however, for managers to be informed. Know something about mental health, mental illness, and the impacts of chronic stress on their employees. There are countless online resources that offer mental health training—something that should be handled right at onboarding and part of an overall well-being strategy. Every employee should know the fundamentals of dealing with mental health at work for their benefit and the benefit of their peers.

The Canadian Centre for Occupational Health and Safety suggests the following tips for effective verbal communication when addressing mental health concerns.[20] It also offers tips for how we can present more effective nonverbal cues:

- Use calm body language. Unclench hands and be attentive.

- Position yourself at a right angle to the person, rather than directly in front of them.

- Give the person enough physical space. Normally between two and four feet is considered appropriate.

- Get on the other person's physical level. If they are seated, try kneeling or bending rather than standing over them.

- Pay attention to the person. Do not do anything else at the same time, such as answer phone calls, read emails, and so on.

- Do not appear challenging or threatening, for example, standing directly opposite someone, putting your hands on your hips, pointing your finger, or waving or crossing your arms.

After we engage in a conversation about mental health with someone on our team, the next steps should include providing access to support tools that may reside in an employee assistance program or elsewhere. Make sure you have that follow-up information on hand before you initiate a dialogue about mental health. You want to be ready with help, because the conversation might be difficult. And, remember, if you need help before going down this road, just ask. Your HR team can provide suggestions for how to lead through these types of scenarios.

What If I'm Overworking?

What if you're a leader who is struggling to balance your workload? You're definitely not alone. In our survey data, we found that leaders are burning out at alarming rates.

As a good leader, when you are mostly accountable to yourself, you have to walk the walk, which can be challenging if you're a high performer who loves the work. I remember one day in May 2020 when I was trying to get some space to write this book. My family of five was feeling tired of each other. We'd been in lockdown since March, with three kids homeschooling.

There is nothing more humiliating than realizing you are definitely not smarter than a fifth grader. My ten-year-old daughter had received a note from her teacher saying she didn't seem to understand the last assignment and wanted to offer some assistance. I had to write back that actually I had poorly advised her.

I switched over to my six-year-old, who was completely disengaged from school and would sometimes cry because she missed her old life so deeply—her friends, her teachers. It was all a bit much. Then my thirteen-year-old, who was struggling and had suddenly become nocturnal, was a challenge to get going in the morning. He'd be sullen and frustrated. I didn't blame him. Keeping a teen from friends is like separating meerkats from the drongos.

My husband had been thrust into a new role and was working in the basement. We were privileged to have separate spaces, but it was still chaotic. I had gone from writing the book at home in my happy quiet space to feeling as if I was in a real-life version of *The Loud House*.

That space had been all mine during the day, and I loved it. I am someone who loves working remotely and thrives in the work-from-home world. My husband is the opposite. He likes people and collaborating with his staff. He enjoys feeling that energy that can come with being in person with coworkers. So, adjustments had to be made all around. I often had to write in my bedroom. That felt so tiring, I just wanted to go back to sleep.

The reality was, everything had changed, but the expectations hadn't. We still needed to hit deadlines, meet goals, learn, execute, and deliver. Yet, we were all stuck in one house, under extreme circumstances, glued to the news, fearing for our health and the health of our loved ones. No wonder I started to burn out while writing a book on burnout. Oh, the irony.

But I figured it out, as you can tell because you're reading the final product of those intense and emotional months. The one and perhaps most paramount practice while writing the book and keeping up my speaking engagements, strategy work, and research was to cut the guilt.

The stories we gathered from respondents around the world repeatedly echoed mine. Here is one example, taken from hundreds just like it: "There is no semblance of balance or separation in the structure. Now my work is literally in my living room and my parenting is happening in my 'office' (which is on the kitchen table). Roles collided and it makes for an almost comical impossibility (taking important meetings from the floor of my closet while my daughter passes me notes under the door telling me she needs a snack)."

I had the privilege of being my own boss (as many of you know, there are pros and cons to that). But, reporting to a boss while leading others adds complexity to the role. As a manager, we feel we have to put our emotions aside to quash uncertainty during times of change and stress. We often have to be the harbinger of bad news, which can be taxing. That role threatens us with blame for the changes.

As leaders, we are so prone to burnout. We often feel pressured to move constantly at breakneck speed. We fail to recognize when to take the jet packs off and slow down. Yet, if we want to protect our employees from burnout, we had better start modeling the behaviors we want to see in others. Employees can't be what they can't see.

Palena Neale, in an article for *Harvard Business Review*, "'Serious' Leaders Need Self-Care, Too," writes that when she suggests that her leadership clients take a break, she's constantly met with, "I don't have time!" Or something along the version of, "Are you kidding me?! I'm already way beyond capacity looking after my team and my family, trying to organize home schooling, emotionally supporting my friends, colleagues, family . . . I don't have time for that!"[21]

I have said these words before. It wasn't until I actually experienced burnout personally that I stopped saying them. I urge you—do not take that route. It's so much easier to find the time now, before you burn out—even fifteen minutes each day—for self-care. We can't be successful leaders if we don't take time to recharge.

Neale points to an abundance of research that reinforces this point. "Studies show that taking breaks can help prevent decision fatigue, renew and strengthen motivation, increase productivity and creativity, and consolidate memory and improve learning," she says. "Even short 'microbreaks' can improve focus and productivity."[22]

Neale also suggests that leaders consider the "I don't have time" objection with some introspection questions:

- What are the key priorities in your life? Can you achieve them without health and well-being?

- How much time can you save by responding from a place of control rather than reacting from a place of stress?

- What is one thing you can choose to say no to today that will give you back at least five minutes? (Hint: You probably spend longer on social media than you want to.) How can you use this time to improve your own well-being and performance?[23]

There is always time. You just need to prioritize it. And you will be a more effective, efficient, and transformative leader if you stop making the excuse that you have no time.

ROOT CAUSE 2

Perceived Lack of Control

With the juggling demands of work, the expectations of our leadership team, and the need to maintain productivity, it's not surprising that we can fall into micromanaging. But, as it relates to burnout, it is 100 percent the wrong approach.

A Korn Ferry poll of nearly five thousand professionals claims that one of the top reasons people leave a job comes down to lack of novelty, lack of flow, monotony, and lack of autonomy—feeling micromanaged. All of the above increase stress and potential for burnout in the workplace.[24] In the article "6 Causes of Burnout, and How to Avoid Them," Elizabeth Grace Saunders says, "Feeling like you lack autonomy, access to resources, and a say in decisions that impact your professional life can take a toll on your well-being."[25]

Monotony at work is exhausting and predicts burnout, but so is a lack of autonomy. Employees who experience burnout are three times more likely to feel micromanaged.[26] Another study of 8,500 full-time workers in Sweden found that employees who had a higher level of influence and task control:

- Had lower levels of illness symptoms for eleven out of twelve health indicators

- Were absent less frequently

- Experienced less depression[27]

According to the article "Micromanagement—A Costly Management Style," "Micromanagement can be advantageous in certain short-term situations, such as while training new employees, increasing productivity of underperforming employees, controlling high-risk issues, and when there can be no question of who is in charge. However, the costs associated with long-term micromanagement can be exorbitant. Symptoms such as low employee morale, high staff turnover, reduction of productivity . . . can be associated with micromanagement. The negative impacts are so intense that it is labeled among the top three reasons employees resign."[28]

The authors go on to suggest that micromanagers are also at great risk of burnout from failing to effectively delegate tasks. They end up working overtime fulfilling daily obligations versus strategically planning for the future.

Reduce micromanaging by doing these things:

- Hire people with the right skills for the job.

- Have consistent, structured, and informal internal communication channels.

- Make peers accountable to each other more than their boss.

- Don't expect perfection (of yourself, too). Mistakes are an important process in the learning experience and should be valued.

When we are proud of the accomplishments we achieve independently or in a group without constant oversight, we can increase confidence, self-efficacy, and self-worth.

Managers who want to create dialogue without overstepping should try to:

- *Authentically care about someone's learning.* If you do, then you'll be more practical about mistakes and see that the learning has benefits, too.

- *Make it safe to say, "I'm not OK."* If you want to develop people, you need to know when something isn't working for them, or if they are dealing with more they can handle. Don't make "fine" the predictable answer when all signs point to the opposite.

- *Allow people to disagree.* Create opportunities for debate and even set up the space to have employees role-play the dissenting opinion in meetings.

We all need to be heard. Therefore, organizations that sponsor open, collaborative, and most importantly, safe communication cultures are more likely to thrive.

The Role of the Black Hat

Laura Gallaher, CEO and founder of Gallaher Edge, started her career working at NASA. She was highly involved in turning around the culture at NASA after the space shuttle *Columbia* disintegrated upon its return to earth on February 1, 2003, killing the seven astronauts on board. NASA suspended space shuttle flights for more than two years as it investigated the disaster.

"So, it just came down to decision making and communication," said Gallaher in our interview. She said the culture at NASA was to avoid saying something controversial and to stay in your own lane. People were terrified of making mistakes. When they spoke up, they knew they were putting their job in jeopardy, so they stopped speaking up.

Then seven astronauts died. A two-year investigation led to a realization that there were serious cultural issues that contributed to the accident, and Linda Ham, NASA's acting manager for launch integration at the time, became infamous for her role in shutting down lines of communication that, some believe, could have prevented the crash.

Twenty years later, some still put the blame on Ham. But others have come to see her as emblematic of the cultural machinery that supported these behaviors. "It's not like she's a bad person, and I have a lot of empathy and compassion for her actually," Gallaher reflected. "But she was part of a broader, systemic problem."

Gallaher went on to share that the technical and engineering teams didn't have seats at the same table, so there was no voice to push back, but inevitably "she still gave the shuttle a green light, and so of course, it's always complex. [T]here's multiple factors, but because it comes back to human behavior, human decision making that causes errors, it means poor listening and communication is absolutely a cultural problem."

After her years at NASA, Gallaher now has her own consulting firm where she helps organizations solve big cultural problems like this one. I asked her what changed at NASA after she and the team went in to fix some of the issues.

She responded, "They had the engineers and the safety professionals in an organizational design standpoint, buried underneath the program, and so what that means is we've got the senior leadership sitting around the table without equal representation. So, they pulled safety and engineering out of the program and gave them their own departments instead. Now they have their own senior leadership with their own seat at the table, always. They were able to own that responsibility, 'I'm there to represent engineering and nothing else. I am here to advocate.'"

NASA implemented its own culture survey and poured over the results, really digging into this specific issue: "I feel comfortable raising a dissenting opinion without a negative impact on my career."

Gallaher recommends that firms that are eager to develop cultures of trust and honest communication set up space to make that happen. She advises her clients to have meetings or organizational exercises where someone has to wear a "black hat" and be the counterpoint in the room who is charged with dissenting.

By tasking someone to disagree, the fear of being "difficult" is taken away. Women, in particular, struggle with pushing back because they can be labeled "disagreeable"; evidence has shown this impacts their career negatively compared to men who are less affected.[29] What is most important is that we need to create environments where speaking up is celebrated.

In an interview with the *Baltimore Sun*, Ham described how a year after the accident, she still felt haunted by it, her life changed forever. "There isn't a day that goes by that I don't think about *Columbia* and the accident," Ham said softly. "I am accountable and fully responsible for any decisions made at the MMT [mission management team]."[30]

This lesson is important for all of us. We may not be making life-or-death decisions, but regardless, the domino effect of leaving someone out of important conversations can have major implications. We need to strive for healthy debate and critical feedback so at any time we feel empowered to raise our voices and potentially mitigate disaster.

Giving Employees More Autonomy

Shahram Heshmat, an associate professor emeritus at the University of Illinois at Springfield, claims that workplace monotony can be caused by people's belief that they lack agency or autonomy in their choices about what they work on, who they work with, and so on, whereas autonomy in the workplace refers to how much personal freedom employees have to make these same decisions. Autonomy can range from setting schedules to how goals are met to what type of work an employee engages in from one day to the next. Higher levels of autonomy tend to result in an increase in job satisfaction, while lower levels of autonomy increase stress and can lead to burnout.[31]

These findings clearly indicate that a lack of meaning in employees' work, limited agency over how they achieve their goals, and insufficient novelty in the tasks they engage in every day can have serious negative impacts on their mental and physical health. But we can prevent that.

Studies show that about 40 percent of our daily activities are performed each day in almost the same situations. Subconscious behaviors allow our conscious brain to be more mindful and feel more psychologically safe. The tradeoff for the comfort of routine can mean a less enjoyable experience when we engage in these tasks.[32]

So, what if we could make small tweaks to how employees perform those actions or change the way they perceive these tasks so they stop seeing the tasks as monotonous and instead see them as novel and purposeful? This is the magic of job crafting. It transforms parts of work that once felt meaningless into something that feels valued. Employees can feel these small shifts in big ways. Work becomes a place of flourishing and engagement, instead of task mastering and boredom.

Job Crafting to Avoid Burnout

In 2001, Jane Dutton, professor emerita of business administration and psychology at the University of Michigan, and Amy Wrzesniewski, professor of management at Yale, conceptualized and defined the idea of job crafting. They proposed that for employees to craft their jobs, they should practice "changing cognitive, task, and/or relational boundaries to shape interactions and relationships with others at work. These altered task and relational configurations change the design and social environment of the job, which, in turn, alters work meanings and work identity."[33]

Dutton, Wrzesniewski, and Gelaye Debebe, assistant professor at George Washington University, in a paper entitled "Being Valued and Devalued at Work: A Social Valuing Perspective," found that cleaners who enjoyed their interpretation of work included details like interacting with patients and visitors in their job descriptions and believed their work was of high value. They also referred to themselves as "ambassadors and healers" and would seek out assignments to support that self-title—like spending more time with patients who seemed lonely and regularly changing the pictures on the walls where patients were comatose to make the room feel nicer and maybe help them revive.[34]

The most critical piece here is that employers have to give permission to employees to craft their roles. They have to figure out what inspires one person—which may be totally different from what inspires their peers—to tweak each role in the most optimal way. Often, it's all about perspective, changing the filter in which workers see the significance of their roles. This takes a culture of openness and integrity versus compliance-based leadership.

As Mae West said, "I never said it would be easy. I only said it would be worth it."

ROOT CAUSE 3

Lack of Reward or Recognition

"I'm overworked and underpaid." Sounds like a line out of a movie script or something you'd see on a bumper sticker. People joke about this phenomenon despite it being the reality for employees in numerous industries. Worse, it's a central cause of burnout.

The results of a research study involving two hundred US police officers found that "overcommitment at work [is a determinant] of higher cynicism and exhaustion" and that extreme involvement in work may negatively affect their ability to do their jobs. According to the authors, "Overcommitment may be related to a need for approval and inability of officers to withdraw from work, even in an off-duty status."[35]

The effort-reward gap crops up frequently in studies of nurses. In one study of 204 German nurses, when high job demands were met with poor promotion prospects, there was a significant depletion of the nurses' emotional resources and increase in symptoms of burnout.[36]

Another study of 263 nurses in Poland yielded similar results. Within this group, nurses experienced the largest deficiencies in salary and prestige. Exhaustion was explained by stronger demands and lack of respect (large effect). The study also found the nurses were experiencing depersonalization as a result of stronger demands and a lack of respect. This reinforces other evidence that claims excessive demands and lack of esteem are key reasons for burnout among surgical nurses.[37]

"We're very desperate," said Haverhill, Massachusetts, Chief of Police Alan Denaro in an interview with *Boston 25 News*. "It literally keeps me awake at night because if I have officers working 70–80 hours a week, I don't want officers at 4 o'clock in the morning . . . hitting a tree or another car. It's very frightening for me that our officers have to work this amount of hours to get the job done."[38] In the interview with

25 Investigates, physicians said that if these overworked officers didn't catch up on their sleep, the results could be dangerous.

For both police officers and nurses, sleep debt poses serious health risks. Some of the most serious potential problems associated with chronic sleep deprivation are high blood pressure, diabetes, heart attack, heart failure, or stroke. It also can impair decision making and judgment—highly consequential for people in lifesaving roles.

One study found that moderate sleep deprivation produces impairments equivalent to those of alcohol intoxication. After seventeen to nineteen hours without sleep, performance was equivalent to or worse than that of a blood alcohol concentration (BAC) level of 0.05 percent. After longer periods without sleep, performance reached levels equivalent to a BAC of 0.1 percent.[39] Most of North America and Europe have set their driving-under-the-influence (DUI) limits at a BAC of 0.08 percent, with some places even lower; Scotland, for example, has a BAC of 0.05. One all-nighter, and we're legally incapable of driving.

Imagine you're leading a team of police officers, firefighters, first responders, or nurses with chronic sleep deprivation, and their job is to constantly make split-second decisions that can mean the difference between preventing harm or causing it. We have to make some adjustments here, rewarding these employees with both the appropriate compensation packages and opportunity for upward advancement. But we need to go beyond those measures and have caps on hours worked. We need to follow protocols similar to those of airlines for pilots.

According to the US Federal Aviation Association, pilots must have the opportunity for eight hours of sleep during their rest break. The rest period does not begin until the pilot is released from duty, and it ends when they report back for duty. The new rules also require airlines to ensure that pilots are free from duty for a minimum of thirty consecutive hours per week.[40]

Why shouldn't other industries have similar guidelines when a professional's lack of sleep means risking lives? Leaders must step up, particularly in industries where roles are becoming more challenging.

With more scrutiny, particularly in policing, why not control what we can control? If sleep deprivation has taken even one life, that is one too many. Both the public and the police officers are at risk when we over-commit our employees to long hours with no protective guidelines.

With more instability in our global economy and job numbers plummeting, then rebounding, and then falling again, younger workers are at risk of employers taking advantage of them. Combine that with massive student debt, and we're seeing more of our younger workforce chronically overqualified, taking on jobs that don't match their education and skills. It's the reason lawmakers are starting to push for legislation to curb unpaid labor—starting on Capitol Hill.

"Will Work for Free!" . . . Said No One and Meant It

Unpaid internships are a perfect example of exploitative behavior, particularly of vulnerable groups of people from low-income households who cannot afford to work for free. Meanwhile, employers see them as a way to receive services while avoiding overhead costs.

Carlos Mark Vera has become a well-known name on Capitol Hill for his lobbying efforts for Pay Our Interns, a nonprofit Vera founded in October 2016 with the goal of getting Washington organizations (and all corporations) to pay their interns.

In my interview with Vera, he shared that it was his personal burnout story that kick-started the mission. He said, "My freshman year of college, I had an unpaid congressional internship that was thirty hours per week. I worked twenty hours a week at a side job and took six courses. Rather than trying to be fully present in my internship, I was fighting not to fall asleep. This is still the reality for many college students across the country, and it isn't hard to see how burnout happens."

Vera sees burnout as a "confluence of unsustainable economic realities that are pushed on young people. First, college is unaffordable, with more students working on the side to cover costs. Second, unpaid internships only exacerbate inequality. Third, employers are asking for more experience for entry-level positions, which creates a cycle like the one I found myself trying to fill every hour of every day." Vera argues that if employers really want to invest in the future, they need to pay with actual money because "experience doesn't pay the bills, and internships are work, after all."

Michael Gaynor, writer for the *Washington Post*, agrees: "Unpaid internships create one of those vicious cycles of the modern economy. Many entry-level jobs today require some previous experience (ironically), and often the only way to get that is through an internship. If it doesn't pay—and 43 percent of internships at for-profit companies do not, according to the National Association of Colleges and Employers—then the only people who can afford to take them are those with means. That leaves underprivileged students out of the internship pipeline, and starkly disadvantaged when it comes to job hunting."[41]

Professor of Economics Nicolas A. Pologeorgis explains, "Historically speaking, apprenticeships date back to medieval times when an inexperienced person—the apprentice—would work for a length of time learning a trade at the hands and tutelage of a master. In this early version of on-the-job training, the apprentice often lived a meager existence at the home of the master or even at the workplace. Hours were long, the pay was nonexistent, and the apprentice was at the mercy of their teacher."[42]

Vera continued, "And of course, Covid-19 exacerbated all of this. As soon as the pandemic hit, cities started shutting down. Employers across the country began to eliminate summer internships, and students lost their housing when schools closed. Despite not being a direct service provider, Pay Our Interns received over 150 messages from distraught students asking if we knew of any resources to help fund various expenses, including rent and flights back home. In dealing with this, all our in-person programming was canceled, and we lost the majority of our revenue."

In response to the need, Vera put together the Intern Relief Fund, which, in the first round, generated more than a thousand applicants in less than five days. Many of the applicants were college students whose paid internships had been canceled or who were told their internships would no longer be paid. Vera shared the story of Nandini, a summer grantee: "Nandini is a student at Stony Brook. For months, Nandini and her family have faced the possibility of homelessness. She told us in May that her parents had been unemployed for over a year and had nearly lost their house multiple times. Prior to the pandemic, Nandini was getting paid for her internship at an international NGO, but they'd canceled her funding. Thanks to our grant, her family was able to pay their mortgage by the deadline set by the bank."

But Vera soon realized that this passion-driven effort was putting him at risk for burnout, again: "The irony is that, in working to help unpaid interns through their crises, I was, once again, contributing to my own burnout. I woke up at 3:30 every single morning and stopped taking care of myself. After a month of this schedule, I told myself the same thing nearly every applicant of the Intern Relief Fund had told Pay Our Interns: this is unsustainable. I realized that I needed to pace myself, which is, I'm certain, a luxury most unpaid interns can't afford."

So far, Vera and his team have raised $200,000 for the Intern Relief Fund—grants that allow young people to pay rent, buy groceries, and contribute to their households, in addition to covering college expenses.

"It's Not Our Money"

We need to do more than pay people what they're worth and for their time. One company is ensuring that access to pay is a priority as well. Elaine Davis, chief human resources officer at Continuum Global Solutions, leads an organization of seventeen thousand mostly hourly workers based in call centers.

In mid-March 2020, she moved all the workers to remote work, no small feat. And although she tracked the mental health of her employees consistently and tried to provide them support in as many ways possible—even going so far as to send the working mothers kits for the kids to help them stay busy while they were quarantined at home—she focused more on the most important needs her staff required to get through each day. And that included getting paid.

Right at the onset of our conversation, Davis said emphatically that pay is the biggest need for her employees. When she switched roles from leading HR for a *Fortune* 1000 company, she realized quickly that the needs of this workforce were quite different from her previous one. According to Davis, the majority of her employees are women, many of them single mothers. Some have a pattern of unemployment or have struggled in the past to find work. For most, this is their first job or will be their last.

Obviously, in any organization, appropriate compensation is a top priority. But, for many hourly workers, getting paid can mean the difference between getting access to medical care, keeping the lights on, eating properly, even preventing eviction. Adding even more stress to an otherwise challenging situation, there is no plan B for most employees in this position, as they lack credit or savings to lean on.

According to a survey of more than three thousand hourly workers by Branch, a wellness platform turned challenger bank, approximately 80 percent of hourly workers had less than $500 saved for an emergency and 52 percent had nothing saved, which was up 12 percent from the previous year. Seventy-six percent had already delayed or missed a bill payment, with another 10 percent expecting to in the following month. Basic living costs continued to rank among hourly workers' top concerns.[43]

In light of this reality, Davis partnered with the CEO of Branch, Atif Siddiqi, whose company partners with employers who want to give their employees access to a portion (50 percent) of their pay before payday. It gives those employees who've been hit with an unplanned medical bill or the threat of utility shutoff a chance to keep their heads above water. Sometimes, Davis told me, "It's now a school trip that they can pay for, giving their child more opportunities to learn and keeps them from being singled out."

Does the plan involve interest, penalties, or other costs? Is it like a payday loan scheme? The answer is no. It just allows you to get paid right after you've earned it instead of every two weeks. It's simple but so meaningful for Davis's workforce. This highlights her empathy and a deep awareness of the needs of her people.

Davis said, "I always remind the people who work for me that this is *their* money that *they* earn and we're just giving it to them when they need it, not when we feel like giving it to them."

"So, Thank You!"

In Herzberg's two-factor theory of motivation, paying people what they're worth is simply appropriate corporate hygiene. But what is often missed is the impact of social rewards like recognition and feedback. Part of early childhood development is based on positive feedback that reinforces healthy actions and subsequent long-term behaviors. That remains part of our learned behaviors. Consistent recognition for doing a good job only reinforces an intrinsic motivation to do more of that good thing.

On the flip side, when we don't acknowledge each other, both as peers and leaders, we lose our sense of value to the greater organizational mission and we stop feeling good about ourselves. But it's important to make sure we recognize others who are demonstrating empathy.

TinyPulse, an employee insights company, shared in its blog post, "The Most Embarrassing Employee Recognition Stories We've Heard," examples of good intentions with wrong results. One story described an employee whose boss had posted his picture in the company's lobby as their "Number One Salesman." The employee shared that he'd spent his career trying to prove to prospects and customers that he was concerned with solving their problems and helping them succeed: "But with one glance, that picture destroyed all that work: turning me, in their eyes, into someone whose goal was to sell to them rather than someone trying to help them buy what they needed."[44]

Employee recognition is valuable in the workplace. But first consider the way you're doing it. Be thoughtful in your recognition methods and, of course, reward equally.

Alan May, executive vice president and chief people officer for Hewlett Packard Enterprise (HPE), said that recognition was instrumental when the company was entering the height of the pandemic. He wanted to recognize employees across its global workforce for living out the values and culture of the organization but, moreover, remind them of their value to the company as well. During our interview, May discussed the surprise recognition calls from members of HPE's executive committee.

It all started with a request from corporate executives for specific employees to be interviewed for a story that would appear in the internal vlog, HPE Insider. The employees had no idea that they would be "Zoom bombed" by one of their executive team members. C-level executives worldwide jumped on to surprise each employee with a one-on-one thank-you meeting.

I saw some of the reactions on the internal vlog. One global legal and administrative services buyer based in HPE's Dalian, China, office received a video surprise from John Schultz, HPE's chief operating officer. Schultz said, "I just want to recognize your contribution and thank you for it, so thank you!" The employee was so surprised, excited, and proud that she couldn't even catch her breath. It took a moment before she could say, "Oh, thank you. It's my great honor . . . oh, OK, oh my God, I'm so happy! I need to take a picture!"

Such a simple gesture has enormous benefits to well-being. May shared how much he loved reaching out in this way. The benefits go both ways. "It sounds simple," he said, "but I've seen this many times in my career, where you feel like you have to dominate the airwaves rather than listening, but we just really focused on listening, and it's been so critical to employee mental health."

May also focused on employee needs through empathetic listening and rewarding people's good ideas by implementing them: "We have a segmented audience from the mental health perspective; some people are living alone and they're starting to feel isolated, some people are at home taking care of an elderly parent or someone who is potentially compromised or has an additional condition that might be a concern; obviously, the parenting concern is a big one. We have some people who frankly have got very nice facilities to work from home, and we've got others that are literally working out of their kitchen in a very, very small flat somewhere in Bangalore."

After that realization, May went on to create social chat groups for peer-to-peer communication, bringing together like-minded individuals with no real objectives. "We didn't proctor the groups, but we did participate to some extent by listening," said May. "And then, if they started providing specific tools for people working at home, specific suggestions for those that were homebound and lonely, things along those lines, it just became all about lifting up the good ideas that we heard in a number of those chat rooms and executing on them."

This is how to recognize people. We let them know that they've been heard and that their voice matters. It's important when we call out someone for doing good work to recognize specific actions, results, or behaviors. For example, when someone goes above and beyond for a customer or a coworker or overdelivers on a project, share their stories, too, not just feedback. The final video that the HPE executive team engaged in was highlighted across all sixty thousand staff members so others could see how valuable the employees were to the greater organization.

There are also other ways to create a network effect of recognition in the workplace, particularly when sharing stories of peers:

- *Start positive gossip.* It sounds like an oxymoron but is such a powerful way to switch the mindset in the office from focusing on what we don't have to what we do have. It kick-starts more thank-yous and appreciation for good work and pushes unproductive complaining to the background.

- *Gather feedback by sharing gratitude.* Tell stories about your peers on gratitude walls. The wall can be as simple as a blank space, sticky notes, and a sharpie set up in a common area. Have your weekly stand-up meeting include the sharing of one nice thing about someone from the week before. Include questions like "Who was helpful?" "How did it make your experience of work a bit better this week?"

- *Set a recurring thank-you meeting.* Have a weekly two-minute reminder set up on your calendar that reminds you to acknowledge someone's good job in two sentences or less.

ROOT CAUSE 4

Poor Relationships

According to social psychologists, "Groups that provide us with a sense of place, purpose, and belonging tend to be good for us psychologically. They give us a sense of grounding and imbue our lives with meaning. They make us feel distinctive and special, efficacious and successful. They enhance our self-esteem and sense of worth."[45]

The antithesis of this feeling is isolation, loneliness, lack of meaning in our lives, loss of healthy attachments, and burnout. In the article "Psychological Sense of Community and Burnout," the researchers shared that in their study of undergraduate students, subjects who experienced a strong psychological sense of community in their living environment reported lower burnout on the MBI and the Meier Burnout Assessment, a twenty-three-item, true-false burnout test that complements the MBI, compared with those without a strong sense of community.[46] Since people spend 50 percent of their waking hours each day at work, healthy workplace relationships are vital to mental health.[47]

And, community drives belonging. Belonging, along with well-being, is at the top of Deloitte's Global Human Capital Trends survey as one of the most important human capital issues. According to the survey, "79% of survey respondents said that fostering a sense of belonging in the workforce was important to their organization's success in the next 12–18 months, and 93 percent agreed that a sense of belonging drives organizational performance—one of the highest rates of consensus on importance the company has seen in a decade of *Global Human Capital Trends* reports."[48]

The Deloitte survey cites a BetterUp study that analyzed the value of diversity and inclusion and found that "workplace belonging can lead to an estimated 56 percent increase in job performance, a 50 percent reduction in turnover risk, and a 75 percent decrease in employee sick days. The study found that a single incidence of 'micro-exclusion' can lead to an immediate 25 percent decline in an individual's performance on a team project."[49]

With more individualism, nationalism, and polarization dividing us, our respect for each other's differences is eroding. Despite all the tools available to us to stay connected and our rapidly expanding global workforce, it feels as if the more we need to belong, the more we're growing apart. And that has to change.

We're seeing more arguments about politics in the workplace, increased racial tensions, and gaps in equality and pay. We're on either one side or the other. For organizations and leaders, this is a major threat to healthy cultures and inevitably the success of our overall business goals.

Along with some of the other solutions we explored earlier in the chapter, like NASA's approach to the *Columbia* catastrophe, dissenting opinions and open discussions foster a stronger, higher-performing, healthier culture. By advancing psychological safety strategies, we build healthy communities. And that means building trust.

Trust, however, is rooted in honesty. In complex and delicate workplace environments, honesty can be tricky. To successfully share feedback across the table, empathy (once again) must be at the root of our communication to ensure that feedback is helpful rather than painfully critical.

Jim Moss, executive director of YMCA WorkWell and a nationally recognized expert in well-being who also happens to be my spouse, believes that to build a healthy community culture, we must value honest feedback. He believes feedback is the best tool for recognizing the most critical behaviors that accomplish individual and organizational goals. He also confirms that when it comes to providing feedback, empathy should be foundational to those conversations. He said, "To find that balance between health and performance, it requires measuring and adjusting to the ebbs and flows of the world around and within our workplace. Yet, never willing to sacrifice all or too much of either, and leaders have to hold ourselves accountable to that notion. This is the kind of organization that thrives over the longer term and is more 'self-healing' and functionally resilient."[50]

When it comes to burnout, Moss suggests that the organization is leaning toward being high performing. not realizing that it is fueled by, or coming at the cost of, individuals' health within its social community. "And, we can't take a gamble on that," Moss said. "Having a strong sense of community is really powerful. It can give us a feeling of being part of something larger and important or, without it, can make us feel alone, isolated, and left out."

Moss claims that the moment someone perceives that the community they once relied on for social support and psychological safety has abandoned them, it can have substantial negative rippling effects. He said, "As an injured athlete forced into early retirement due to health reasons, I felt pushed into the shadows for a while. It was challenging to see how the community I had relied on at work was not there in the same way they had been before. But, not being able to label it, but instead just feeling this loss, it was hard on my mental health."

Moss shared that it can take just a few individuals to drive the change, but the community has to be genuine before it will grow in a healthy way. He said that this is why values have to be aligned, and the workplace is somewhere we can bring our authentic selves to work. "We need a space—whether it's physically or virtually—that allows us to contribute in meaningful ways and grow and develop as individuals. Only then can we contribute in meaningful ways as an entire organization."

Have Trust. Grow Friends.

There's a good reason why Gallup includes the "I have a best friend at work" item in its Q12 survey. According to Gallup, we are social animals and work is a social institution; therefore, "the evolution of quality relationships is very normal and an important part of a healthy workplace."

Its decision to include this item came from years of research in workplaces with high levels of employee retention, customer metrics, productivity, and profitability: "The research identified 12 dimensions that consistently correlate with these four outcomes—dimensions Gallup now uses to measure the health of a workplace. An associated research effort, in which Gallup studied more than 80,000 managers, focused on discovering what great managers do to create quality workplaces."[51]

Gallup observed that employees who report having a best friend at work were:

- Forty-three percent more likely to report having received praise or recognition for their work in the last seven days

- Thirty-seven percent more likely to report that someone at work encourages their development

- Thirty-five percent more likely to report coworker commitment to quality

- Twenty-eight percent more likely to report that in the last six months, someone at work has talked to them about their progress

- Twenty-seven percent more likely to report that the mission of their company makes them feel their job is important

- Twenty-seven percent more likely to report that their opinions seem to count at work

- Twenty-one percent more likely to report that at work, they have the opportunity to do what they do best every day[52]

According to Gallup's research, "This item also points to the issue of trust between coworkers. When strong engagement is felt in a work-group, employees believe that their coworkers will help them during times of stress and challenge. Employees who have best friends at work identify significantly higher levels of healthy stress management, even though they experience the same levels of stress."[53] However, when Gallup surveyed more than 15 million employees worldwide, less than a third reported having a best friend at work.[54]

A fascinating twenty-year study led by researchers at Tel Aviv University found that people who have a good peer support system at work may live longer than people who don't. They discovered that coworkers had the biggest impact on our health: "Peer social support was rated as being high if participants reported that their co-workers were helpful in solving problems and that they were friendly."

The participants were asked questions about the behavior of their boss, their relationship with their colleagues, and their work environment, all while their health was monitored. What the researchers found was that the factor most closely linked to health was the support of coworkers. Middle-aged workers with little or no "peer social support" in the workplace were 2.4 times more likely to die during the study.[55] So, basically, the meaner a colleague was, the higher the risk of the subject dying.

When I read this study, all I could think of was, whoever is leaving passive-aggressive notes above the sink really should stop doing that. The study also made me think about how important it is for leaders to have strong relationships with their peers. Sometimes our roles can feel isolating, but having at least one person to call and bounce ideas off of or to gain perspective is valuable. This is difficult, however, when we're becoming more disconnected from the people we work with. Isolation increased as a result of the explosion of remote work in 2020.

One of the outcomes from our research was the finding that it was hard for peers to maintain a strong connection with their colleagues while working remotely. Nearly 40 percent of respondents said they struggled with being so disconnected. Maintaining a healthy remote culture takes specific strategies, which include getting people physically together as much as possible.

One respondent shared how they felt about that separation and its impact on the company culture: "It's become wholly virtual. I work for a company that has topped Glassdoor's Best Place to Work list multiple times, a company that is known for its culture—a culture I love. But it is not the same. All the fun stuff and connection is so hard to replicate virtually that work life now feels like it is all about work, and not much else. I have struggled to balance my personal needs to keep mentally well and healthy with my work life."

In 2020, we saw a massive shift from working from home sometimes to working from home always. This shift was permanent for many companies. And, for some, this was a good-news story. They'd been hoping to work from home for years, and this forced a workplace experiment that became a wish come true.

As I've mentioned before, I love working from home; not everyone does. I am urging leaders to consider that hybrid offerings are the best approach to promoting healthy relationships in the workplace. That means offering physical spaces where people can come together for in-person collaboration when they want. And they can also choose to work from home to get personal space.

When we are remote, random lunchroom run-ins and deskside drop-bys are no longer a given. That means leaders need to find alternative ways to cause innovation collisions—the moments of spontaneity that can solve big problems.

In *Back to Human: How Great Leaders Create Connection in the Age of Isolation*, Dan Schawbel tackles the impact of loneliness and disconnection in the workplace.[56] Schawbel urges people to "use technology as a bridge" to further human interaction. He advises individuals not to let technology be a barrier between them and those they need to connect with most. He also encourages leaders to take the necessary time to get to know their teams. "By solving someone's human needs, you're also solving their work needs," he says.

Schawbel's recent research, in collaboration with Virgin Pulse, was aimed at determining the best ways to enable stronger human relationships. His survey of two thousand managers and employees across different age groups and world geographies found that off-site meetings were a helpful strategy for enabling human relationships. Schawbel learned that by gathering in environments away from work, employees were better able to escape the office talk and engage in more personal conversations. Following the off-site events, participant data showed that productivity and engagement among the group increased, while feelings of isolation and loneliness decreased.

"Really, it's about trust," Schawbel shared in our interview, "because if you have never seen someone's face, you don't trust them as much. The second you meet someone, everything changes, everything."

The problem is compounded by the increasing number of people who live alone, which was once rare. Now, single-person households are the second-most-common type of US household—just behind married couples without minor children and even more prevalent than married couples with children under eighteen. In many urban centers, roughly 40 percent of households are single-occupant dwellings.

The trend to live alone raises concerns among mental health experts. Studies have found that it is linked to depression, lower quality of life, and health problems. Millennials, who make up the largest segment of the workforce, are the loneliest generation. Three in ten millennials always or often feel lonely, according to a poll by YouGov, a London-based research and analytics company.[57] At work, 66 percent of millennials found it hard to make friends, compared to less than 23 percent of baby boomers, according to a 2018 survey from UK-based Milkround, a student and graduate career resources company.[58]

Personal connection isn't just good for engagement and happiness at work; it's what makes us human. It's part of our genetic makeup. This deeply ingrained evolutionary legacy goes back to the days when our survival depended on safety in numbers. Today, work is where we often find our tribe.

In addition to getting people physically together, there are other ways leaders and managers can help nurture healthy relationships at work:

- *Give people places where they can connect about nonwork-related topics.* Have Slack or Teams channels—whatever your organization uses as a social collaboration tool—that discuss a range of topics, from quilting to ax throwing to parenting. Don't worry about people engaging on these channels during work hours; supporting its usage means you trust that your people can handle their workload.

- *Connect people across the entire organization.* Support collaborative projects that energize the team and connect them to the organization's mission and values. Employees that have purpose and meaning in their experience of work is a huge contributor to well-being. Dopamine plays an extremely important role in the creative process—particularly upon completion. Throughout the process of creative collaboration, we experience healthy doses of dopamine, but when we finish the project, our brains are flooded with dopamine, so that feel-good chemical actually helps motivate us.[59] It is also the chemical that allows our brains to wonder and think up new ideas. Not only is this healthy for forming bonds at work, it increases opportunities for innovation.

- *Perform acts of altruism.* Another way to increase that happy chemistry is to engage employees in volunteering. People who have volunteered have been shown to self-report a higher quality of life and healthier relationships than those who don't commit acts of altruism.

- *Monitor unhealthy competition.* On one hand, competition can be healthy. According to research published in the *Academy of Management Journal*, "It can increase an individual's motivation and effort to produce results."[60] But overly competitive work environments can cause stress, secrecy, defensiveness, and predatory behaviors. Too much competitiveness can also lead to feelings of isolation among coworkers and an "every person for themselves" culture. While strategies such as cooperative sales targets and team metrics can help, the best way to encourage healthy competition and mitigate feelings of loneliness among workers is to have employees focus on shared goals.

- *Build inclusive cultures.* Feelings of inclusion drive what we call a "virtuous loop" that energizes employees to "do for others" in that group. This encourages them to work harder for their teams and for the whole organization. In contrast, individualism can cause social isolation that inevitably causes changes in brain functionality, leading to diminished learning capacity, poor decision making, and an elevated threat response.[61] We need to drive a culture based on inclusionary group goals rather than the "survival of the fittest" strategies too often seen in production-focused environments.

What happens when employees can't connect authentically to the organization? How do mismatched values force them to hide who they truly are and want to be at work and, subsequently, put them at risk for burnout? Lack of fairness.

ROOT CAUSE 5

Lack of Fairness

Unfair treatment, also described as a lack of organizational justice, can result from a variety of conditions including but not limited to bias, favoritism, mistreatment by a coworker or supervisor, and unfair compensation and/or corporate policies.

According to Gallup, "When employees do not trust their manager, teammates or executive leadership, it breaks the psychological bond that makes work meaningful."[62] Employees who perceive they are being unfairly treated in the workplace are at increased risk of taking sick days and remaining out sick for longer, according to research by the University of East Anglia and Stockholm University.

Constanze Eib, a lecturer in organizational behavior at Norwich Business School and coauthor of the study, found that "while shorter, but more frequent periods of sickness absence might be a chance for the individual to get relief from high levels of strain or stress, long-term sickness absence might be a sign of more serious health problems."[63]

The study's lead author, Constanze Leineweber, from the Stress Research Institute, said, "Perceived fairness at work is a modifiable aspect of the work environment, as is job insecurity. Organisations have significant control over both . . . Organisations might also gain from the selection of managers for their qualities associated with fair practices, training them in justice principles, and implementing performance management practices for them that consider their use of organisational justice."[64]

If leaders want to reduce unfair treatment at work, they need to follow similar standards to those found across human rights commissions globally. The researchers describe the following as a better mechanism for employees to report unfair treatment at work:

• Have a complaint mechanism in place.

- Have a shared corporate awareness of what constitutes unfair treatment.

- Respond to every grievance.

- Take the matter seriously.

- Act promptly.

- Provide a healthy work environment while the event is under investigation.[65]

In my interview with Christina Maslach, she shared that lack of fairness is an ever-increasing issue that predicts burnout. In one of her examples, lack of fairness turned out to be a huge issue. Yet, it took Maslach and the leadership team a while to realize what was really bothering people. Where did people feel the practices were actually unfair? When the leaders finally discovered what it was, they were completely surprised.

Maslach learned that the type of practice the leadership team thought was "wonderful," like awards for distinguished service, ended up being the problem. At first, they questioned what could be wrong with handing out awards.

Maslach explained to the leadership team that it wasn't the handing out of the awards but *who* they were recognizing. What she learned from the survey responses was that most of the employees felt the recognition and awards were going to people who didn't deserve them.

Maslach found that most of the time, these awards went to someone who didn't get a pay raise that year as an offset for not paying them enough. "This is the kind of thing that really just eats at a person's soul—their craw, you know," Maslach said.

I was nodding my head vigorously as Maslach spoke. Everything she was saying aligned with my intellectual and emotional brain. As Maslach explains, these are the pebbles. The irritants. The small stressors that grow into major causes of burnout. And all it takes is asking, getting into the small yet most meaningful data to actually fix it.

Yes, it's frustrating and tiring when we see people getting recognized for sloppy work. It's unfair and dissatisfying, particularly if you're in a vulnerable group during a time of a major societal uprising and you're burned out from a global pandemic. That's when lack of fairness moves to injustice—a space not all of us can understand. This is when leaders must stop what they are doing to listen and learn.

The Layers of Inequity

According to research by Adia Harvey Wingfield, associate dean at Washington University, "The conditions under which many Black health care providers are working produces a specific kind of burn-out, stress, and exhaustion. Frequently, this happens not only because many are working in under-resourced public facilities, but because they are also dealing with the racial implications of their work—caring for low-income patients of color whom even many of their white colleagues view through a racially stereotyped lens as drug abusers, noncompliant patients, or irresponsible parents."[66]

Another important voice on the topic of Black burnout comes from award-winning author and poet Tiana Clark, who also teaches creative writing at Southern Illinois University at Edwardsville. She wrote a counterargument to an article on millennial burnout that left out the Black experience of burnout. She claims, when it comes to burnout for Black Americans, "the data is bleak." Getting paid sixty-one cents for every dollar a white male counterpart makes is already disturbingly unjust, but compound that with the stress of everyday racism; for the Black workforce, it is exhausting. Clark said, "Burnout for white, upper-middle-class millennials might be taxing mentally, but the consequences of being overworked and underpaid while managing microaggressions toward marginalized groups damages our bodies by the minute with greater intensity."[67]

The story of Abena Anim-Somuah that first appeared in *The Cut* in August 2020 described the additional pressure placed on people of color in the workplace. Add in social unrest, and it can be a recipe for total exhaustion and burnout.

Abena shared, "I think when you're a Black woman, you always feel like you have to work twice as hard to get half as far. So, you constantly put things on your plate because you say, oh, if I take on this project, when my performance review comes up, they'll see I'm a valuable asset to the company, and maybe that will lead to something more."[68]

She also realized that the quarantine had contributed to her burnout, but it was when the Black Lives Matter protests began that she became overwhelmed. "I felt this exhaustion from working at a predominantly white company, being one of the few Black people or people of color, and having to sit through meetings, knowing that people who looked like me and my family are being mercilessly killed," she revealed. "I told myself, No, I'm going to take some time off to recoup and rejuvenate."[69]

Getting to the root of this burnout story is so critical—finding the actions that are hidden behind the ones that look like the opposite of burnout. Or the person who takes on project after project, increasing workload under severe emotional unrest to assuage someone else's unjustified bias, the kind that has been unfairly propagated over hundreds of years.

We need to dig deeper. We can do better.

We must ensure the questions we ask are nuanced and inclusive. And understand that even asking questions at all can be rooted in mistrust. For certain groups, being surveyed may feel threatening, as historically, those surveys were used with malicious intent. Open and transparent conversations that commit to sharing the data after it's gathered are critical.

If we gather data with bias, we don't get the full picture of burnout in our organizations. Ensuring there are experts on our teams who truly understand the needs of a diverse and inclusive work community will be a good first step.

Unfair treatment at work is a major contributor to burnout and therefore must be a priority for leadership. The added negative impact on employee health, combined with the potential for the unfair treatment to be seen as a threat to human rights, makes it even more critical for leadership to tackle the issue immediately.

ROOT CAUSE 6

Values Mismatch

According to author Elizabeth Grace Saunders, if employees aren't valuing the same goals of the organization, then "motivation to work hard and persevere can significantly drop."[70]

Arne L. Kalleberg, professor of sociology at the University of North Carolina at Chapel Hill, analyzed some of the most common mismatches and their outcomes. He discusses why overqualification can lead to dissatisfaction at work and, inevitably, unhealthy consequences for the employee. When he first started his research, the number of people in the labor force who were overqualified for a job was one in five.[71] That number grew after the Great Recession in 2008; now that number has increased to one in four.[72] For new graduates, that number is even higher, with one in three considered to be overqualified for their roles.[73]

One reason economists and HR experts are highlighting this is that not enough job options match educational attainment. So we're seeing too many college graduates, particularly those with massive student loan debt, lowering the bar just so they have a paycheck—even if they are overqualified.

According to research from Deloitte, as of 2015, a reported 17 percent of waiters and waitresses and 33 percent of retail salespeople held a bachelor's degree or higher. Both are examples of occupations that classify as requiring no formal educational credentials and are unlikely to provide long-term satisfaction or occupation advancement to those with advanced degrees.[74]

Overqualification rates are substantial even for occupations requiring bachelor's degrees. In 2015, 100 percent of actuaries, 58 percent of personal financial advisers, 47 percent of financial analysts, and 42 percent of mechanical engineers in this cohort held master's degrees in those occupations, all of which (according to the Bureau of Labor Statistics) require no more than a bachelor's degree. According to the Deloitte study, "This is an alarming reality for college-educated millennials, who may find themselves competing with others who have more advanced degrees. An 'inadequate' candidate is left to do one of two things: pursue a higher degree themselves or find another occupation."[75]

How did this trend begin? The Pew Research Center found that unstable job markets encouraged young adults to go back to school or pursue more-advanced degrees, effectively prolonging their college career.[76] Added to that, college tuition has grown at an annual rate of 4.8 percent. Plus, the slow recovery that followed the recession also encouraged new graduates to continue obtaining degrees for some time, resulting in a continuous influx of highly educated new workers.[77]

A study by Michael Harari of Florida Atlantic University examined twenty-five years of research on the impact of perceived overqualification.[78] He found that overqualified employees experience psychological strains, such as depression, anxiety, and job burnout (even when statistically controlling for general negative affective tendencies). Overqualified employees are also less likely to experience positive psychological well-being. For example, they report lower levels of life satisfaction.

Perceived overqualification occurs when an employee is expecting a job in which they can use their credentials and skills but does not actually work in such a position, leaving them feeling essentially deprived.

"That deprivation is what is theorized to result in these negative job attitudes," Harari said. "There's a discrepancy between expectation and reality. Because of this, you're angry, you're frustrated, and as a result you don't much care for the job that you have and feel unsatisfied."[79]

According to Harari, "Employees experience psychological strain when they invest effort at work and expect rewards in return, such as esteem and career opportunities. For an overqualified employee, that expectation has been violated."[80]

The pandemic, as part of a more recent workforce disruptor, exacerbated these issues, leaving millions in the workforce either returning to attain more schooling, or out of desperation, taking on jobs that don't meet their qualifications.

There are two key points here:

1. We can't take advantage of overqualified talent by hiring them into inferior roles; this will only lead to dissatisfaction and burnout.

2. However, we can't stop hiring overqualified talent because we will then just keep new grads out of work.

What do we do?

-   *Find the path.* We need to reassure overqualified hires that they will not get stuck. Develop a strategy that includes a plan for development and training.

-   *Communicate the plan.* To minimize dissatisfaction and increase retention, routinely communicate how their skills, talent, and education are being developed and how—even if it isn't right now—there is still a plan in place to get them to where they want to be.

-   *Realize the goal.* Make sure that this plan isn't a dangling carrot or even a pacifier. We need to make sure that the plan is going to actually realize the goal. It demonstrates to the entire organization that we stick to our promises.

Do We Fit?

According to Terrence Jermyn Porter from the University of St. Thomas, Minnesota, "Applicants want to work in organizational cultures that provide them the best opportunities to be successful based on their perception of a culture match with their personal values and needs."[81] Porter goes on to claim that during the initial stages of researching information about organizations, job seekers often develop strong beliefs about the culture of organizations. This is where an applicant tries to determine if there is person-organization fit (POF). The POF theory is the concept that describes the compatibility between people and organizations. As expected, candidates tend to be attracted to organizations that share similar values and goals.

However, if someone discovers the mismatch between their initial perceptions of an organization's culture and its reality, the difference between the two can be very harmful to everyone involved. Hiring someone whose values and goals do not align with the values and goals of the organization's culture may result in lower job satisfaction and negatively impact mental health. This in turn will lead to lower rates of productivity and a higher turnover rate.

Some other consequences could include:

- Increased physical and mental exhaustion and stress

- Low morale within the team

- Lack of individual and team motivation

- Low productivity or unsatisfactory work

- Increased costs for hiring and training

- Burnout

This doesn't mean we should follow the old way of recruiting for "fit." As human resources consultant and Netflix's former chief talent officer Patty McCord shares when describing the pitfalls of hiring for fit, "What most people mean by culture fit is hiring people they'd like to have a beer with. Then you end up with this big, homogenous culture where everybody looks alike, everybody thinks alike, and everybody likes drinking beer at 3 o'clock in the afternoon with the bros."

Obviously, this isn't the right way of thinking when attracting or hiring talent. We want people to know what they're getting into. So, if your culture is all about having beers at 3:00 p.m. and your workforce lacks diversity, don't claim the opposite. That just ticks people off.

Either get the culture you want and promote that, or change your culture. But be warned, you may not be hiring for diversity and are missing out on talent because of blind spots around a false perception of fit.

Wall Street Journal columnist Sue Shellenbarger wrote that "employees err in taking a job because it offers office ping pong, free lunches or heated toilet seats." Her article suggests that "hiring managers need to go deeper and figure out whether applicants are in sync with more fundamental elements of their culture."

She suggests that leaders should consider right at the hiring stage whether candidates "are . . . excited about how the company innovates, serves customers or makes a social impact? Will they mesh with the way individuals and teams at the company work, by collaborating or competing? And will they naturally make decisions the way the employer wants—individually or as a group, embracing or avoiding risk?"[82]

Leaders should strive for a culture that encourages shared values, beliefs, and behaviors between employees and the company itself. When these features are aligned, it enhances overall performance and reduces burnout. Not only because purpose-driven work can act as a barrier to burnout, feeling connected to a mission can fuel engagement—a counterpoint to burnout, according to Maslach and Leiter.

. . .

I've only scratched the surface on how workload, autonomy, reward and recognition, community, fairness, and values alignment can impact our risk of burnout, and conversely, when handled well in organizations, can be a recipe for the healthiest and highest-performing cultures.

We can't only assume that by managing for the root causes of burnout, we'll prevent people from getting sick. We need to build a culture focused on upstream interventions, one where the hygiene is healthy and therefore culture can flourish.

Empathy in leadership will be the way forward. Ask people how they're feeling and listen to their needs. Invite people to share their feelings anonymously so they have no fear of repercussion.

- Assess workload. Is it manageable?

- Are people feeling aligned with the company's values?

- Assess compensation structures. Do people think they are being paid fairly?

- Which groups aren't feeling recognized?

- What could we do to ensure people feel more valued?

- Are people feeling micromanaged? How?

- Are we properly tackling the impact that the pandemic has had on marginalized communities? Has it impacted people's feeling of inclusion?

- If we ask these questions and get answers, how are we going to respond?

Here is where we get to work. Take that learning and put it into action. If we're not ready to tackle everything at once, prioritize. What can we realistically get done and what is our time frame? Just commit to a future where more will be accomplished and communicate that out loud. Stay accountable to the commitment.

Although we can concurrently tackle hygiene while working on strategies that increase motivation, burnout remains a threat when hygiene is not the first priority. When solutions are simple and pain is preventable, it just makes it worse when problems are left unsolved and sores fester.

The effort isn't as overwhelming as one might think. Simple actions done with repetition create positive benefits. There are hundreds, maybe thousands, of ways we can acknowledge others for doing great work. We just have to be intentional about it. No excuses.

Right now, by placing just a few selective support boats in the water upstream, you won't have to dive in and pull your people out of the water downstream.

Remember: the examples included in this chapter are all starting-off points for further conversations. Instead of tackling everything at once, choose a focus and invest time for problem solving. Even then, it will take time to turn the ship around.

Burnout is real and evolving, but there are solutions. It may feel like a heavy lift, and I can't lie and say that it won't be a challenge. But the time for questioning the need is gone. It all really boils down to intentionality and following through.

I'm assuming you're up for it. So, let's keep going.

2

The Most Vulnerable among Us

As I've said before, burnout is a "we" problem to solve. There are systemic problems within the organization that are causing people to get sick. But specific roles and sectors are more prone to burnout. And certain personalities put someone at further risk. It's important to identify that multiple factors are at play, because when they're combined, they can be catastrophic.

In his article, "Staff Burn-out," Herbert J. Freudenberger lists personality factors that may mean that one person will suffer burnout more than another. He claimed in his early research that employees who are more "dedicated" and "committed" could be more at risk.[1] A workplace environment that requires more emotional involvement, empathy, and personal investment, combined with an intrinsic motivation versus extrinsic rewards, can further increase the risk. For example, healthcare professionals are especially prone to burnout, particularly staff who work in patient care. Other high-risk professions include teachers and educators—specifically those working directly with students—and mission-driven nonprofit employees. There's something to be said about that adage, "It's lonely at the top"; C-level executives and startup founders are also known to disproportionately suffer from burnout as a result of high-achieving personalities, isolation, and stoicism.

In this chapter, we'll look at problematic industries in more detail, including health care, education, and tech. Though some of us don't work in these industries, the problems we'll uncover point to infrastructure failures that are likely present in your organization. But, first, we'll analyze three personality traits that are linked to increased burnout risk.

Personalities at Risk

People that exhibit neuroticism, introversion, or most significantly, perfectionism are prone to burnout. This makes it critical for us to identify areas of weakness and subsequently create the systems to help support the people we lead who may also be at risk.

Neuroticism

Neuroticism is one of the "big five" higher-order personality traits in the study of psychology. If you dig into the definition, it makes sense that this trait correlates to higher rates of burnout. Individuals who score high on the neuroticism scales are more likely than average to be moody and to experience such feelings as anxiety, worry, fear, anger, frustration, envy, jealousy, guilt, depressed mood, and loneliness. People who are neurotic respond worse to stressors and are more likely to interpret ordinary situations as threatening and minor frustrations as hopelessly difficult.[2]

In her 2018 dissertation, "The Relationship Between Big Five Personality Traits and Burnout: A Study Among Correctional Personnel," Sharon Maylor of Walden University suggests that individuals possessing the personality trait neuroticism experienced high levels of emotional exhaustion and depersonalization. In her study of 112 correctional staff, the length of years employed, years worked, type of work, and marital status on their own did not have any relationship with burnout. However, when coupled with personality traits, the findings showed that neuroticism was the only personality trait that was associated with all three dimensions of burnout.[3]

A recent study from researchers at UC Irvine, the MIT Media Lab, and Microsoft found that employees who display neuroticism have a harder time at work than people who do not display neurotic tendencies. Specifically, they struggle with multitasking and focus, according to Gloria Mark of UC Irvine and colleagues. "Forty information workers' online activity was tracked over two workweeks. The median duration of online screen focus was 40 seconds. The personality trait of Neuroticism was associated with shorter online focus duration."[4]

Conversely, it's important to see the value in this personality type. We tend to give personality traits like these a bad rap, but there are upsides. People with the neuroticism trait tend to be:

- Highly analytical and hyperaware of threats or dangers

- Cautious and less likely to make impulsive decisions

- More accountable and will take personal responsibility for errors

In certain roles, this may help them to perform better at work, as long as we're watching for burnout. It is critical that the appropriate well-being policies be put in place, particularly because this group is statistically more likely to end up working for less compensation.[5]

Additionally, people high in conscientiousness and neuroticism have an even greater ability to channel their anxieties into positive behaviors. Managers can leverage these strengths by doing the following:

- Place employees with these traits in roles that require a high attention to detail or where they assess and manage risk.

- Provide plenty of positive feedback—this should be table stakes regardless of personality type, but it is particularly helpful within a group that has to overcome deficits in self-efficacy.

- Establish less pressured deadlines and have a longer window (plan ahead).

- Give them space to work alone; make sure they get uninterrupted chunks of time to focus.

- Pull them into group tasks because they work better with a team-oriented goal.

There are obvious potential benefits to having someone with neuroticism on the team, but we need to be mindful of how we lead to avoid burnout.

Introversion

Introversion is another big-five dimension that defines what we consider as personalities; introversion is polar to extroversion. It is a myth that introverts fear or dislike others and are shy and lonely. This is not the case. They simply have nervous systems more suited to spending time in a calm environment with one or a few friends.

Evidence from a study conducted by researchers at Stony Brook University, Southwest University, and the Chinese Academy of Sciences found that the brains of introverts do not react strongly to viewing novel human faces; in such situations, they produce less dopamine, a neurotransmitter associated with reward. Conversely, the results show that the brains of extroverts pay more attention to human faces, whereas introverts' brains don't seem to distinguish between inanimate objects and human faces.[6]

Although their nervous systems may be dissimilar to those of extroverts, that doesn't mean that introverts aren't just as effective. "Extroverts are routinely chosen for leadership positions and introverts are looked over, although introverts often deliver better outcomes. They're not perceived as leadership material," says Susan Cain, bestselling author of *Quiet: The Power of Introverts in a World That Can't Stop Talking*, and a frequent speaker on introversion and extroversion in the workplace.[7]

The leader prototype trends toward a dominant vocalizer who holds the attention of the room. This attention equivocates power. Introverts are perceived as weak leaders, and as such, they earn 20 percent less than their counterparts and manage half as many people as extroverts.[8] Yet, we miss the potential of introverts if we don't figure out how to lead this group most effectively.

According to Cain's research, the power of introverts can be identified in the following behaviors. They:

- Tend to be more productive than extroverts and less likely to become distracted

- Explore subjects in more depth

- Are great listeners, which helps them in problem-solving scenarios

- Are often creators; writers and artists are more likely to identify as introverted

- Have a strong capacity for empathy

- Are moderators and can calm stressful situations

- Are more cautious and better at managing risk

However, since the physical office can be a highly social place, research suggests that introverted people are at greater risk of developing burnout than extroverted people.[9]

Although working remotely was already on the rise, 2020 exploded that trend wide open. Pre-Covid-19 lockdown, working from home was a perk, available to a select few who worked in progressive organizations. But that changed. And, you could almost hear introverts' collective sigh of relief.

Introverts working virtually in most situations, minus a global lockdown, are removed from the noise, the hustle and bustle of a buzzing office, the potential disruptions that cause a lack of psychological safety, and the pressure to conform to those office norms. What if we made workplaces free of these kinds of strain? With some simple shifts, we could leverage introverts' strengths instead of draining them of mental resources.

We had to make sweeping changes to follow health and safety protocols during the pandemic, so why don't we consider designing our office spaces to increase psychological safety? This seems like a no-brainer, but it hasn't been a big priority for most organizations. The open office continues to be the norm, yet, it's proven to hinder productivity in countless cases.

Just ask Cain, who shared in our interview, "The best workspaces allow people to move freely between solo and shared spaces. Sometimes we want to work alone. Sometimes we crave company. Sometimes we want both of these things in the space of a single morning. Why not design around these natural preferences? Radically open office plans don't actually increase collaboration or decrease loneliness. On the contrary, they create giant rooms full of worker bees wearing headphones."

Cain's work with Steelcase, an office space and furniture design company, is part of her effort to educate employers about the best ways to leverage the powers of introverts. Appropriate workspaces play a big part in that effort. Cain cites a few design principles with introversion in mind, including:

- *Permission to be alone.* This means offering workers a private, interruption-free space and the ability to remove themselves from an otherwise highly stimulating workplace.

- *Control over the environment.* Cain's research shows that introverts are more sensitive to stimulation and have a greater need for control over their environment. They also have a lower tolerance for external forces such as noise and light.

- *Sensory balance.* Calming influences found in organic materials help introverts manage their sensory needs.

- *Psychological safety.* Introverts need spaces where they feel unseen as respite from feeling perpetually noticed by their peers.

"There's a big difference between happily seeking out solo time (for getting into a flow state, or simply to recharge) versus unhappily feeling lonely (because of social isolation or toxic interpersonal dynamics)," Cain contends. "The best workplaces maximize the former and minimize the latter."

Perfectionism

If you're prone to perfectionism—specifically, perfectionism concerns—you run a high risk of burning out. Even more worrisome, the professions with a legacy of burnout are attracting personalities more at risk of burnout. This combination is highly toxic and has proven to be fatal.

Broadly defined, perfectionism is a combination of exceedingly high standards and a preoccupation with extreme self-critical evaluation. Scientists Joachim Stoeber from the University of Kent and Kathleen Otto from the University of Leipzig suggest in a narrative review that perfectionism consists of two main dimensions: perfectionistic strivings and perfectionistic concerns. Perfectionistic strivings are associated with positive aspects of perfectionism; perfectionistic concerns are associated with negative aspects.[10]

Essentially, they discovered that our desire and subsequent efforts to achieve perfectionism are acceptable as long as we can emotionally handle scenarios when we don't achieve it. When we start to believe that everything we do must be perfect and anything less means a failure, or that others may judge us as a failure, then this becomes detrimental to our mental health.

Someone who struggles with perfectionist concerns may exhibit the following traits:

- Maintaining a rigid self-evaluative style that looks at events in all-or-nothing terms, for example, you're either a winner or a loser.

- Overgeneralizing negative events by making a rule after a single event or a series of coincidences. For example, an argument with a friend or coworker that has occurred a few times becomes "We always fight about the same thing." Or, someone is passed over for a promotion, and the narrative is now, "I will never move up in this company." These "always" or "never" statements frequently appear in a perfectionist's vocabulary.

- Ruminating about past failures. Being unable to let go of mistakes and assuming they will come up again in the future.

- Having a strong need for self-validation, for example, always questioning their self-worth. In some situations, they will sub-consciously seek out ways to prove they are "right." They believe their self-worth is constantly threatened.

According to researchers Andrew Hill and Thomas Curra in their article "Multidimensional Perfectionism and Burnout: A Meta-Analysis," "Perfectionistic concerns are associated with considerable strain that render individuals vulnerable to the accrual of stress and subsequent burnout. In summarizing current understanding of the perfectionism–burnout relationship, then, it is the harsh self-evaluative processes central to perfectionistic concerns that are understood to fuel the perfectionism–burnout relationship, rather than perfectionistic strivings."[11]

Cognitive behavioral psychologists have characterized these harsh evaluative processes as "cognitive distortions or patterns of erroneous thoughts," which is essentially a lie our brain sends to our conscious mind.[12]

According to David Burns, Professor Emeritus of Psychiatry and Behavioral Sciences at the Stanford University School of Medicine, examples of cognitive distortions found in someone with perfectionist concerns may include:

- *All-or-nothing thinking.* "I didn't get an A. I must be stupid." "I didn't save the patient. I shouldn't be a doctor." "I lost a client. I'm going to get fired."

- *Overgeneralization.* "I never get this right."

- *Mental filter.* You focus only on the negative, ignoring the positives.

- *Discounting the positives.* "Ninety-nine people thought my presentation was great, but one didn't. I must have messed something up."

- *Jumping to conclusions.* You assume people think negatively of your abilities, or you predict events will turn out poorly.

- *Magnification or minimization.* A life event is either blown out of proportion or completely pointless.

- *Emotional reasoning.* "I have no confidence in my abilities. I must be a terrible manager."

- *"Should" statements.* "I should be a department head by now." Such a statement can lead to guilt, frustration, or unnecessary pressure and stress.

- *Labeling.* You base your identity on one minor error.

- *Personalization and blame.* "This was all my fault."[13]

When it comes specifically to health-care professionals, particularly physicians, research finds these perfectionist concerns are rampant. This can be exacerbated by the stressors they face each day, including the loss of autonomy associated with hospital-based practice, the restrictions on practice associated with managed care, the ongoing escalation of liability lawsuits, and the maintenance of competency in a rapidly changing specialty. According to an article published in the *Bulletin of the American College of Physicians*, "These stressors can interact with pre-existing psychological characteristics typical of surgeons."[14]

Authors Mick Oreskovich and James Anderson wrote, "Surgeons are trained to never make mistakes, so when they do occur, the surgeon may be tormented by their own sense of perfectionism, resulting in self-incrimination and even self-loathing. An exaggerated sense of responsibility coupled with guilt and self-doubt adds stress to an already difficult situation. Unfortunately, some surgeons are unable to differentiate perfectionism from the aspiration to excel. Numerous authors have demonstrated that perfectionism is a vulnerability factor for depression, anxiety, burnout, and suicide."

The research highlights that as perfectionists, "surgeons often suffer from numerous cognitive distortions: that they are valued only for their performance; that the better they do, the better they are expected to do; and that, if they lose the 'edge,' they will lose their colleagues' support. The consequences of this perfectionism include only short-lived satisfaction with achievements; a sense that awards and accolades are unmerited; and striving to excel not for personal and professional satisfaction or pleasure, but rather to relieve the tormented psyche."

We don't just see perfectionism show up in a physician's psychology; this tends to be a trapping of other roles at risk. According to Oreskovich and Anderson, "Perfectionism is one of the major precursors for burnout because it is often accompanied by an exaggerated sense of responsibility that leads to self-doubt and guilt, which then leads to rigidity, stubbornness, and the inability to delegate. These behaviors, in turn, may result in a devotion to, and identification with, work to the exclusion of relationships and self-care."

Oreskovich and Anderson suggest that we need to consider the following, if we experience perfectionist concerns:

1. Identify the difference between power versus powerlessness over people, places, things, and situations; if we stop trying to control everything, we will find more joy. It may be a challenge to surrender, but it is necessary to prevent burnout.

2. Understand the differences between self-knowledge and self-awareness (self-knowledge is what we believe to be true about ourselves; self-awareness is seeing ourselves as others see us). These insights are rarely the same yet are equally important.

3. Accept help.

4. Take care of ourselves so that we can take care of others.

Perfectionists are not limited to certain roles, but there are sectors that seem to attract this persona. Health care is perhaps where this matchup occurs most commonly. Unfortunately, health care has a legacy of burnout, where overwork is a badge of honor and running on empty is the norm.

Unhealthiness in Health Care

It has been hard to watch the frequency with which corporate leaders in health care turn a blind eye to the rampant human and financial costs that burnout is causing. I was fortunate enough to speak to several advocates who've been sounding the alarm on this issue for some time. Their stories follow. But they even admit that the shift has been slow, despite the astronomical rise and deadly consequences of burnout in the field of medicine.

Dr. Corey Feist is the CEO of the University of Virginia Physicians Group and cofounder of the Dr. Lorna Breen Heroes' Foundation. He suggests that certain personality types are drawn to medicine—a personal reflection that is backed up by research related to perfectionism. He says that the bravado inherent to the culture has a lot to do with a need to be perfect, and that means never asking for help or admitting defeat.

The health-care industry has a long-standing problem with burnout that is encoded in the culture. For myriad reasons including excessive workload, stigma, post-traumatic stress, and learned helplessness, we see a major threat that has only gotten worse. But, when these broken cultures are normalized and somehow celebrated, this makes it hard to unwind the clock.

In health care, overwork may be one of the most damaging and yet tolerated problems. Nurses and physicians notoriously work long shifts—often up to sixteen hours or more at a time—despite the stats that errors in patient care increase threefold when nurses work twelve-hour shifts compared to eight-and-a-half-hour shifts.[15]

A study published in *Health Affairs* found that the longer the shifts for hospital nurses, the higher the levels of burnout and patient dissatisfaction.[16] Another study found that "both longer shifts and working overtime were significantly associated with lower quality of care, worse patient safety reports and more care left undone."[17] Compared with nurses who were working eight hours or less, the odds of nurses who worked twelve hours or more on their most recent shift describing the quality of nursing care in their unit as "poor" or "fair" increased by 30 percent, and the odds of them reporting "failing" or "poor" patient safety in their units increased by 41 percent.[18]

Another study by scientists in China noted that physicians who reported sixty or more work hours per week and physicians who reported serious burnout were independently associated with a higher incidence of medical mistakes.[19] A study published in the *Journal of the American College of Surgeons* showed similar findings. It found that surgeons involved in recent malpractice worked longer hours and had more night calls.[20]

What we find consistently is that burnout from workload is often preventable. The issue in health care is the same. Unfortunately, over the last decade, this group has witnessed the increase of mostly tedious, unnecessary, and highly administrative activities adding to workload and causing burnout.

Are EHRs to Blame?

According to research led by Edward R. Melnick, assistant professor of emergency medicine at Yale, what was supposed to improve the quality and efficiency of health care for doctors and patients has instead become a source of high rates of professional burnout.[21] The study reports that physicians spend one to two hours on electronic health records (EHRs) and other desk work for every hour spent with patients, and an additional one to two hours daily of personal time on EHR-related activities. It also indicates that the lower physicians rated their EHRs, the higher the likelihood that they also reported symptoms of burnout.[22]

Melnick's study also found that EHR technologies were rated "F" for usability. Compare that to Google's search engine receiving an "A" and ATMs a "B" in similar but separate studies. It demonstrates a solvable problem. Make them easier to use. Unfortunately, herein lies the problem. The technology's potential limits its usability. "A Google search is easy," says Melnick. "There's not a lot of learning or memorization; it's not very error-prone. Excel, on the other hand, is a super-powerful platform, but you really have to study how to use it. EHRs mimic that."[23]

In "The Rapid Rollout of EHRs Following the Health Information Technology for Economic and Clinical Health Act of 2009," published by Yale University, the authors suggest that the "$27 billion of federal incentives into the adoption of EHRs in the US forced doctors to adapt quickly to often complex systems, leading to increasing frustration."[24] This doesn't seem to be improving patient care, according to Melnick; instead it's used for billing, and worse, the patient's health story is lost.

Corey Feist strongly believes that the addition of the EHRs has dramatically impacted physician workload and is a major cause of their burnout. "EHRs remove the joy in practice," Feist explained in our interview. "The reasons doctors and nurses go to school is to take care of patients, not to be data entry clerks. And patients see doctors for the medical expertise, not their typing acumen. I know that these records are intended to improve quality of patient care—so patients can go between hospitals and their history goes with them—but this unintended consequence of the electronic medical record has instead just been this incredible burnout."

Feist suggests that to help fix the workload issue, fix the EHR issue. Reduce "pajama hours"—the number of hours that people spend working at home after hours. Feist references the addition of more scribes for anyone who has to input data more than they should. He says he's getting into artificial intelligence and using virtual scribes, a new technology that needs "to come along," but he sees as a good path forward to making the technology more usable.

In addition, programs to train physicians better on the technology and keep increasing proficiency helps. Feist also says that team-based care is a strong tool for preventing burnout: "In a team-based care model, we share the data entry work across a number of people on the team based on goals and responsibilities."

Most importantly, Feist said that we can use data to see how many pajama hours are being spent by monitoring and checking in: "These large electronic medical record companies are now producing reports that identify physicians and the number of hours they're spending before and after work on administrative work. With that information, you can now make sure individuals have the training and the help they need to reduce the workload."

An excessive workload from preventable stresses, like practicing data management instead of practicing medicine, along with the already grueling hours most health-care staff have to endure, plus the exposure to death and dying, all have a dangerous impact on well-being.

The American Medical Association, along with researchers at Mayo Clinic and Stanford University, surveyed over five thousand physicians on topics related to burnout. In 2017, the burnout rate was 43.9 percent.[25] In September 2020, in a study by the American Association of Family Physicians, almost two-thirds (64 percent) of the US physicians surveyed said the pandemic had intensified their sense of burnout. About half said they had personally treated patients with Covid-19.[26]

When asked about the sources of stress caused by the pandemic, some responders cited treating patients who were likely to die, and others cited being exposed to Covid-19 without being given the proper personal protective equipment. When asked about the ways they're coping with the stress of the pandemic, 29 percent of US doctors said they were eating more, 19 percent said they were drinking more alcohol, and 2 percent said they were taking more prescription stimulants and medications.

Dr. Edward Ellison, a medical doctor and former co-CEO of the Permanente Federation, wrote about the massive negative impacts of physician burnout in the *Annals of Internal Medicine*: "Beyond the anxiety, depression, insomnia, emotional and physical exhaustion, and loss of cognitive focus associated with physician burnout," he noted, "an estimated 300 to 400 US physicians take their own lives every year"—a suicide rate dramatically higher than that of the general public, 40 percent higher for men and 130 percent higher for women.[27] A Dutch study found that female physicians experience more patient empathy and as a consequence, higher levels and deeper experiences of burnout—one hypothesis for the alarmingly high suicide rates.[28]

I spoke again with Ellison in October 2020 as his hospitals were fighting another Covid-19 surge and the California wildfires were ravaging around them. He described the pain his staff faced day in and day out: "I think that one of the challenges we'll face at some point is post-traumatic stress disorder after we get through the crisis, particularly physicians and staff who worked in the ICU and the Covid-19 cohort units. They're caring for patients and losing patients at a different rate than they did before, and young patients; that's just emotionally devastating because your job is to save lives and every life lost to tragedy is horrific. It's all around you, that grief and loss."

Ellison realized they were in a rapidly evolving situation with too many unknowns, so he made communication a top priority. "You can't communicate enough," he said. Ellison initiated daily town halls for all physicians to call in, which were mostly quick debriefs followed by a lengthy opportunity for Q&A. The Permanente Medical Group sent out daily emails with a cascade of offerings to every service group and unit managers. Ellison wanted to be visible, so he toured the different units and met with the staff in the ICU to see firsthand what they were dealing with. He said that every day was all about: "This is what we know. What are your questions? How can we answer your questions?"

Ellison is describing the practice of management by walking around, a fairly self-explanatory concept developed by management consultants Tom Peters and Robert H. Waterman in 1982. This leadership method has been widely embraced by the health-care industry for some time, particularly as private practices have been increasingly absorbed by larger consortiums and CEOs, not physicians, that run hospitals. As Ellison is both a medical doctor and a co-CEO of the Southern California Permanente Medical Group, he's indicative of a return to more physician-run versus executive-run hospital syndicates.

Peters and Waterman's analyses found that in successful companies, CEOs and managers spent much of their time in the field instead of being confined to their office. Peters and Waterman noticed these managers were more aware of the operations and, in general, had a better ability to solve problems.

The theory became popular when Hewlett Packard and Disney implemented this particular management style of deploying managers to work shifts alongside their staff.

By walking around, Ellison was able to hear stories of physicians, nurses, and health-care staff who were not going home, or they were going home and sleeping in the garage or had sent their children to live with grandparents. That deeper understanding of how his staff was being affected by the crisis created better supports.

There were additional peer-to-peer groups and second-victim groups that were bolstered, so that one hospital group, perhaps slightly less hard hit than another, could reach out to those in harder-hit hospitals with mental and emotional support. The Permanente Medical Group also put in place some benefits that provided separate housing and childcare services. Ellison said, "I just want to reduce the stigma and to say it's OK to ask for help—that it's healthy. And this is where the resources exist if you need them."

Some of those supports include therapists available for drop-in calls when needed. A portal with different resources and applications is available to help with mental health and addiction and access to spiritual care. The Permanente Medical Group is leveraging a burnout inventory and monitoring physicians over time to see what interventions are helpful. Ellison believes first and foremost that humanity and hope will be the answer to weathering a crisis, especially for the health-care industry and beyond in a post-Covid world. He said, "I think the idea of staying connected and listening is really important, and then how do we take what we're learning and do something with it? Because part [of] our job is to talk about hope for the future, and that hope has to be grounded in reality."

Ellison shared how the company started a campaign called #55WordsStories. It was to address the humanity and to hear from the people on the front lines and how they were feeling. There were a few that broke my heart, but this one really hit home:

> **A LOOK INTO THE EYES**
> Everyone is masked: me, RNs, EVS, even all the patients. All we can see are each other's eyes. Perhaps the eyes are the window to the soul? In them, I see pain, anguish, and fear. But I also see love, compassion, and hope. Be safe everyone.

But what happens when it all becomes just too much to bear?

When You Just Can't Leave

Corey Feist had already been an outspoken critic of the causes related to physician burnout, but it was his sister-in-law Lorna Breen's tragic suicide that would ultimately drive Corey and his wife, Jennifer Feist—Lorna's sister—to take on the topic of physician burnout in a substantial way. It became their mission to educate the health-care industry about the realities of burnout from the background to the foreground of their day-to-day lives.

Dr. Lorna Breen was the medical director of the emergency department at New York–Presbyterian Allen Hospital and an assistant professor at Columbia University. She was working on the front lines, deep into the first surge of a locked-down New York City as the virus ravaged her city. Breen had just recovered from Covid-19 herself when she returned to work, only three days after her fever subsided. The virus was new to the medical community; health-care staff were contracting the virus—about 20 percent of her colleagues were already infected at the time—and were much too quick to return to work. Now we know that even though you test negative for the virus, there is no way to know how long the illness can continue to exhaust your body and fog your mind.

Feist remembers how Lorna described the hospital as "Armageddon" on her first day back to work. When I spoke to him, only six months after his sister-in-law's death, he was still grief-stricken, as expected. He was also determined to ensure that her narrative and the impact of burnout on her life would be accurate. Within two days of a story about Lorna Breen in the *New York Times*, he and his wife, Jennifer, established the Dr. Lorna Breen Heroes Foundation as a means to control the narrative of Lorna's death.[29] Although Breen instinctively and naturally cared for her patients—which was most definitely imbedded in who she was—that would not be the sole reason she'd burned out. A combination of events and the broken culture in health care ultimately caused her death.

"The culture in medicine is that physicians don't ask for help, and they really don't receive help because there's an appearance of weakness," says Feist. Lorna would say she was overwhelmed, and yet she never felt like she could take a break because of fear of retribution and the impact on the colleague, so it's just . . . there's a lot of layers here to this."

Corey described how Lorna's burnout timeline was highly compressed. Only five months earlier, she'd published a journal article on how to mitigate burnout in the emergency room. Flash-forward to April 2020, and burnout would take her life.

The factors that played a role in her death, according to Feist, were multifold:

> First, Lorna contracted Covid-19 and became exhausted,
> depleted, and probably dealing with the brain fog and other
> contributors that we now know impacts people with the virus.
> Then she went back into the workforce way too fast because
> she'd been very sick. She was completely wiped out. And, on
> top of still being sick and exhausted, she would have to face
> this volume of death and dying that she'd never seen before,
> even though she had been a career physician in New York
> City. Add in feelings around not being able to contribute and

not being able to take care of your patients, because they were dying, and doctors are used to being trained to fix people and when they don't have those tools—it was all so overwhelming.

Only a few days after she was back at work, her family pulled her out and admitted her to the inpatient psychiatric unit at the University of Virginia. For a person who'd had no prior history of mental health issues or depression, this was jarring. Breen immediately assumed that her peers would observe her not being able to keep up, which she thought to be "a career killer." While undergoing care in Virginia, "she was convinced that her medical license in New York would be revoked and she would never be able to work again," Feist said.

Maureen O'Connor, contributing editor to *Vanity Fair* and author of the article "A Doctor's Emergency," wrote about Breen's story: "In her 49 years, Dr. Lorna Breen did everything that could have been expected of her. She was the kind of person you'd invent if you were trying to describe a platonically good person: a literally lifesaving, straight-A student who loved her family, ran marathons, and went to church. She played by the rules. She used education as a ladder. She knew that doing everything means risking burnout and took action to avoid that too—in the final years of her life, Breen studied burnout. And she still burned out."[30]

Feist believes that the feeling of professional failure and the perception by colleagues and the overlaying impact of it on a doctor's license all contribute to those in the medical field not getting help and reinforce suffering in silence. He said, "I cannot tell you how many physicians have told me about when they were on the brink of—whatever, fill in the blank—maybe not necessarily suicide, but some kind of a mental break, and they'll say, 'Hey, if you look at my CV, you see a gap here and it says that I did a fellowship somewhere but really, I just couldn't share that I had to take time away because I was having, or about to have, a breakdown.' So, I think that there's a pattern here. And now, obviously, this is magnified across the country."

Ellison says that even before the pandemic, those in health care were expected by others—and expected of themselves—to be superhuman.

He said, "But they're human and we need to let them be human. I think that's the key to all of this. That's the dichotomy that we have to address."

Ellison shared that this is why we need to train for a philosophy of self-care, and that asking for help is OK, at the onset of a physician's training. The year 2020 was the opening of the Kaiser Permanente Bernard J. Tyson School of Medicine, hosting its first class of fifty students. Baked into the curriculum is a four-year *required* course named REACH. The letters stand for reflection, education, assessment, coaching, and health and wellness. REACH was created as a way to build wellness into the curriculum; it is intended to provide students with space for reflection of experiences and learnings. It includes education in positive psychology.

This course, which occurs for a full week every six weeks during the academic year, includes the following:

- Each student has a physician REACH coach (formally trained as a coach) who will help students identify goals and strategies to meet their goals.

- Students are offered free individual counseling. They are required to engage in at least three sessions. The school has an on-site clinical psychologist as well as a health and wellness director who does special programs for students.

- Since the school has an integrated curriculum, professors try to reinforce and connect concepts in several places within the curriculum. For example, students study nutrition in an integrated science course as well as in REACH and also in health promotion. All these courses are required. The school is in the process of developing third- and fourth-year electives that likely will offer deeper levels of complexity on these topics.

"We want to break that cycle of a hundred years of medical education in which mental health was not talked about or emphasized," said Ellison. "We want to make sure that we begin to train new generations of physicians who can now not only take great care of their patients but understand the importance of taking care of themselves to do that."

Lessons on Burnout

In 2018, there were 84.3 million teachers in the world, yet in various surveys and studies, a significant number of teachers are considering leaving the profession. The *Economic Policy Report* in 2019 claimed that barring any major changes, the annual teacher shortage would reach about 110,000 by the 2017–2018 school year.[31]

Not only is it challenging for students when teachers leave the profession, but schools lose between $1 billion and $2.2 billion in attrition costs yearly from teachers switching schools or leaving the profession altogether.[32] Although it appears that recruitment numbers for this sector have increased, employers (predominantly the government) suffer from retention issues.

The data shows that over the next five years, almost half of those teachers will either transfer to a new school or give up teaching completely. The teacher shortage is such a massive global employment issue that UNESCO claims the world must recruit 69 million new teachers to reach 2030 education goals. Although there are many complex issues related to the teacher shortage, one of the most cited reasons in the OECD countries is the lack of ability to recruit young people to the profession and the burnout of current teachers. In developing countries, teacher status and lack of training are the most highly cited reasons for attrition.[33]

Supporting teacher welfare is a critical issue for me. Not only is burnout extremely high in this profession, but the number of teachers experiencing burnout hit an all-time high as a result of the pandemic. At the height of the virus, while a majority of schools in the United States were engaged in remote learning, an extensive survey of K–12 teachers found that that they feel "somewhat" or "extremely" uncertain (81 percent), stressed (77 percent), anxious (75 percent), overwhelmed (74 percent), sad (60 percent), and lonely (54 percent).[34]

Mary, an English-as-a-second-language teacher based in Canada, was dealing with a challenging year. She had a student with special needs in her class—not unusual for her—but given this particular student's age and the increase in needs in the school and the lack of human resources, it became extremely draining. Mary said, "I had little help from special education and little support from my principal. There were many days that forty-five minutes would go by as I tried to deescalate the child's behavior and had really no idea what the rest of my class was doing during that time (even though I was in the room)."

Mary struggled to balance the needs of the other students and constantly felt as if she was letting everyone down. Even the parent of the special needs student blamed Mary for her child's behavior. Mary said, "I was verbally attacked on a daily basis by the student and regularly by the parent as well."

It isn't unusual to hear stories like Mary's. When we don't have the right ingredients for a healthy culture, we see these kinds of mental breaks. What happens is that Mary becomes a single complainant, othered, bucketized, an anomaly.

But this is inaccurate. Among educators, burnout is becoming more prevalent. With the increase in students with special needs matched with a reduction in support for teachers, their workload has reached epic proportions.

Systems are breaking, and therefore the culture is failing Mary, not the other way around. Here, burnout is caused by the workplace, not the employee. And, when it comes to pay—a root cause of burnout—teachers are not in a good place.

Under most countries' labor standards, teachers are considered non-exempt salary employees, meaning they cannot earn overtime. But that doesn't mean they aren't working more than forty hours a week. The US Bureau of Labor Statistics conducted a recent study that found that teachers are more likely to put in work over the weekend—roughly 1,900 hours a year—than the average American.[35]

One report found that teachers earn 18.7 percent less than other college-educated professionals, which forces at least one in five teachers to also hold down a part-time job.[36]

The story of Hope Brown made headlines when it appeared in *Time* magazine in 2018. It shone a light on the pay disparities teachers face in the United States. Entitled "'I Work 3 Jobs and Donate Blood Plasma to Pay the Bills.' This Is What It's Like to Be a Teacher in America," the article says, "Hope Brown can make $60 donating plasma from her blood cells twice in one week, and a little more if she sells some of her clothes at a consignment store. It's usually just enough to cover an electric bill or a car payment. This financial juggling is now a part of her everyday life—something she never expected almost two decades ago when she earned a master's degree in secondary education and became a high school history teacher."[37]

A 2017 report by the Economic Policy Institute shows that education and health industry workers are the third most likely group to experience a minimum wage theft violation, in which their employers paid for fewer than the number of hours worked or didn't pay for overtime (behind only retail and food and drink service industry workers).[38] According to the National Education Association, "Teachers spend an average of 50 hours per week on instructional duties, including an average of 12 hours each week on non-compensated school-related activities such as grading papers, bus duty, and club advising."[39]

Because of my time spent researching and working with professionals in education, I've had the opportunity to learn, firsthand, the experience of teachers in the classroom. I had a healthy respect for their work before starting the research. But that respect turned into awe as I witnessed the workload and the above-and-beyond culture that permeates every single classroom.

When classrooms suddenly went virtual, teacher burnout was rampant. It was like expecting a front-end designer to suddenly start writing back-end code, a doctor to become a nurse, or a nonfiction writer to begin writing fiction. It all seems as if it's similar enough, right? There shouldn't be a real leap, but ask any teacher and they will attest that teaching virtually is nothing like teaching in person.

"I started feeling burned out around November of that school year," said one Canadian teacher we'll call Anne to protect her anonymity and her employment. "I kept pushing through, using alcohol to help cope. I drank more than I usually would (that is, on work nights versus weekends only). I told myself it was 'just to take the edge off.' I thought it would get better, but combined with family issues—a son that is on the autism spectrum—it increased tenfold."

Anne went on, "I continued to work and push through. I hit a bump in February after some major blowups from the student and parent, with my son who was in the ER several times. I took three days off in a row (very uncommon for me). I needed to reset and start fresh. By March I needed permission to take a break. I was exhausted, not sleeping, not taking care of myself, and drinking too much to cope. I ended up taking a medical leave. I needed to feel like I wasn't letting anyone down, that I had tried my best. I didn't want to feel like I failed the students, my colleagues, my family, and myself."

Anne felt reset after taking a two-month break, but that didn't last long. She said, "HR was questioning my leave and whether or not it was legitimate. Even with a doctor's note. Going back to work after two months brought on a lot of anxiety again, but I finished the year. In retrospect, I shouldn't have gone back until the following year."

Once again, systems are failing people—not the other way around. These are unresolved problems rooted in antiquated thinking.

Anne said that over her seventeen years in the profession, she's witnessed an increase in burnout in education. She shared that during Covid-19, the number of hours spent online with students or receiving emails from students and parents at all hours of the day and night was exhausting. Some teachers were really good at setting "office hours," but others (like her) had difficulty setting those boundaries, which in turn, she believes, contributed to her burnout. "What is being asked of us is beyond reasonable at times. Dealing with mental illness and behavior challenges is difficult as we are not trained or supported enough. The demands on teachers are quite high. While I know we have plenty of breaks and time off, the time we are at work is very high stress."

Anne also described the physical impacts of her burnout: "I was constantly nauseous, not sleeping, making terrible food choices, and drinking too much alcohol; I had headaches. My weight would fluctuate too for no reason, gain a few pounds, lose seven pounds, then repeat."

The shame may have been the hardest part for Anne. It keeps coming up from the many people I've spoken to about their burnout: "I felt ashamed of it. I was ashamed for taking time off. I felt like a failure, to be honest, but I needed it. I know that now. And I knew it once I was home for a few weeks. It's so awful that I felt that way. We shouldn't feel the pressure to do it all, but I did and still do."

Preventing Burnout in Education Using Small Data: A Case Study

Before I begin this case study, I want to reinforce that although the example here is centered around the education system, we've tested these interventions in multiple industries outside of education with similar results.

The main goal was to understand how purpose in our work promotes a healthier outlook at work, and that spills over into performance. The interventions were focused on promoting well-being and targeting hygiene issues that came up in the data.

The project began with a single intervention focused on one psychological trait for three weeks. And, in line with the most enlightening research projects, we started by analyzing kids.

We asked students in grades four through eight to share, through words, art, or in whatever ways the teacher believed would be most engaging, "What made you smile today?" We prompted the students with this question for twenty-one days to see what would happen. The students completed pre- and post-surveys to determine the impact.

In comparison to before the program, after just three weeks, the students experienced the following:

- Overall appreciation of school increased by 20 percent.

- They were 11 percent happier and 10 percent more grateful.

- They were 8 percent more engaged in their schoolwork (liked school, interested in schoolwork, paid attention in class).

- They were 7 percent more socially engaged (felt like they had more friends, felt more connected to others).

- This was the most exciting data point—after only twenty-one days, they were able to identify twice as many things they were grateful for in the same amount of time, demonstrating a major increase in gratitude fluency. From a neuroscience point of view—in simplified terms—this means that they were essentially wiring cognitive gratitude into their developing brains.

What is so special about this research and the preceding analyses that occurred across 8,000 staff serving 63,000 students throughout 120 schools was in the small data. It wasn't just that kids were happier in the school; it was the conversations that those daily interactions ignited. Teachers found out little things about what made the students happy and excited. These moments each day also told the teachers a story of struggle at home. It gave them insight into the students' emotional IQs and where the teachers could draw a spark.

Teachers and staff shared story after story of children who'd written or drawn their superhero figurines, their trampoline, their family, or their family pets as part of the exercise. As the weeks went on, the children got more specific, with stories of migrant parents who'd brought them to Canada for a better life, or how the trampoline was a way to let out frustrations when tensions got high in the house, or that the dog was more than just a family pet but a therapy dog for her brother. And the superhero figurine? Well, it had special powers that kept one child feeling safe during chemo and radiation.

Most classrooms in the research project kept a "gratitude wall" all year—for kids to get up anytime and share what had made them smile that day or that week. We toured one school where, on their gratitude wall, was a child's note that was both heartbreaking and encouraging: "I'm grateful that my mom got out of jail this week."

At the time, the teacher had no idea what this child was going through. But this small piece of data now explained some of the student's behavioral problems. It also increased compassion and patience as the child worked through their issues in the classroom. This same school once had lines out the door of the principal's office. After two years of interventions focused on empathetic listening and developing emotional intelligence in staff and students, the principal had free time, time that translated into helping "fail to fills"—classrooms that were missing teachers because resources were unavailable. Spending time listening to the small data allowed him to resource his staff and enjoy his role again. He used to be a phys ed teacher, so getting to run the gym was his favorite part of the day.

Finally, violence in the playground had decreased by over 80 percent. Kids were working through their issues in nonviolent ways. Everything was changing for the better.

There were so many lessons these stories offered about how to drive a healthy, happy, and high-performing culture for both teachers and students. Enhance staff well-being, enhance student well-being. Enhance student well-being, enhance staff well-being. The virtuous circle.

To better understand this phenomenon in the education industry overall, we assembled a team of researchers, consultants, and subjects to determine how to prevent burnout, while improving well-being in all staff. Would the same interventions hold true for school board CFOs and the executive team? What about accounting or IT? We needed to find out. Most importantly, we hypothesized that if all systems were working more efficiently—particularly at the corporate level—it would spill over into teacher well-being.

Long before the pandemic hit, teacher burnout was a massive problem. When we started our research in 2012, we had no idea what was on the horizon. Flash-forward to 2020 and burnout followed the trajectory of Covid-19 and has arguably become an epidemic in many countries globally. At this rate, it should be on track to hit pandemic status in no time.

Yet, pre-pandemic, our goal was to take some of these early learnings about well-being in the field of education and see if we could apply them across other industries and sectors. But first, we needed to see how the hypotheses translated into various roles, teams, departments, and stakeholders that fit within a school ecosystem.

We started with a team that consisted of scientists from different areas of focus: David Whiteside, organizational behavior; Vanessa Buote, social psychology; and Rodrigo Araujo, mathematics and machine learning (data scientist).

To identify the causes of burnout and the interventions that would most likely increase social well-being in staff, students, *and* parents, we initiated a multiyear research project that culminated in the paper "An Ecosystem Approach to Staff Well-being in the Education Sector: A Case Study" that was presented at the 2019 World Government Summit in Dubai and appeared in the *Global Happiness Policy Report* by the Global Happiness Council, led by world-renowned economist Jeffrey Sachs.[40]

Before any interventions took place, we gathered baseline measures. Surveys gathered data on engagement, sense of community, inspiration, satisfaction, predicted satisfaction, culture, trust, recognition, communication, upward feedback, stress, well-being, hope, efficacy, resilience, optimism, gratitude, performance, citizenship behaviors, and net promoter scores. Data provided key insight on the areas for improvement, most notably communication, recognition, and upward feedback—or key drivers of culture.

Within a school board environment, where staff are decentralized, widely dispersed across hundreds of locations, and fill a wide range of roles and responsibilities, we determined that we would develop benchmarking tools to identify "at risk," "average," and "healthy" scores for each survey response.

After we saw the first round of data, we swiftly engaged training and programming to address these areas for improvement. Budgets and resources directed at well-being were increased 300 percent, with a commitment to ongoing data collection at both the department and school levels.

Over four years, interventions varied in size and intensification across 125 schools and eight support departments. Schools identified groups across three cities; the Education Center (board office), broken out by departments (e.g., HR, finance, executive, IT); and parents, also considered a distinct group.

The team began with a goal to educate the senior leadership about the benefits of seven social-emotional skills that have been empirically

shown to increase happiness and performance: hope, efficacy, resilience, optimism, gratitude, empathy, and mindfulness. The goal was
to incorporate these seven traits as the new values framework for well-
being across all staff, then to expand to students, and eventually outward to parents and the broader community.

The interventions began methodically with an aim to create a shared
language with the seven traits at the core of all interventions. Education consisted of one-hour talks at annual events, full-day training and
workshops at regional and provincial conferences, and speaking with
staff during mandatory professional development days. After one year
of pure education at the leadership level, phase two began.

This is when the "ecosystem theory" was engaged. Teachers and all
staff, including custodial, part-time, early childhood educators, leadership and administrative, plus students and parents were invited to employ the seven traits into routine practice in school, at work, and at home.
The goal was focused on improving workplace culture among staff to
subsequently improve conditions for learning for students. Schools were
provided an exploratory framework for staff and students to utilize.

Interventions for students and staff based in schools included:

- Student and staff cocreated mantras to read aloud daily.

- Mindfulness exercises were held in class and before staff
  meetings.

- Curated music played as students were entering the classrooms at
  the start and leaving at the end of the day.

- There were monthly, student-led, public assemblies (community
  was invited to attend).

- Priming, which occurs when exposure to one thing can later alter
  behavior or thoughts, was created using gratitude walls, hope
  trees, trait-focused art, mantras at all entrances of the school, and
  posters with three intervention examples related to each trait,
  written in multiple languages located in staff lunchrooms and in
  all staff and student school bathrooms.

- Online employee portals were cocreated with staff, education consultants, and consulting firm Plasticity Labs internal teams for digital collaboration and curriculum guidance. None of the framework was programmatic; it was tool and resource agnostic and showed up differently in each group or school.

- Most notably, staff would get three hours every month of paid time off for professional development in positive psychology.

- Each school identified two leaders who would both gather monthly to learn, ideate plans, and then return to their individual schools and train other staff.

The research and consulting team worked with departments to understand their daily experiences and personas and target specific programming: custodial staff, finance, marketing, HR, union groups, and parent councils.

Interventions for corporate staff in education included:

- Using empathy in communication

- Building resiliency for frontline staff

- Creating a well-being portal; programming resources were propped up with an exponential budget increase

- Improving physical health

- Focusing on diversity and inclusion. One example (among others) was the raising of Pride flags at all 125 schools during Pride Month, with supporting conversations of empathy and inclusion related to the LGBTQ+ community. There was a significant increase in diversity and inclusion work or learning performed in schools and in corporate offices throughout the project and after the project was complete.

Researchers from Plasticity Labs, Wilfrid Laurier University, and the Waterloo Region District School Board worked together to measure three times throughout the year to identify outcomes. Phase three expanded the research to control schools; these insights were cross-referenced with the entire school board's data, and a full report was developed to capture the outcomes from phase zero data gathering, phase one piloting, and phase two expansion.

We drew some major takeaways from the learning. One was the "proximity to purpose," defined by Whiteside in his paper, which argues the pros and cons of engagement and refers to it as an incomplete measure when it comes to the mission-driven workforce.

Notably in this group, engagement scores were high across almost all subjects. Purpose-driven people remain engaged, despite being at risk of burnout. It is still valuable to track engagement, but I believe we need other measures to establish whether engagement is high and passion is harmonious or engagement is high and passion is obsessive.

This critical data came out of this multiyear research, ethics, and peer-reviewed research project. It validated a gut feeling that many of us working in the practice of improving organizational culture had been feeling for years.

We also found that the real driver of well-being is the school's culture: trust, community (peer relationships) recognition, communication, and feedback. If we consider again the root causes of burnout, we can mitigate the risk if we invest in culture and the list of well-being drivers cited earlier.

Harmonious passion, however, is a major driver of well-being. As patients are to those in health-care roles, students drive purpose for staff in education.

From the research, we learned that the groups at the education center that were furthest from students (IT, finance, etc.) did not have strong engagement and well-being scores, despite stating nearly identical problems with their workplace culture. Because their "proximity to purpose" is significantly lower, it pales in comparison to the engagement and happiness levels of teaching and teaching staff in schools.

And, in the control schools, where staff were not able to engage in any of the interventions, the scores were, on average, fourteen points lower on recognition, communication, and feedback. Whiteside claimed that through teaching the importance of traits such as gratitude, empathy, and optimism to students, there is a boomerang effect where staff are cultivating the strengths required to foster and build strong cultures at the same time.

Nicholas Christakis and James Fowler's work on the social contagion of happiness provides evidence of this. Christakis, a physician and medical sociologist, and political scientist James H. Fowler coauthored a study that examined the relationships of nearly five thousand people who were tracked for decades as part of the landmark Framingham Heart Study.

Cool fact: happiness spreads like a contagious disease. They found that happiness (well-being) moves readily through social networks of family members, friends, and neighbors. Knowing someone who is happy makes you 15.3 percent more likely to be happy yourself, the study found. A happy friend who lives within a half mile makes you 42 percent more likely to be happy. Yet, if that same friend lives two miles away, their impact drops to 22 percent. Next-door neighbors who are happy make you 34 percent more likely to be happy too, but no other neighbors have an effect, even if they live on the same block.[41]

This isn't the first evidence showing that emotions can spread like a virus. Studies have found that waiters who offer service with a smile are rewarded with bigger tips. On the flip side, mental health can also spread like a virus when it comes to depression, loneliness, anxiety, and suicide. One research study analyzed college freshmen and found that having a mildly depressed roommate increased depression in those also residing in the same room.[42]

This research also points to why in-person teaching may be a better option for some students over others, particularly as homeschooling and virtual learning proved to be challenging during lockdown for both teachers and students alike.

The most critical takeaway from the research is that when we invest in a common shared language that supports trusted relationships, then we can bridge the divide between the multiple stakeholders that education professionals have to juggle. Perhaps, a bit more uncondi-tional support from her employers to increase trust and less siloed rela-tionships could be just what Anne needed to avert burnout.

Although the education and health-care industries are at the head of the pack when it comes to burnout, tech companies are battling for the baton.

Burnout in the Tech Industry

We see workload creep occur because of the always-connected culture and the life on-site "perks" these companies offer, but it's what these practices emphasize that really tell the tale. To be successful in tech, you need to remain available at all hours and try not to go home. As the oft-admired Elon Musk famously tweeted, "There are way easier places to work, but nobody ever changed the world on 40 hours a week."

What may have been even more alarming is the subsequent thread that resulted from Musk's tweet.

> @margrethmpossi
> Replying to @elonmusk
> What's the correct number of hours a week to change the world?

> Elon Musk
> @elonmusk
> Varies per person, but about 80 sustained, peaking above 100 at times. Pain level increases exponentially above 80.

This is a problem. Gallup analytics show that occupational burnout risk increases significantly when employees exceed an average of fifty hours per week and escalates even more substantially at sixty hours per week.

Meanwhile, back in Silicon Valley, employees at Uber shared that working until 2:00 a.m. was typical. A *New York Times* article about

Amazon described "marathon conference calls on Easter Sunday and Thanksgiving, criticism from bosses for spotty Internet access on vacation, and hours spent working at home most nights or weekends, as well as employees being given low-performance ratings directly after cancer treatment, major surgeries, or giving birth to a stillborn child."[43]

The tech industry is now facing the aftershocks of the global pandemic and will feel that for years to come. The year 2020 was a tipping point for 226 Google employees. On January 4, 2021, for the first time in big tech, employees formed a union. This small group of employees signed union cards with the Communications Workers of America, one of the country's largest labor unions.

A *New York Times* op-ed claimed that the formation started as a result of increasing tensions surrounding Google's "business and operational decisions." The departure of Timnit Gebru has added momentum to the union's formation. Gebru is a world-renowned ethics researcher who highlighted the risks of large language models, which are key to Google's business. This sparked a massive but important debate that would inevitably force Gebru to exit the company. It also questioned the lack of diversity in tech productization and whether the voices behind these innovations were being quieted.[44]

This is not an issue that just lives in one company. Unfortunately, lack of diversity throughout the entire global workforce is a long-standing and pervasive issue and disproportionately impacts the burnout of all vulnerable groups. However, the tech industry is particularly lopsided when it comes to gender diversity in leadership.

In my article for the Society of Human Resource Management, "Disrupting the Tech Profession's Gender Gap," I wrote that women make up over half the US workforce, but in the male-dominated tech industry, they hold a disproportionate 26 percent of computing roles—a number that has been steadily declining for years, according to the National Center for Women & Information Technology. Women represent a minority of the workforces at the top-eleven US tech giants, making up an average of roughly 16 percent of the technical roles at those companies. Their rate of turnover is double that of men, and 56 percent of women in tech leave their employers midcareer, according to the National Council of Women in Technology.[45]

Despite fewer than 8 percent of women owning tech-related patents, when women develop products and lead their companies, those organizations not only hire more women and increase diversity but also perform three times better than those with male CEOs, according to Quantopian, an investment platform. More-diverse companies also have 22 percent lower turnover.

Yet, "you can't be what you can't see," said Dorothy Hisgrove, former partner and chief people officer at consultancy PwC in Australia. In our interview, she shared that when women leave tech, they often are not opting out for family reasons. "Data shows us that many of those women go on to start their own businesses. That's why PwC is focusing on the bigger issue of retention by ensuring equity in access to leadership development opportunities, transparency in performance outcomes, and particularly promotion opportunities," Hisgrove said.

When an individual can't see themselves modeled at the leadership level, their sense of value diminishes. The tech industry is already pushing unsustainable hours and celebrating that women can freeze their eggs to prevent missing out on advancement opportunities—aka, keep working unsustainable hours—yet, there is only an 11 percent chance that a woman will make it into a senior position in this industry.

This is tragic. A real prevention strategy here would be to swap out egg freezing and make paid family leave a priority. Some of you may be asking, How could parental leave be considered a perk? Isn't it mandatory?

A 2019 report by UNICEF analyzed which of the world's richest countries are most family friendly. The report, which used data from the forty-one countries in the Organisation for Economic Co-operation and Development and the European Union, found that only half offered mothers a minimum of six months' full pay. And the United States was the only one *without* national statutory paid maternity, paternity, or parental leave. So, then it becomes a perk, which, simply stated, is not good. Suggesting that parental leave is the norm throughout the world would be untrue. In the cases where leave is protected, mothers get time to bond with their babies, but fathers do not. If they do, again in most cases, this is a perk.

Alan May, executive vice president and chief people officer for Hewlett Packard Enterprise (HPE), is attempting to lead the charge here. He implemented a fully paid, six-month leave for all men and women to either have children or adopt children. Although it isn't as big a deal in some countries, May hopes it will eventually become the status quo in the United States, not just because a company is progressive, but because it's the right thing to do. To expand the policy, HPE added three years to return on a part-time basis (for both men and women) with full job security. For May, it was critical to target the opportunity to both males and females. He told me, "The well-known medical and psychological evidence around the nurturing of young people in the first year or two of their lives makes this policy essential for all groups."

When it comes to preventing burnout for women in tech, we need to make our culture inclusive. By encouraging both mothers and fathers to take a paid family leave, we reduce the stigma for any woman who's felt that taking time off to have a child means a lack of ambition. It also reduces the stigma for men who are interested in being the primary caregiver.

Isaura Gaeta, vice president of security research at Intel, echoes the importance of role modeling and mentorship. During our discussion, she asserted that the industry suffers from an "institutional bias" because engineering systems have been set up in a very gendered way: "At Intel, there are two career ladders. One is the managerial ladder that leads all the way up to vice president, and the other is the technical ladder. The most senior role on the technical ladder is called the Intel Fellow—you can tell just by the name that it's gendered. So we have to address the issue of how to start removing the assignment of what a technical leader looks like to be more inclusive of all behaviors."

Jill Larsen, executive vice president and chief people officer at Medidata Solutions, believes that the key to retention lies in a strong culture of learning and pursuing stretch goals. Larsen said the company provides support and guidance as needed to those in the stretch assignments "and we make their successes in these roles visible to highlight their achievements."

On top of modeling and mentoring, women need peer supports to prevent burnout in the tech industry. Gaeta credits informal and formal networking for keeping her in tech after a lonely and challenging first decade of her career. It wasn't until she found female allies in her field that she finally felt like she belonged and that her voice was being heard.

Not all leaders in tech, however, feel the same way as Elon Musk. In an interview with podcast host Rich Kleiman, cofounder of Thirty-Five Ventures, Jack Dorsey, founder and CEO of Twitter and Square, was asked whether young startup founders need to be worried about burning themselves out. Dorsey answered definitively: "100 percent."

He also shared that Musk's suggestion that twenty hours on with a four-hour sleep schedule is "bullshit" and limits personal growth. Dorsey said, "Working nonstop can take options off the table—you're so determined to work hard that you don't notice opportunities coming your way."[46]

We need more leaders in all industries to push back on the glamorization of sixty-hour workweeks. This cavalier attitude toward burnout is dangerous. It's time for the cult of overwork as a sign of high performance to end.

We Actually *Can't* Do It All

In an article I wrote for *Harvard Business Review*, "When Passion Leads to Burnout," I questioned the old adage that if you do what you love, you'll never work a day in your life.[47] I concluded that it's a nice idea but a total myth. I am highly aware of how easy it is for me to be a walking irony. As a person writing a book about burnout during a pandemic, I must admit there were a few times I worried about my personal risk for burnout.

As I previously mentioned, one of the biggest hurdles for me is stepping outside myself and becoming my boss. When you're deep into a project, you can lose that self-awareness and that means using tools and reminders to pull you away from the work. When you love what you do, you may not clearly see the line between overworking and just loving the work. According to a study published in the *Journal of Personality*, this type of labor can breed obsessive—versus harmonious—passion, which predicts an increase of conflict and thus burnout.[48]

We want to be able to find that harmonious passion and instill that in every organizational culture, because purpose and passion are highly correlated to workplace happiness and increased employee well-being. Although there is a risk for burnout, it is imperative that we don't try to quash the joy we feel when we engage in purpose-driven work.

We need to become aware of who is most at risk for burnout and nurture that balance between loving what we do and becoming obsessed with work.

I really don't like getting asked, "How do you do it all?" Not only is it extremely sexist, because the question is almost always directed at women, but I dislike having to answer it honestly. Truthfully? I'm not doing it all. Most of us aren't. The majority of us are in triage mode far too often, using criteria like "Who or what is bleeding the most?" to decide what we're going to attend to first. Not sustainable in the least.

Whether or not we deal with perfectionist concerns, we are all at risk from overwork. In all cases of workload, we need to ask ourselves, has my workload become unsustainable solely for reasons out of my control or do I also play a role? Ask yourself:

- Do I continue to raise my hand even though I know I should focus on accomplishing my current workload?

- Do I communicate to others when it feels like it's too much?

- Do I delegate well?

- Have I identified what gives me energy and what drains me?

- Do I manage my distractions?

- Do I have outside interests or do I give my life to work?

- Do I have a close friend at work who I can lean on for support?

If you find yourself acknowledging that you engage in a few of the less-healthy actions, you're likely realizing the role you play in increasing your own workload. Watch yourself for a few days to see when and where these actions and behaviors show up, the first step in better managing them.

1. *Check your fear of missing out.* Review your schedule for the next few weeks. How many of those obligations are work-related and which ones are work-expected? It may feel like we need to be seen at a networking event or to join a community board, but if we are dealing with consistently challenging workloads, something has to give. To be frank, this was me. I felt pressure to "show up" for my community, so I took on every request. Looking back, I should have picked one or two commitments with high fidelity instead of giving only 50 percent of my capacity to everyone who asked.

2. *Protect your time.* Make sure that you are doing more of what you're good at and less of the stuff that drains you. If you're burned out from Zoom, take a call and make it half the time. If you're exhausted from digital interruptions, turn on your out-of-office message and give yourself protected time. If you need more creative time, block off space in your day to accomplish it. You'll find flow and less stress and subsequently decrease the risk of burnout.

3. *Find a friend.* Discover people to lean on, both at work and at home. We need healthy relationships for a healthier, higher-performing life both personally and professionally. We also need to ensure there is a significant investment in those relationships to help them flourish. You can't give them the time they need to develop and grow if you are only at work.

Friends at work are also important; we discussed their value in the last chapter, but we also need peers we can trust who will help when we ask. We need reciprocal relationships at work that are fostered through teamwork and trust. Having the psychological safety to know that if you're in a crunch, you can lean on your coworker helps mitigate stress and burnout.

Although I've highlighted only a few sectors at risk for burnout, this does not mean other roles and industries are exempt. To the contrary. Even burnout experts can suffer from burnout. Every role takes on different shapes at different times. It will be our self-knowledge, self-awareness, and self-compassion that will hold the key to prevention.

Perhaps most importantly, battling burnout requires teamwork. It requires partnerships between organizations and their people. Partnerships among peers. And a partnership internally where good intentions are met with authentic action. We need to notice the roles we play and the moments they get too big for us to handle. We need others to look out for us and protect us from the worst. When all of that fails, it's now a life-and-death situation.

When I said goodbye to Corey Feist on our call, I told him how sorry I was for his loss. He shared with me that his grief is still fresh, but he always has hope. He has to have hope. His work has garnered the attention of 60 million people and growing, so that gives rise to hope. He said, "We need to start taking care of each other. And that means recognizing the culture has to change. We can't change it for them. I can work to try to change every law in every state and I can help in any supportive way, but I cannot do it alone, and it's not appropriate for me to do."

As we're crowdsourcing culture, we need an individual desire, but it's the contagion piece—the collective will—that generates an impact. It's a hard thing to do. It takes a lot of time and a ton of tiny movements that spiral outward until it catches. But when it does, the effect is powerful.

PART TWO

Strategies

3

Good Intentions Gone Bad

Sometimes we don't do a great job at reading the room. It isn't for a lack of compassion or a real desire to impact our teams and our company in a positive way. It really comes down to authentic empathy. The Golden Rule 2.0 can be applied here. Don't just do unto others as you would have done unto you. Do unto others as they would have done unto *themselves*.

From a new policy to a calming speech during a time of crisis to a single tweet—the way we decide strategy, inform a new program, or communicate to our teams must always keep the receiver's interpretation of that message in mind. We can have the best intentions, but if they're not infused with empathetic leadership, then they will miss the mark. Or worse, make a small, exclusive group happy, while the rest of our employees feel left behind.

Cultures Gone Wild

Early in my career, I worked briefly at a company that was known for its amazing culture—part of its brand. It sold the culture in its recruiting, during the interviews, in the awards hung on its walls. The office itself was stunning—picture perfect—ready for the "best places to work" photo shoot.

But upon a closer look, you saw that the awards were decades old, achieved under different leadership; you learned that beauty is only skin-deep and that culture can feel like a washed-up prom king.

I'd been observing this fall-from-grace sentiment in the staff for a while. Many had enjoyed the heyday and now felt adrift. One senior leader said, "We have peaks and valleys here. It'll come back." It was good to hear from a tenured person that this was normal; it gave me hope. But, a year later, the culture hadn't improved; it was so much worse.

The company had made a series of hires that were out of its comfort zone, but most didn't last long. Its aspirational culture was not the reality that new employees walked into, and fit became a major issue. People would onboard, but like scratchy clothing you just can't wait to take off, they felt too uncomfortable staying. And in truth, the executive team was happy to see them go.

One day, near the end of my tenure there, I walked past the games room, and I stopped. I'd repeated this action many times, but today it was as if I noticed the room for the first time. It was all glass, so you could be witness to how much fun everyone was having and be prompted to join in. There were plenty of things you could do—there was a Ping-Pong table and a pool table, a couch and chairs for reading or hanging out, and an assortment of worn-out board games stacked slightly askew as if they'd been loved just a bit too much.

This moment symbolized everything that was wrong about the culture. As I approached the glass, I could see that the pool table was dusty. The cues were missing. The Ping-Pong table was pushed against the wall, buried behind a graveyard of abandoned and broken chairs. The games were old and outdated. And I'd only witnessed that room used as it was intended twice in two years.

People never went in there because they never had any time to use it. Workloads were so insane that even thinking about playing a game seemed out of the question. The room became a symbol for me that the company's aspirations didn't match its reality. It screamed at me as I walked by, "We lied!"

Bad cultures are like dusty pool tables. When they are inauthentic, they fail.

It's OK if you are not a Ping-Pong-playing company. You're better off being honest with your hires, your staff, and your brand. Plenty of companies that have terrific cultures don't include a games room. They have great cultures because they have trust. They are what they said they would be; that is critical to establishing trust right from the onset. It means practicing radical honesty, even if looking inward is the toughest thing they've done as a company.

The way we build cultures free from games-room-turned-graveyards is to establish what we want to be. When we fully understand that, then we will find the people who fit those core beliefs. Aspirational cultures are only good if they are real. If not, they turn into promises undelivered.

When we are authentic about our values, we stop wasting money on a fake culture. Rather, we finance what really matters. Gone are the pool tables and expensive decor; in with the resources to help manage workload. Again, good intentions are not prevention. The following are some of the good intentions gone awry that can end up being of less benefit and more burnout if they aren't underscored with good cultural hygiene.

Perks and Benefits

I've had conversations with several employees who've worked for decades in companies that promote perks like a badge of honor. Perks aren't always the golden ticket to well-being, and they don't prevent burnout.

A former Silicon Valley–based employee of a large global enterprise anonymously shared that it was time to leave the program manager role after eight years because the cons had outweighed the pros. He loved the free food, free 24/7 gym access, free (self-service) laundry, the bowling alley and volleyball pit, and the custom-built and exclusive, employees-only outdoor sport park. He also liked the pay. But, in the end, he felt that "the perks don't outweigh the burnout rate. All those perks and benefits are an illusion. They keep you at work and they help you to be more productive. I've never met anybody who actually took time off on weekends or on vacations." He described a challenging environment where marriages are "falling apart" and the norm is "colleagues choosing work and projects over family, colleagues getting physically sick and ill because of stress, colleagues crying while at work because of the stress, colleagues shooting out emails at midnight."

Technology companies are notorious for innovating massively disruptive products and services and being first to the market with nearly everything we use in our day-to-day lives. To acquire and compete for talent, they've had to become extremely aggressive, which includes perks that can sometimes feel over the top.

On-site perks don't work because they just keep employees away from their personal lives. Although having a meal made for you can feel like a luxury, it stops being valuable if you rarely get to enjoy it with family and friends outside of work. Preparing food and eating with loved ones are critical to our health and longevity, improving our overall diet and longevity.[1]

Before the pandemic, the amount of money the average American spent on eating out surpassed what US consumers spent on food at home. Pre-Covid-19, the average American ate roughly 4.5 restaurant or takeout meals every week.[2] But studies suggest cooking at home is healthier for us. One study looked at the cooking habits of men and women in Taiwan and Australia and found that cooking at home up to five times per week increased the odds of being alive in ten years by 47 percent.[3] And, since healthy relationships also correlate to higher levels of happiness and increased longevity, eating at home can provide that time to come together.

One study claims that dinner with your kids at least four days a week can increase their vocabulary by a thousand new words, and regular mealtime is an even more powerful predictor of high achievement scores than time spent in school, doing homework, playing sports, or doing art.[4]

All of this is a clear signal that life on-site doesn't look at the overall picture of employee well-being. And, when the majority of staff stay on-site after hours, it can create a culture of guilt where employees feel like they have to show they are working by being seen. In the end, this isn't all that helpful for the bottom line because more hours do not mean more productivity. And if employees' dietary health is declining along with their relationships, it ends up working against the effort to promote well-being. These so-called perks create the artifice of trust and support, but in too many instances, they just lead to burnout.

The pandemic thrust these companies out of their on-site comfort zone and into a virtual testing ground. The result? A mostly remote workforce could still be just as productive as if they were on-site—perhaps even more so.

As workplaces became safer and restrictions were lifted, some companies continued their remote work policy indefinitely, while others were eager to get back employees back to the office.

According to a CNBC report, Google employees who want to work remotely for more than fourteen additional days per year post-Covid can formally apply for it. Although the company didn't go remote first, it will assess a flexible workweek in which employees work at least three days a week in the office and other days at home.[5]

"We are testing a hypothesis that a flexible work model will lead to greater productivity, collaboration, and well-being," Sundar Pichai, CEO of Alphabet and its subsidiary Google, wrote in an email. "No company at our scale has ever created a fully hybrid workforce model—though a few are starting to test it—so it will be interesting to try."

NBC News reported that other companies followed suit. Microsoft will tinker with a flexible workplace solution, while Facebook CEO Mark Zuckerberg suggested that half of all employees will work remotely over the next decade. Twitter confirmed it will offer a permanent work-from-home option for all employees.[6]

The tech industry is setting a great example by offering hybrid and flexible working options. Workplace experts have long argued for a more fluid consideration of where we are most productive. These changes should significantly reduce the risk of burnout.

When it comes to workplace well-being, having the agency to choose what work environment makes us most productive is critical. And these hybrid solutions are a healthy compromise between employer and employee.

More flexible and hybrid options came as a result of testing something new and realizing that it works. But it's easy to fall back into old patterns. To make employees want to go back to work after the pandemic, some firms announced more perks to being at the office. If we want to realize good intentions, the key here is to make these options available but not culturally expected. That means modeling healthy behaviors at all levels of leadership:

- Managers should check in when employees are eating every meal on-site or staying consistently later than they should. It may be ideal for some members of the team, but not for all.

- Ensure that if someone wants to stay at work longer or use the facilities, they aren't rewarded as a team player for making those choices.

- Celebrate people going home to their families and social lives as a sign of good corporate citizenship.

The physical location of work has dramatically shifted for knowledge-based workers and, in turn, changed the meaning of life on-site considerably. In "Three Tips to Avoid WFH Burnout," Laura Giurge and Vanessa Bohns suggest how we can avoid living at work versus working from home.

They highlight the importance of maintaining physical and social boundaries, referencing a paper by Blake Ashforth of Arizona State University who "described the ways in which people demarcate the transition from work to non-work roles via 'boundary-crossing activities.'

Putting on your work clothes, commuting from home to work—these are physical and social indicators that something has changed."[7]

As managers, we need to ensure that people aren't forgoing their morning commute to just start work earlier—something that we saw increase in 2020. Remote employees need to maintain some of those boundary-crossing activities. We need to notice when they are online much too early and staying online far too late.

Create a team rule that notifications from work are turned off at a specific time of day and that employees can use an out-of-office message to indicate that they have officially left the building. If parents need time for familial issues, that should be the rule rather than the exception. All employees should have the autonomy to make those in-the-moment decisions to pick up a sick child from school or attend a doctor's appointment.

To actualize good intentions, success is rooted in human-centered outcomes first, and performance metrics second. That may be challenging to accept, because for centuries, the relationships between leaders and employees have been transactional. Employers hire an employee to do a job. They do it. Employers pay them. They come back to do the job again the next day.

This is hygiene. It's not motivation. Today, the relationship between leaders and their teams is much more complex and nuanced. When that relationship is optimized and running efficiently, it's the super fuel that gives companies a massive competitive edge.

We need to trust that externally perceived measures of success will come. But we can't start with them first. The upstream interventions should have only one goal in mind—the health and well-being of employees as a first priority. Productivity, sales, fundraising, growth, shareholder value, and so on are just slightly behind that goal, but that is where they permanently live.

It is a total myth that one has to come at the expense of the other. Rather, if you get the first goal right, the following goals are certain to exceed your expectations.

As a well-being expert with many years of experience, I can tell you that both anecdotally and from the evidence, happier employees are simply more effective, and a happier culture creates a network effect of healthier workplaces overall.

In a study conducted at the University of Warwick, individuals who were made happier by various interventions exhibited around 12 percent higher levels of productivity. The research also discovered that lower happiness levels reduced productivity, leading the researchers to conclude there's a causal link between happiness and performance.[8]

Other research by David Wyld found that increased employee well-being is tied to retention, while another study by Claudia M. Haase and colleagues found that when individuals felt happy, they exhibited greater levels of motivation and were more likely to achieve their goals.[9]

We also know that leaders with higher well-being have a greater impact on the success of the people they lead. A study of 357 managers looked at how mood states correlated to transformational leadership and found that leaders with higher positive affect were more transformational within their organizations. Among the benefits of transformational leadership is its tendency to be associated with higher levels of creativity, performance, and organizational citizenship.[10]

In "Does Happiness Promote Career Success?" Julia Boehm and Sonja Lyubomirsky say that "taken together, evidence from cross-sectional, longitudinal, and experimental studies supports the hypothesis that positive affect can bring about successful outcomes in the workplace. Happy people are more satisfied with their jobs and report having greater autonomy in their duties. They perform better on assigned tasks than their less happy peers and are more likely to take on extra tasks such as helping others. They receive more social support from their co-workers and tend to use more cooperative approaches when interacting with others."[11]

The authors also share that "happy individuals are less likely to exhibit withdrawal behaviors, such as absenteeism, and are less likely to be unemployed. Accordingly, overall, happy people enjoy greater workplace success."

When we think about the impacts of well-being as a causal relationship to success, this should compel us to lead accordingly. With well-being as our priority, we'll radically decrease burnout. It's a simple equation. Augmenting human-centered strategies equals overall organizational success and a reduction in burnout. Good intentions combined with an authentic mission are how we'll succeed with burnout prevention.

Unlimited Vacations

In 2017, Netflix, Virgin, and Kronos announced that they would have an unlimited vacation policy. After their announcements, hundreds of other companies fell in line, including Glassdoor, Dropbox, and Kickstarter, among others large and small. The idea was dazzling. But the results have been less so.

Unlimited paid time off (PTO) means that employees under these policies are permitted to take as much time off as they need with the expectation that they will get their work done in a timely manner. The policy is intended to demonstrate trust, a critical component to preventing burnout. But if the envisioned benefit isn't realized—people actually taking reasonable time off—then it ends up achieving the opposite.

In the report "HR MythBusters" that analyzed the data of 125,000 customers, HR software company Namely shares that Americans leave nearly 700 million vacation days on the table each year. It cites one study that found 80 percent of workers believed they would be more comfortable taking time off if their manager encouraged them to. Since unlimited vacation policies were implemented, studies continue to show that employees are taking fewer annual vacation days. Employees with unlimited vacation plans take off an average of only thirteen days per year, whereas traditional plan employees average fifteen days annually.[12]

Yet, if you want to protect your employees' well-being and in turn enhance high performance, the data shows that performance is correlated to taking more, not fewer, vacation days. Namely's study reported that "high performers tended to take an average of 19 vacation days per year, while individuals who scored lower took only 14 days." A study conducted by the University in Mannheim in 2012 found that "psychological detachment from work"—that is, a vacation absent of work in any form, including passively receiving emails—had a marked impact on well-being and job performance.[13]

Authentic human-centered cultures are the critical component to ensuring that unlimited vacation policies work and inevitably prevent burnout. This means that policies have to align with core values.

An example of flexible PTO done right can be found at Electric, a New York–based IT solutions company made up of 200 people globally with roughly 165 in New York full-time. I spoke with Jamie Coakley, vice president of people for Electric, who shared that what she quickly realized during Covid was how many employees, herself included, weren't using PTO. Early on during the pandemic, around March 2020, Coakley looked at the figures for the company's PTO and saw that they were reduced because of travel restrictions and nobody was able to go anywhere. But when she looked at the numbers again in May, she noticed 70 percent of the staff had only taken two days off in five months. For her, this was a red alert: "I think it was a chronic notion of a few things; trips getting canceled and not rebooked; people thinking they'll just keep working through it: 'I can go on a trip when this whole thing is over.' Additionally, I think there was just a lot of fear."

Coakley sat down with the leadership team to come up with an alternative plan for people who just weren't ready to take restful time off. She implemented programs to support well-being like meditation and yoga and engaged speakers focused on well-being, learning, and development. The first meditation class was a hit. Eighty-five people joined. But the next time the program came around, only ten people showed up. The third time, the same ten people appeared. This is when the really honest, strategic decisions took shape.

"I don't think the events we were offering were bad events; it was just that the reality is, people were starting to live at work. Being on Zoom calls all day, it was just too much," shared Coakley. "You have thirty minutes to yourself to go make a sandwich, or you put in the laundry, or you sit down with your partner and your kids. You don't want to have to be on yet another Zoom meeting."

This is when Coakley truly dug into how she could help her people in the ways they really needed it. She asked her entire team to evaluate the programming to find out what people were feeling. The staff was honest and embraced it. Coakley heard, "I don't want to meditate, but I want to continue to invest in my personal development," to "I don't feel like I can take breaks throughout the day because my meetings are back-to-back."

Coakley and her leadership team also tried to identify how this all contributed to the risk of her staff burning out. She categorized the biggest threats to burnout into three different buckets. One was to figure out how to still be that highly social workplace that everyone loved when people weren't connecting anymore. The second was to stop feeling like everything was a priority, which Coakley shared was in a constant state of adjustment. The third was to provide some space and flexibility to people and, most importantly, give time back to people.

The final piece was how Coakley and her leadership team at Electric fostered a more sustainable and realistic expectation of time off, particularly during a pandemic. They started to take the company offline once per month so no one was working; it was a time when everyone could just shut down collectively. They removed the mental blockers of workload if days were being taken off by ensuring that days off matched deliverables. They gave flexible PTO so no one would feel like it had to be planned—a challenge during Covid-19.

Leaders also helped the nonexempt workers who were primarily on the service desk teams. Since this group was ticketing eight hours a day, they implemented project plan hours to offer some different types of structures throughout other days. As Coakley said, "I think it's really hard right now to be engaged for eight full hours in a queue. We need to ask ourselves how we can still give flexibility to different types of workers."

Most importantly, managers sent surveys asking staff to share what they thought of the former PTO policy and what they thought of the new one. They asked, "Are people actually resting? Are they planning further out in the future regardless of if they can go anywhere?" The new policy helped shape an uptick in PTO. Coakley reported that more people are taking much needed time away from work.

Communicate the value of time

Plenty of research supports the idea that taking time off is good for us. This way of thinking should be imbedded in the culture. To get everyone on board, it's key to communicate the evidence that backs up the theory.

The physical benefits of taking time off are substantial. A study sponsored by the Heart, Lung, and Blood Institute at the National Institute of Health followed, over a nine-year period, twelve thousand men who had a high risk for coronary heart disease. The study found that those who took frequent annual vacations were 21 percent less likely to die from any cause and were 32 percent less likely to die from heart disease.[14]

According to a Gallup study, people who always make time for regular vacations had a 68.4 score on the Gallup-Healthway Well-Being Index, in comparison to a 51.4 Well-Being score for less frequent travelers.[15] Professional services firm Ernst & Young conducted an internal study of its employees and found that, for each additional ten hours of vacation employees took, their year-end performance ratings improved 8 percent.[16]

One study found that three days after vacation, subjects' physical complaints, quality of sleep, and mood had improved as compared to before vacation.[17] And, vacations are good for relationships, too. A study published in the *Wisconsin Medical Journal* found that women who took vacations were more satisfied with their marriages.[18]

All of these benefits—the ones that come with getting more time to rest, recuperate, spend with family and friends outside work—also help to prevent burnout.

Model the behavior. In our organizations, leaders need to be open and enthusiastic about taking time off. We need to be totally inaccessible, not just pay lip service to being out of contact and then continue to answer emails the entire time we're away. Laura M. Giurge and Kaitlin Woolley in "Don't Work on Vacation. Seriously," write that as a result of the Covid-19 crisis, "how and when we work is fundamentally changing." With evidence pointing to more people working on weekends and during holidays during the crisis, it's coming at a major cost to employers and employees alike.[19]

According to the authors' research, "Spending weekends or holidays working undermines one of the most important factors that determines whether people persist in their work: intrinsic motivation." So not only are people overworking, they are winnowing the kind of motivation that prevents burnout. It's a double whammy.

So, how can we reinforce the importance for all of us to get time away from work? If leaders really want to make an impact, we must heed our own advice.

Redefine high performance. The antiquated belief that long hours equal higher productivity has been proven untrue in a series of studies. A Stanford University study by economics professor John Pencavel discovered that productivity per hour declines sharply when a person works more than fifty hours a week.[20] After fifty-five hours, productivity drops so significantly that there is no value in putting in any more hours. If someone works seventy hours per week, they are just as productive as the person who put in fifty-five hours.[21]

This emphasizes the need to redefine what it means to be high-performing. Just as Arianna Huffington emphasizes getting more sleep, we need to make it cool to work fewer unproductive hours. I've mentioned this before but focusing on manageable goals versus number of hours worked is how we can prevent burnout. And if you want your employees to take a vacation without burning out, have them follow some simple protocols:

- *Distribute the weight.* Make sure the people employees are tagging to be their support systems can handle responsibilities when they are away. Managers should assist by checking in on the bandwidth of the team so no major project lands in a coworker's lap right before their teammate leaves. This helps employees go on vacation without a pervasive feeling of anxiety about overwhelming their peers while they're away.

- *Support expectation management.* Have a rule that employees set an out-of-office message before departure. This may seem like common knowledge, but in some workplaces, it may not be. The message must be clear that employees will *not* be checking emails or answering calls while they are away. Have your staff add a one-day buffer on the return date to give them a way to regroup on their first day back. And suggest they send out an email to their stakeholders before their departure so they don't get surprised with a last-minute request just before they're about to leave.

Walk the walk. A good intention gone bad includes providing all these supports and then still emailing your staff while they are away or allowing them to email you. It is paramount that you give all the space required *no matter what* goes on at work. Managers may find this challenging because they think that no one else can handle their job. However, this is a myth. If we set up the supports before anyone on our team leaves, we will be fine.

We all need to recognize that in most cases, lives will not be lost if an email wasn't sent that day. Sometimes we just have to accept that a client may be frustrated, or a project will be late, or some person is going to be upset, but as leaders, our job is to protect our people. We are not meant to be leaders if we're unable to be that buffer.

Personally, I have fallen short of this a few times in my career, and I regretted not prioritizing my team over the needs of the company. This seemed to happen most when the client had an urgent need; we would drop everything for that one request. It would often end up not all that urgent, but our mental health still suffered. It was not sustainable.

Part of leadership is knowing the difference between perceived and real. I came to realize that everyone sees their need as urgent. As soon as you assume an employee-first strategy, it's easy to assess how you'll tackle a real emergency when it arises.

What happens when we feel as if something (or someone) is stealing our time? Called time theft, it's a cause of chronic stress at work. When well-being becomes part of the workload, that can also make us feel as if we're not spending our time wisely. Here's how that can happen inside our organizations.

Well-Intended Wellness Programs

If you looked at a statistical analysis of stress and compared those graphs to a similar graph of the growth of the wellness industry, you would assume that stress would be going down as the wellness industry rose. Unfortunately, the data and the graphs tell a different story.

In 2021, the global health and wellness industry grew to US$4.5 trillion. The international corporate wellness sector owned a large share of the output with a US$57.2 billion market share that should reach $97.4 billion by 2027.[22]

Mental wellness added a $121 billion market share in 2020. That same year, health and fitness apps generated 656 million downloads and growing, which most experts contributed to the pandemic that caused "consumers to stay at home and restructure their exercise regimen and general lifestyle practices."[23]

Unfortunately, tech burnout became a rapidly evolving problem as companies shifted to new ways of communicating virtually. As the pandemic wore on, the interest in well-being apps grew, but stress continued to increase exponentially. Something wasn't translating.

Long before the pandemic, fitness trackers and subsequent steps competitions or challenges were hugely popular. These products are expected to hit $48.2 billion in annual revenue by 2023, claiming that the reason for their rapid growth is owed to the "increasing prevalence of chronic diseases."[24] Some say the apps are great for team bonding; some claim they're simply good for the bottom line when employees are physically healthy.

This is true. Physical well-being plays a valuable role in mental health, and it makes sense to connect that to building positive relationships.

Yet, it's critical that organizations ensure that the programming is well executed, not just well intended.

One example can be found in a randomized trial coauthored by Zirui Song, assistant professor at Harvard Medical School, along with Katherine Baicker, dean at the University of Chicago. The research team studied the efficacy of a fitness-specific wellness program imbedded at a large US warehouse retail company. The study of nearly thirty-three thousand employees found that although there was a measurable increase in self-reported healthy behaviors, there were "no significant differences in clinical markers of health; health care spending or utilization; or absenteeism, tenure, or job performance after 18 months."[25]

Another randomized controlled trial published in the *Lancet Diabetes and Endocrinology* analyzed eight hundred participants using a fitness tracker to improve their health over fourteen months. Researchers found that by the end of the trial, the fitness tracker had no effect on test subjects' overall health and fitness—even when it was combined with a financial incentive.[26]

We may not all be going back to work as usual, but as we look to reshape the way we engage these types of perks or wellness tactics, we need to consider, first, if they work, and second, if they are inclusive. Well-being programs can be well intentioned, but if they hold an inherent bias, they can have harmful effects.

Does what we're suggesting fit the times? Have we left anyone out? Are we engaging in these practices for the right reasons? Are we being authentic?

In some cases, employees can feel shame or guilt if they don't engage in activity challenges. While some employees score big points for their teams and get access to better parking spaces or free lunches, others feel singled out and left behind. A steps challenge can make a person with limited mobility or weight problems feel as if they're under a microscope. For some, this major blow to self-esteem can have long-lasting impacts.

Take the story of Emily and her coworkers, who were introduced by their HR leadership team to a consultant from a popular weight-loss program. During the initial consultation, along with the list of benefits for joining the program, they learned that they could receive a reduced rate when a threshold of employees joined. When they didn't meet the threshold, HR summoned Emily to the office to express frustration and disappointment that she hadn't joined.

Emily shared that as an overweight woman, she felt embarrassed. When she was criticized for "not caring about the health of her fellow teammates, or her own—clearly," she felt harassed. Emily left eight months later, but five years later, she still recalls the incident as painful, with "a lasting effect on her self-esteem."

In another example, former HR leader Darin Phillips described working at an organization that was consistently engaging in poor wellness practices because the CEO and COO "were concerned about the cost of health insurance." Phillips shared that they specifically "targeted groups that included smokers and people who did not regularly exercise" by monitoring their fitness trackers. Fitness trackers were a mandatory part of the steps campaign, which also included a $500 incentive to participate. According to Phillips, "People were trying to recruit the heavier people to join their team so they could show better weight-loss results." Phillips explained that if these targeted employees stayed in the program, they often felt peer pressure to participate in the weight-loss challenge. Yet, if they pulled out, they'd lose all the other benefits that the program offered, including the $500. He soon left the company for another role.

However, good intentions gone awry can always be remedied. As long as we're actively listening, we can learn and then adjust course. It's about leveraging new information, research, and data to make changes to our current way of thinking about well-being. We need to rethink how we use these tools in more meaningful and sustainable ways.

Researcher Andrew Campbell, a professor of computer science at Dartmouth College, set out to understand how fitness trackers can be used in the most optimal way. He developed "a system that monitors physical and emotional signals that employees produce during the day and correlates that data to performance."

Campbell shares that he knows when he is stressed, but he doesn't always know how that stress is impacting his work. Quoted in the *Washington Post*, Campbell says that he and his team "want to use that information to empower workers to tell them whether they're being influenced by levels of stress or sleep or other factors that may not be immediately obvious to them."

To make that happen, Campbell gathered a team of researchers. They analyzed the "passive sensing data" of 750 employees representing various levels and roles within a high-tech firm. Subjects wore wearable fitness trackers that monitored heart functions, sleep, stress, and measurements such as weight and calorie consumption, as well as a smartphone app that tracked their physical activity, location, phone usage, and ambient light.

They found:

- High performers tended to have lower rates of phone usage.

- They also experienced deeper periods of sustained sleep and were more physically active than their lower-performing colleagues.

- High-performing supervisors tended to be more mobile during the day, but they visited a smaller number of distinct places during their working hours.[27]

In our interview, Campbell shared that he believes there is value in wearables providing real-time feedback on stress. He said, "However, most vendors don't publish their algorithms, which are mostly based on heart rate variability. No randomized control trials and black-box algorithms mean few research scientists trust the stress measures." Campbell recommends that companies need to open up the box and explain how they built their models and validated them or else giving people feedback from commercial wearables is worthless. He added, "There is more noise than signal."

In my interview with James Park, CEO of Fitbit, he shared that thinking with me. Park believes that for the last thirteen years, Fitbit has stayed true to its mission: a holistic approach to helping people understand how exercise, nutrition, and sleep tie together for increased wellness. However, when it introduced Fitbit Sense, it brought an entirely new level of understanding of how stress intersects with all of it.

"Our commitment to helping people get and stay healthy has never been stronger," said Park. "The future for wearables is about making the invisible, visible—unlocking even more information about our bodies to take better control of our health and wellness."

To see how Fitbit was using its wearables to get more signal and less noise, I connected with Conor Heneghan, Fitbit's director of research and algorithms, who explained how it's done. "To understand the importance of tracking stress," Heneghan clarified, "we first have to define what it means to be stressed and understand the ways it can impact our physical and mental health."

Heneghan reminded me about how stress is processed in our bodies, that when we are faced with a stressor, our sympathetic nervous system releases stress hormones, like adrenaline and cortisol, to prepare us for a fight-or-flight response. This is why Fitbit invested in metrics like heart rate variability and electrodermal activity. "Tracking these 'invisible' metrics can help us recognize when our body is stressed, even when there are no obvious signs," said Heneghan.

I was pleased to learn that Fitbit saw tracking stress as part of its future strategy. Personally, I see this as a more holistic way of looking at our overall health. Fitness is a valuable part of our well-being, but it doesn't make up the entire picture. While this gets us closer to a full picture, it's definitely not all the way. It *may*, however, be able to track whether the fitness campaign is stressing us out.

The trackers, the wearables, or the apps aren't to blame if everyone refuses to adopt them, or if someone feels excluded or embarrassed. That is an organizational failure. It's authentic versus inauthentic intentions that will promote or prevent their acceptance and subsequent success.

As with anything new, we have a long way to go before we see the long-term impacts. For example, it's helpful for employees to know their stress levels and manage their responses to stress. But, once again, we've just given individuals more data to solve these problems on their own. How does that really help? People are now forced to say, "So, now I know I'm stressed, but is that all on me? What am I supposed to do with that information?" We're just pushing the expectation for self-care back on the individual.

Yet, leaders are in the middle of a quagmire. To help, we have to know that employees are stressed. That means accessing the data. That means not protecting their privacy. This is a conundrum, wrapped in an enigma.

Here is how one company is tackling that question. Beyond offering mental health days and meditation and wellness apps, San Francisco–based startup ProductBoard created a Slackbot named Freud that acts almost like a member of the team, except it's not human. It can join channels, upload files, send messages, and so forth, providing an anonymous way for people to discuss mental health in the social collaboration platform Slack. When someone writes a direct message to Freud, the message is anonymously posted in the #talk-mental-health channel, where advice, feedback, and empathy can be shared in response.

According to Maurice Klein, who is the engineering manager overseeing the project, Freud has been a helpful way for new employees to ask questions and get recommendations without the fear of judgment.

"A lot of people are still scared, ashamed, or embarrassed to talk about mental health issues. In a perfect world, no one should have to feel like this; most people will experience mental health issues at some point in their lifetime. Unfortunately, we're not there yet, and the stigma around these issues still exists," says Klein. "I introduced Freud because I wanted everyone to be able to share what they are struggling with, even when they feel scared, ashamed, or embarrassed, because I believe that opening up about your struggles is the first step toward improvement."

Freud promises a positive shift toward more access to mental health supports in a workforce filled with stigma. But the ideal would include both mental health offerings and open conversations free from shame.

One leader, Edward Ellison of the Permanente Federation, is making destigmatizing mental illness a priority. He shared with me that employers need to first centralize communication about their wellness and mental health support tools and programs, and then regularly let employees know what is available and how to access it.

The company intended to provide all its staff and patients with two apps: Calm, a sleep and meditation tool, and My Strength, a support tool for managing depression, anxiety, stress, and sleep, but first a robust plan to enhance well-being had to be put in place. If not, the big announcements about the new apps might feel tone-deaf. Adoption of apps and tools occurs when there's trust—when good intentions are authentic and intentionally delivered.

According to the company's usage data, that trust led to more adoption. Anecdotal feedback showed that during times of extreme stress, these apps proved useful for physicians working at hospitals during Covid-19 to get emotionally regulated before entering the chaos. They were grateful for the array of tools offered to them.

Trust in leadership makes it easier for people to believe that wellness technology, wearables, apps, and other virtual and in-person services are there to help them. With trust, employees give leaders the benefit of the doubt rather than questioning their motives. Employees more readily leverage the benefits of these tools because they assume that leadership is looking out for their best interests. They also feel that their ability to use them is supported. They aren't dusty pool tables. And, healthy cultures offer more than one well-being initiative. They don't serve up silver bullets.

In our conversation, Ellison listed how he's trying to support well-being with various strategies. Some of those supports included:

- Drop-ins with therapists are offered at lunchtime; call-ins with therapists are available throughout the day.

- The chief wellness officer created a page on the company portal that outlined the different resources available to staff.

- A multidisciplinary, psychological support team was set up as a peer support tool within the employee assistance program.

- The company set up the second-victim grief group (people suffering the impact of loss within the hospital).

- A program that has been running for years, "Finding Meaning in Medicine," helps staff maintain resilience to stay connected to the joy—to the meaning—of why they do what they do every day.

- In 2020, the company started research on burnout with the Institute for Healthcare Improvement that includes monitoring for burnout to see what interventions are helpful.

Ellison consistently emphasized in our conversations that it has to come back to a positive culture and trust: "I think what is encouraging to people is to help them know that they're not alone, and that everyone does recognize the effort and the sacrifices that they're making. I remind them, you're going to make a difference, you're going to make lives better. You're here to save lives, to reassure and restore families. It's why you do what you do."

Team Building and Forced Fun

I connected with Louise Lambert, psychologist and editor of the *Middle East Journal of Positive Psychology*, who is currently working and living in Dubai. We spoke during the Covid-19 pandemic, and both of us had witnessed the massive increase in well-being becoming part of the workload.

"I had organizations asking me to do Zoom webinars with no real goal other than talk to us about something on mental health," said Lambert. "I didn't always get the sense that people needed or even wanted it; it seemed to come from the pressure managers felt to do something. While well intentioned, sitting in endless webinars didn't add to anyone's well-being; it added to ill-being by producing Zoom fatigue, body aches, demands on attention that are unsustainable in any other context, and a feeling of being chained to one's chair because it must be 'good for them.'"

People felt forced to participate in virtual yoga or exercise classes; some felt uncomfortable sweating on screen and seeing coworkers watching them work out. One woman who identified as introverted shared with me that "doing those kinds of bends and stretches in front of my boss was so unbelievably embarrassing. I hated every minute of it. But I also felt like if I didn't join in, I was basically saying it's OK to not have a good culture at work—because this had become our new culture in the pandemic."

Lambert suggested that managers risk two things if the notion of well-being isn't clear in their minds. She said, "First, well-being becomes an additional job that employees must do on top of an already stressful day. Secondly, it gives the impression that work cannot be enjoyed in itself and requires frills to be enjoyed. Like putting ketchup on perfectly good beans!"

I loved that analogy (and now understand why I've never put ketchup on beans). I agree with Lambert that in our work, we often feel a need to do more or make the effort more complicated to demonstrate its value or its fidelity. But there is power in simplicity.

We also used to think we were "always on" before the pandemic. We can safely say that "always" then was nothing to our "always" today. Dialing down the tech is going to be critical to maintain a sustainable workload and healthy digital practices at work.

Fortunately, as 2020 evolved, more managers realized these programs were helping some but not all their staff. In a crisis with no frame of reference, we threw everything at the problem and hoped some good thing stuck. But all that did was burn people out. It was an instance of trial and error, which I will say emphatically is totally forgivable.

As leaders, it is OK to give ourselves some room for error here. There was no frame of reference from which to draw the protocols and strategies. Every moment was an opportunity to learn, but it sometimes got exhausting, too. Actually, one executive vice president of a multinational corporation said to me eighteen months into the pandemic, "I feel like right now it's just exhausted leaders leading exhausted teams."

Some years, the learning curve will be astronomically higher than in other years. In those first months of the pandemic, my self-efficacy was at an all-time low.

Leaders who demonstrate a natural instinct or developed skill for empathy tend to better handle times of crisis and change, primarily because they are better at asking and reacting quickly. During rapidly shifting times when outside forces are causing everyone to feel out of control, offering that control back to people in whatever ways we can will improve trust and prevent burnout.

In the everyday moments at work, leaders should still be asking and reacting. This is how those good intentions, like the seemingly innocuous company picnics or holiday parties, end up being the tiny pebbles that become boulders.

Some of you may be wondering how holiday parties and picnics can be a bad thing. The truth is, the stats on these good intentions are actually quite bleak. A 2018 survey by the staffing service OfficeTeam claimed that 93 percent of US companies planned to host a holiday party.[28] A Randstad USA survey found 90 percent of workers would rather get a bonus or extra vacation days than attend a company holiday party.[29] The average cost of a holiday party is $75 to upward of $150 per person if you work in any of the Silicon Valley tech companies. But where should we be investing? What is the impact of $75 or $150 if we spend it on something else?

In my article "Holidays Can Be Stressful. They Don't Have to Stress Out Your Team," I suggest that the annual holiday party is great, only if people want to attend.[30] Some of the reasons nearly 40 percent of employees end up declining an invitation can be attributed to the increased anxiety that goes with the holiday season.[31] The American Psychological Association found that 38 percent of people say their stress increases during the holidays—only 8 percent say they feel happier.[32] Employees are often contending with shortened deadlines, meeting expectations for the end of the fiscal year, and coping with stressed-out customers, which are just a few of the reasons for their increased anxiety. The resulting costs for employers can be quite significant.

The slew of tools to help introverts make it through the holiday office party says a lot about who is attracted to these events and who is not. The Muse put out "An Office Holiday Party Survival Guide for Introverts and Shy People" with the assertion that it's challenging for introverts to truly enjoy a holiday party: "Many people who are introverted or shy, like me, dread holiday party season. All that socializing is draining for introverts, who often feel overstimulated, even anxious, in large groups. Shy people, too, may feel anxious at office holiday parties but for different reasons; it comes from a place of fear rather than a depletion of energy."[33]

Yet, most people can't say no. Further research from OfficeTeam claims that 66 percent of managers say there's an unwritten rule that employees should attend parties: "Basically, it looks good to the higher-ups when you make the effort to celebrate with the team."

The most cited reason for not attending was that the holiday parties, which are typically held in the evenings, clash with family duties at home, once again proving that it's stressful for people when well-being becomes workload. Additionally, for those who do attend the holiday party, there is a 77 percent drop in productivity the next day, with more than half of the staff wasting the first four hours of the following day because they're recovering from the night before—which is slightly better than the 20 percent who call in sick. Employee stress and lost productivity due to the holiday party cost UK companies roughly £11 billion, according to a 2016 report.[34]

I'm going to recommend that we leverage the small data here. Start by taking a referendum on all your events to ensure they aren't just forced "fun." Ask your employees if they like the holiday party or the annual picnic, the Friday "Happy Hours," or even the yoga classes or fitness campaigns. What should we keep? What should we change? Is this actually contributing to well-being and preventing burnout or is it just good for branding?

Acknowledge that team building is an important aspect of celebrating culture and shouldn't be eliminated. There just needs to be a high level of consideration for how it is planned and implemented. In my interview with Dan Schawbel, author of the best-seller *Back to Human*, he said he believes off-sites are a key component to healthy workplace cultures. In his work with Virgin Pulse, he measured the responses of two thousand managers and employees on how to enable more human relationships—it was categorically a win for off-sites. Schawbel explains that because you can "escape the work talk and engage in more personal conversations, feelings of isolation and loneliness were reduced and therefore productivity increased."

This is the key. Allow for fun. Support fun. Create fun. Just don't force fun.

Plenty of people still love these events, so it's OK to maintain them as part of the tradition. Some people *really* love holiday parties (cheeks redden as hand goes up). However, despite my personal love of getting dressed up once a year for the big holiday hoopla, I still say we need to ask, "Is there something else that we should do with that money or is this event worth keeping?"

In the following ways we can reduce burnout due to forced fun and instead build an authentic culture in which everyone at any time feels welcome.

Be inclusive

In my interview with Ben-Saba Hasan, senior vice president and chief culture, diversity, and inclusion officer at Walmart, he shared that leaders must recognize the different ways people celebrate holidays: "As leaders, we need to create an environment where our team members feel comfortable and safe, so that we foster greater awareness among those in the dominant culture for those whose holiday observances look different from their own."

Mini Khroad, vice president of people operations at Splunk, told me in a recent interview: "The holidays should always be an important time at companies. Ensuring that employees have the ability to recognize national or other holidays, at work and in their personal lives, helps to make the workplace enjoyable for everyone."

Protect personal time

Why not offer one extra day off leading up to holidays for employees to attend to personal needs like gift shopping, family demands, or down-time to regroup—whatever they need. One mandatory day off can make all the difference in employee stress levels. These small but much-appreciated gestures increase loyalty and gratitude on your staff and offer long-term payoffs. Why does this matter? Research has proven that grateful staff are more engaged, community-minded, and happier at work.

Rebalance workloads

Competing demands sit at the top of employees' stress lists. Work and home pressures converge during holidays, and time seems highly com-pressed. Plan a review of the workload and see if some project deadlines can be extended. "Periods of high stress such as the holiday season rep-resent an opportunity for managers to treat employees as individuals by understanding and appropriately responding to their specific needs," said David Almeda, chief people officer at Ultimate Kronos Group. In our interview, he suggested that "tactics such as rebalancing workload among team members or allowing atypical work hours for a set period of time will deliver results, increase employee commitment, and materi-ally decrease employee stress."

Give time instead of gifts

Research by neuroscientists Jordan Grafman and Jorge Moll demon-strates that we are instinctually made to give. When the subjects donated to what they considered worthy organizations, brain scans revealed that parts of their midbrains lit up—the same region that controls cravings for food and that becomes active when money is added to people's personal reward accounts. Ben-Saba Hasan connected this thinking back to his team as they bonded over volunteering in their community: "I believe one of the best ways to manage stress and care for yourself is when you turn your focus toward caring for others first."

"Well-being can be developed via simple acts, like a biweekly call asking, 'How are you? What's worrying you? How can I help? What has you feeling hopeful?'" said Louise Lambert. "It needn't be costly or complex. Think back to the best job you had; was it the people that made it good, or the 'entertainment?'"

Remember, the good intention goes awry if it's just an expectation.

So, what happens when leaders suggest that they can help delay their employees' child-birthing years? What if that good intention became the expectation? Seems ridiculous, right? Therein lies the rub.

Egg Freezing

I am not lying. The policy of freezing eggs is an actual "good intention," one that is growing in popularity in tech companies in Silicon Valley and beyond. This has so many underlying "isms," it makes my head spin, and as it relates to burnout, it has a major impact.

Although the policy is meant to give employees more freedom to pursue family planning according to their own timeline, critics say the policy sends the message to employees that work is more important than family. Maternity leave is already seen as a perk, which also sends the wrong signal. It should be hygiene and not a perk, in my opinion and that of others in my field, because as a perk, it emphasizes that getting time off to have a baby is a luxury the company is providing you.

So, when egg freezing became a perk open to all staff, not just those who needed it in special medical cases, it reinforced the systemic barriers that have held women back for more than a century. It suggests that work is more important than family, and women can't have both at the same time. It perpetuates a broken system that makes women feel that the older they get, the more obsolete they are. So, work while you're young and do the rest later. This is a perk that is not only sexist but ageist and one to avoid if you want to prevent burnout.

As leaders, we need to strongly push back on these types of corporate decisions.

Rebecca Mead, staff writer for the *New Yorker* and author of *My Life in Middlemarch*, writes, "The difficulties that an American woman continues to face in her efforts to reconcile having a career with being a mother are more than faulty code to be debugged. Rather, they are vast and systemic: the limited availability of subsidized care for preschool children, the resistance of corporate culture to flexible or reduced hours for the parents of young children, the lack of federally mandated, paid family leave . . . while the fortunate employees of Apple and Facebook enjoy relatively generous family-leave packages . . . these are the exception rather than the standard."[35]

Mead goes on to reinforce that there is also "no substitute for policy reform that might, on its own, begin to obviate the need for a young woman to think about whether freezing her eggs is something she should do. There is never a convenient time to have a baby if you also have a job, as anyone who has ever had a job and a baby can attest. But so long as not having a baby yet is presented as a would-be mother's best option, her choices are unlikely to get much easier."

The American College of Obstetricians and Gynecologists and the American Society of Reproductive Medicine (ASRM) do not endorse the use of egg freezing to defer childbearing—otherwise called social egg freezing. The ASRM lifted the "experimental" label in 2012 so it could be applied to a medically indicated need, such as for women with cancer. For most women, egg freezing, whether medical or social, has a low success rate. The latest and most comprehensive data available reveals a 77 percent failure rate of frozen eggs resulting in a live birth in women aged thirty, and a 91 percent failure rate in women aged forty.[36]

Until the workplace (and government) starts to meet the needs of women in a real way, we are going to see more "good intentions" like freezing eggs become commonplace. Yet, these are just bribes wrapped with a bow. Good intentions are not prevention, especially this one.

. . .

If we analyze where good intentions run amok, it often correlates to one fundamental flaw: lack of authentic empathy. When we are preventing burnout from "life on-site" or living at work versus working from home, we must consider that employees immersed totally in their work at their workplace is not healthy for the areas in life that matter most—family, friendships, a personal life. We need people to take vacations without guilt and pressure by supporting them internally and modeling those behaviors ourselves. We need to ask how people want to spend time away from work and ensure that if we ask them to attend a work function, it doesn't create added stress.

We should confirm that well-being isn't part of the workload and that whatever we implement is inclusive, from the policies to the infrastructure to the programming and the perks. We must be inclusive because lack of fairness is a leading cause of burnout.

This is always a two-way street, a "we" problem to solve. To prevent burnout, we have to identify when we've lost self-compassion; when we've stopped giving ourselves enough room for error. We're living beyond our margins. We may be leaders, but we're also human. If we are truly interested in helping others, we have to help ourselves first. Then we'll be ready to do the work.

4

How to Measure Burnout

The word *data* gets thrown around a lot these days. The truth is that data-driven decision making isn't new. The first employee surveys, commonly known as employee-attitude surveys, surfaced in industrial companies in the 1920s. Between 1944 and 1947, the National Industrial Advisory Board saw a 250 percent increase in companies implementing attitude surveys.[1]

I am a firm believer that we need to rely on our intuition as leaders; our gut instincts can play a big role in shaping thriving cultures. But we should always back up our gut instincts with data, more specifically, accurate data.

So, how can data play a role in preventing burnout? To be an empathetic leader, we must always be actively listening. Providing our employees with the ability to share both open and anonymous feedback is key to detecting a problem. When we provide a variety of channels of communication, we're more likely to learn what we're doing right and where we're veering off course.

Additionally, anonymous data tends to be honest and straightforward. And what we want—*need* is more accurate—to make meaningful change requires being open to the unvarnished truth, even if it may be hard to hear.

Honestly, data-based decisions shouldn't be that hard to adopt. We already have the muscle memory to prove it. For example, nurses and physicians analyze data all day, from taking temperatures to reading X-rays and charts. Teachers give tests and assess knowledge through rubrics. Developers test code and measure for accuracy and compliance. We use data to determine whether to use sunblock that day or to fill up our gas tank. There are countless ways we use data in our daily decision-making.

So, why wouldn't culture (the well-being of our organizations) be equally or more important to assess in an ongoing way? We need to make this a habitual part of our organizational behavior. The world shifts. We track the impact. So, how do we ingrain the habits of measuring inside our organization?

We first need to investigate the tools available to us.

Measuring Burnout

The gold standard for measuring burnout has been and still is the Maslach Burnout Inventory (MBI). Created in 1981, the MBI is a psychological inventory consisting of twenty-two items pertaining to occupational burnout. It measures three dimensions of burnout: emotional exhaustion, depersonalization, and personal accomplishment. There are now five versions of the MBI to fit various industries and personnel types, including a general survey that anyone can take.

All MBI items are scored using a seven-point frequency rating from "never" to "daily." The MBI has three component scales: emotional exhaustion (nine items), depersonalization (five items), and personal achievement (eight items). Each scale measures its own unique dimension of burnout. The score ranges define low, moderate, and high levels of each scale based on the zero-to-six scoring.

This breakdown is extremely simplified, but essentially, the more frequently you feel exhaustion, depersonalization, or cynicism, the more likely you are to be experiencing burnout. The more frequently you feel engagement and personal accomplishment, the less likely you are to be experiencing burnout.

The 2019 WHO definition of burnout was based on the MBI. In most cases, researchers leverage this scale when they are analyzing burnout in their work.

What is important about the MBI in burnout research history (among others) is how it "marked a turning point in burnout research, as it was now possible to easily measure the mental state in different populations and professions."[2] In our survey and follow-on research, we included a partial MBI scale, Michael Leiter's Area of Worklife Scale and combined them both into Whiteside's Rethinking Burnout survey.[3] We also asked qualitative questions that Leiter developed specifically to assess well-being during the pandemic.

When the authors of the MBI (and other experts who have developed workplace surveys) spoke about their work, they expressed their desire for organizations to use the data they gather more effectively. The pervasive belief that "people burn out because of flaws in their character, behavior, or productivity . . . that the individual is the problem, and the solutions lie in changing the person, is an incorrect narrative," said the MBI authors. "Rather, burnout is experienced in response to the social and work environment. The structure and functioning of the workplace shape how people interact with each other, carry out their jobs, and how they feel about this environment. The burnout of individual workers often says more about the workplace conditions than it does about the person. It is not the person but the relationship of the organization with people that needs to change."[4]

I spoke with Christina Maslach about her interest in getting more organizations to think inversely about burnout—where accountability lies and how they can start to shift the conversation. "I think part of the challenge is that we look at a phenomenon of burnout and it doesn't fit the usual categories that people are used to," said Maslach. "And so, I think that's part of the difficulty that people have had of really understanding what it is and what they need to do about it."

Maslach here is referring to the WHO definition of burnout that she believes doesn't go quite far enough in helping us to identify, possibly diagnose, and effectively treat burnout. She continued: "When the WHO announcement came out, it was widely misreported as a disease, although they explained that was not the intention of the International

Classification of Diseases (ICD) inclusion. And yet, I think the WHO should classify it more clearly. It's something that I and other researchers have been saying for a long time—this is partly to help people try to understand it. For example, if it is a disease, then we know we have to bring in medical people, or pharmacological treatments, protocols for treating it, and then we can fit it into a health plan."

Maslach warned, however, that its identification as a disease could then place the onus solely back on the person to beat it. She said, "Looking at it from a different angle, however, if it's now a disease . . . it's a problem in that person, they are suffering, they are ill. And then what does that mean within the workplace?"

One thing I know for sure is that the authors of the MBI care deeply about preventing burnout and have dedicated their careers to learning about its impact. It's challenging, however, to measure something that is ill-defined. Should burnout be identified as a disease? Or should we consider it a diagnosable medical condition? Is it chronic stress? Well, then, shouldn't we just call it chronic stress? Is it exhaustion disorder? That's a diagnosable condition.

These questions shake the burnout research community and are just one more reason why burnout has been a tough nut to crack.

You and Me and Five Bucks

Maslach had so many stories of why "ask first" should be the mantra of all organizations, but the following story in particular resonated. "I remember one of the CEOs I worked with decided to put a volleyball court on the top of the building on the roof. You know where this is going," she said. "There are only so many people who will use it, and it just ends up making people feel so cynical and they get so frustrated because they know it costs a lot of money . . . and the CEO's staff are thinking, 'All that money, oh my God, if only I had some of it too. Here's the list of ten, fifteen, twenty things that might have made a difference in my team's every day at work.'"

An example of this misalignment between leadership and staff showed up in my work with a prominent university during our well-being measurement of its departments and faculties. The music faculty chairs decided to put their entire annual improvement budget toward building a soundproof studio. They were certain the rest of the faculty would be thrilled. They were wrong. In reality, the staff just wanted new music stands at a cost of $300. The existing stands were imbalanced, some were broken, and students would often find their sheet music on the floor while practicing their instruments. The ribbon-cutting event was lackluster, and the engagement of the staff was low. Some faculty didn't even show up. The leaders expressed frustration with their staff for being so ungrateful. Neither group shared their dissatisfaction with the other, and over the course of the following year, that seed of anger grew. The nontenured high performers sought out new opportunities, and the faculty lost talented people. If staff had been given a say in how the budget was allocated, for $300 the team might still be intact.

How often do we feel that $100, or even a resource, could solve a problem? If we could just add one more person, the entire team would feel as if a weight was lifted. How much is that worth? Yet, when those needs are unfulfilled, it creates the conditions for burnout. Often, most of these inexpensive problems can be prevented by simply asking people what they need.

One of my favorite lines from the movie *Reality Bites* is when Troy Dyer, played by Ethan Hawke, says to Lelaina Pierce, played by Wynona Ryder, "You see Lainy, this is all we need. A couple smokes, a cup of coffee, and a little bit of conversation. You and me and five bucks."[5]

This is all that really matters to most people, yet we humans love to overcomplicate. Culture thrives in the small stuff. It's the one-on-ones, the fostering of friendships over coffee. It's an effortless state of belonging. It's the feeling when we fall in love with work because it's real, authentic, and meaningful.

This is where simple actions, done with repetition, create positive outcomes. So, it can't be that we grab coffee just once and poof! We're best friends. We need to go further and set a monthly date where we jump on a call, have a videoconference, have breakfast together virtually, or meet in real life whenever possible to establish a long-lasting bond. Remember, it's the best friend at work who is crucial to happiness in the workplace, the kind of friend who'd pick you up from the airport in the middle of the night or bail you out of jail. Hopefully, we never have to test that last one.

It requires time and intention to make that happen. To identify what someone's five-buck solution is, we gather data. We learn through measuring. And to do that, we need to ask questions frequently in ways that can be quickly acted on.

To eliminate the small irritants, ask the same questions over time. This will also help to figure out the ebbs and flows we feel in the culture. We all know in our guts that sometimes it's working, sometimes it's off. To keep culture from flying off the rails, we ask before that happens. We validate our gut feelings. Then we can start to be more preventive versus reactionary, and over time, the data allows us to be predictive.

Survey Fatigue

Maslach suggested that one of the biggest problems in organizations is that, given the overwhelming number of surveys, people are feeling survey fatigue. I get that. The blame, however, should not be placed solely on the abundance of surveys but, instead, on the lack of action taken as a result of the data.

Maslach and I shared how frustrating this has been for both of us. "When I talk to the employees at different levels," she said, "they will say things like, well, the first time they were asking us these questions, it was kind of exciting, like, yeah, they're focusing on engagement. What could make it better? That sounds really cool. That's really great. There were places where you could put down ideas and suggestions of what would make a difference. But after all that, nothing. Nothing happened."

Maslach explained how defeating this is for employees and the negative impact it has on the culture. It also makes the data entirely useless; she described it as "garbage data." "Next year, same questions. But now employees are like, 'The last time they didn't even read what I wrote after putting in all that time and effort and for what?' By the third time, people are saying either they don't answer it if they can get away with it, or they just tick off everything right down the middle. They're thinking, why bother, nothing changes."

It makes no sense. Would you ever go back to a restaurant where the server takes your order and never delivers your food?

The not-so-funny part? People seem to think that measuring is cost prohibitive. Typically, it's just a small fraction of their payroll budget. But it can be a massive blind spot for leaders who don't see the value in investing a nominal amount toward tracking the impact of culture on well-being and performance.

When you invite others to give you their insights and do nothing with them, how can you ever ask them to share their authentic opinions with you again? You were better off not asking in the first place, because trust in the process was lost, and getting it back is lengthy and expensive.

Data-based decision making is the future of work, but until now, it has been executed poorly in far too many organizations. So, before you survey, agree to act on the data. To make data actionable, you need to establish that:

- You have a budget.

- You have resources.

- You have plans and an ecosystem around that assessment (time, energy, commitment, people identified).

- You are willing to be transparent about the results.

- Measurement procedures and consistency matter. Only when we use the same measurement in the same way will the results be comparable.

- You check in regularly. Pulse checks with ongoing communication about the findings can often yield more results than—or at least complement—giant annual surveys.

How to Ask Effectively

Jim Moss, executive director of YMCA WorkWell, a division of the Y that researches and promotes workplace well-being, along with David Whiteside, director of insights for WorkWell, have spent years perfecting their analysis of workplace culture and well-being.

They use a twenty-two-question, evidence-based survey (part of which we pulled into our survey research) combining questions related to engagement, culture, and well-being. Data is also cross-referenced with a Net Promoter Score to help executives understand employee sentiment and its impact on the bottom line. It's necessary for an analysis to share both of these narratives, why they matter, and how they affect business. That knowledge then better directs the programming and strategic investment.

Moss believes that to make a survey functional, it has to give leaders enough insights to be impactful, but not be so lengthy that it stops employees from engaging with it. The average time it takes to answer the WorkWell survey is roughly five minutes. "Fewer and higher-value questions equals a painless experience for employees and deeper knowledge for staff," explained Moss. "The most significant insights rise to the surface. This tells leaders precisely what each group, department, or team needs to maintain or improve their experience and well-being. When it comes to realistically tackling the data, it's important that we're not trying to deal with everything all at once. If we can see which issues are the biggest priorities, we can more easily action those issues."

To make a survey valuable, Whiteside suggested that questions must be highly targeted and specific, with an opportunity for open-ended feedback. "At twenty-two questions, it means that every question is valuable real estate, and a big part of that has been an iterative process around finding the best questions that have the strongest relationship with well-being at work. It's also incredibly important; something that I see is missed in many other assessments," Whiteside emphasized, "is a question around what do employees *need* immediately to feel like they can be healthier at work. Not just looking at the data and looking for lower scores, but actually asking explicitly and then letting the actual needs of employees speak for themselves."

Moss also suggests that a serious blind spot for leaders is the value of data visualization. "How you visualize and share the insights should never be underestimated," said Moss. "Bringing the stories to the surface matters. Most measures lack compelling reports and report designs, which inevitably fails to galvanize stakeholders. You need the stories to build up empathy in the people who are responsible for actioning the change."

Frequency of asking also matters because, for many organizations, anxiety spikes at certain times of the year, just like clockwork. We witnessed this with corporate accountants dealing with year-end audits. For personal accountants, tax season plays a role in their stress. Teachers in June experience a major increase in stress as they try to wrap up one year and plan for the next. Many experience low coping skills and self-report feelings of exhaustion.

WorkWell's survey asks about predicted satisfaction in three months with a 100-point Likert scale. "How likely are you to feel satisfied in your job in three months?" (0–100, highly unlikely to highly likely). This learning tells an important story—whether dissatisfaction is acute or chronic. When chronic workplace stress and dissatisfaction in the workplace are strong predictors for burnout, it's helpful to know if someone believes that their work experience isn't about to get any better. Plus, when you cross-reference the Employee Net Promoter Score (eNPS), a measure of employee loyalty that indicates how willing someone would be to recommend their workplace to friends and family, you often find that low eNPS is correlated with predicted future stress.

These types of data points are helpful for stakeholders who want to see where to place more investment and, perhaps more importantly, where current investments in people are working and where they aren't.

Don't DIY Surveys

Checking in is one thing. Making up a survey that is intended to decide your well-being strategy, that's a whole other story. I've witnessed these "do-it-yourself" surveys too often in my work.

When we were called in to fix a struggling culture (if they measure; many don't), we reviewed the survey data. We often found homemade surveys that were poorly executed and ineffectively analyzed. Worse, we learned that the information leaders gathered about their people set them on a path to fix the wrong problems. By the time we arrived on the scene, we were repairing relationships and trying to reestablish trust.

David Ricardo's classical theory of comparative advantage, developed in 1817 to explain why countries engage in international trade, explains why we shouldn't always do everything ourselves. We may be able to, but why not create efficiencies through cooperation?

The same applies to organizations. When leaders try to do everything themselves to save money, in the end it may cost them more. For example, say you're a candy store and you ask, "Do you like our candies and how they're displayed?" Yes or no? Seventy percent answer no to reflect that they dislike the way they are displayed. The candy store closes because it thinks no one likes the candy.

Data gathering is a critical component for burnout prevention. Asking good questions is paramount. Although there are some organizations assessing burnout through either the MBI or other burnout specific surveys, many are not. And, from what I've witnessed, the homemade surveys, absent of a psychometrist or any real survey science, are cringeworthy.

Whiteside shared an example of surveys gone awry: "I feel burned out at work when I have to deal with frustrating customers or coworkers: 7-point scale from (1) Strongly Disagree to (7) Strongly Agree."

Whiteside emphatically said, "Just about everything is wrong with it. The question is double-barreled, which means it refers to both customers and coworkers in the same question. And how do employees answer this when they deal with customers and coworkers uniquely? It got even more face-palming when they told me that only about half of their employees are customer facing, but all employees were expected to respond to this question."

Whiteside made another great point when he explained that the question "assumes that you experience burnout at the very moment of a frustrating customer interaction, when the actual experience of burn-out isn't something that is acute or immediate."

He went on to explain that when you place a seven-point agreement scale over a question that is really just a true or false question, and yet it's the degree of burnout that is most interesting, it ends up not appropriately tackling either point. He suggested that better question options would be something like the following:

- I feel emotionally drained by difficult customer interactions. (1–7, agreement scale; propensity for burnout)

- I often feel emotionally drained after difficult customer interactions. (1–7, agreement scale; general burnout levels)

- How often do you feel emotionally drained after difficult customer interactions? (1–7, never–always; frequency of the experience of burnout)

He continued, "You can basically take that idea and adapt it to whatever needs you have, whether the researcher is interested in how often you experience burnout, if you're more or less likely to experience burnout from specific events, or general levels of burnout. But if those simple research method foundations aren't in place, you'll fall well short of your goals and get murky data that doesn't really help solve the problem."

Burnout surveys and inventories like the MBI are critical to burnout prevention, yet, when organizations misinterpret the data, the intentionality fails.

To recap, when we measure for burnout, we need to focus on three key points:

- *Prioritize small data.* Get to it by actively listening, scale team size so you can scale the listening, bring in "eavesdroppers"—anthropologists, external resources, outside ears to help you listen and hear better.

- *Prioritize clear data.* Don't do one of the most critical aspects to preventing burnout yourself. This isn't a side table you're upcycling; this data could be the most critical component to employee mental health. The wrong data fueling strategic plans will erode or possibly destroy the investments made in your company's well-being and burnout prevention efforts.

- *Prioritize actioning the data.* You erode trust in leadership when you continue to ask your employees for feedback and do nothing with it. You can always report back how much is within your realm to change or prevent, but you have to manage expectations constantly with feedback. Don't ask unless you're ready to do something with the data.

The Burnout/Engagement Debate

There has been some debate about which scales are the best for measuring burnout. A potential flaw in the MBI, according to some scientists, is that burnout is determined as polar to engagement. These researchers argue that burnout and engagement need to be measured separately to make each distinct from the other and to get a clearer picture of burnout.

According to Wilmar Schaufeli, coauthor of "The Measurement of Engagement and Burnout: A Two Sample Confirmatory Factor Analytic Approach":

> To date, relatively little attention has been paid to concepts that might be considered antipodes [direct opposites] of

burnout . . . Maslach and Leiter . . . assumed that "engagement" is characterized by energy, involvement, and efficacy
which are considered the direct opposites of the three burnout
dimensions exhaustion, cynicism, and lack of professional efficacy, respectively. Engaged employees have a sense of energetic
and effective connection with their work activities and they
see themselves as able to deal completely with the demands of
their job. By implication, engagement in the view of Maslach
and Leiter . . . is assessed by the opposite pattern of scores on
the three MBI dimensions. That is, according to these authors,
low scores on exhaustion and cynicism, and high scores on efficacy are indicative for engagement.[6]

Part of what Schaufeli argues is that the MBI's definition of engagement includes being fully absorbed in one's work—similar to "flow"
state—a theory defined by Mihaly Csikszentmihalyi, a psychologist and
the Distinguished Professor of Psychology and Management at Clare-
mont Graduate University. Flow, according to Csikszentmihalyi, is characterized by focused attention, a clear mind, mind and body in unison,
effortless concentration, complete control, loss of self-consciousness, dis-
tortion of time, and intrinsic enjoyment.

At first blush, it sounds exactly like the opposite of burnout. However, flow tends to be a more complex concept that refers to short-term,
heightened experiences, instead of a more perpetual state of mind, as is
the case with engagement.

Schaufeli and his team initiated two research samples to determine
whether burnout and work engagement should be measured as independent factors or opposite poles. Sample one comprised 314 undergraduate students at the University of Castellon, and sample two comprised
619 employees from private and public companies, employed in various
jobs and occupational fields.

The study compared the MBI, which consists of twenty-two items
that are scored on three scales: exhaustion (EX: five items, e.g., "I feel
emotionally drained from my work/study"); cynicism (CY: five items,

e.g., "I have become less enthusiastic about my study/work"); and efficacy (EF: six items, e.g., "I can effectively solve the problems that arise in my study/work"). All items are scored on a seven-point frequency rating scale ranging from 0 ("never") to 6 ("always"). High scores on EX and CY and low scores on EF indicate burnout (that is, all EF items are reversibly scored). In Schaufeli's scale, "engagement" was assessed with twenty-four self-constructed items and placed into a forty-item questionnaire.

What the researchers learned is that the relationship between burnout and engagement is more like a triangle and less like a straight line. A 2017 study, drawing on cross-sectional survey data from 1,535 Dutch police officers, also showed that the distinction between burnout and engagement is not as clear as is sometimes suggested. The authors concluded that "burnout and engagement are overlapping concepts and that the conceptual and empirical differences should not be overestimated."[7]

Schaufeli and colleagues would then claim that the absence of burnout does not necessarily imply the presence of engagement or vice versa; they subsequently developed the Utrecht Work Engagement Scale (UWES) that now analyzes engagement specifically.

Matt Leon, assistant professor of management at the University of North Florida, wrote "A Dialectical Perspective on Burnout and Engagement," in which he shared why the theory of dialectal tension could provide context for the MBI. He cited the work of Leslie Baxter of the University of Iowa, who founded the theory of relational dialectics along with Barbara Montgomery of Colorado State University–Pueblo. Essentially, relational dialectical tension is rooted in the dynamism of yin and yang. Like the classic yin and yang, any value pushed to its extreme contains the seed of its opposite.[8] Leon assesses that dialectics not only provide a plausible way of thinking about the relationship between burnout and engagement, but better capture the empirical findings regarding the relationship between the two constructs.

Both Leon and Schaufeli are telling us that engagement as the polar to burnout isn't the right measure. We throw around the term "engagement" all the time in corporate speak, but what does it actually mean?

To define, we need to explore the research of William Kahn, essentially the founding father of employee engagement. Kahn's 1990 study, "Psychological Conditions of Personal Engagement and Disengagement at Work," and the basis of his research into human motivation was inspired by psychologist Frederick Herzberg.

Kahn's research involved two workplace studies: the first in a summer camp and the second in an architecture firm. Through his time in these organizations, he defined engagement as an employee's ability to harness their "full self" at work and identified three psychological conditions that enable it:

- *Meaningfulness.* Does an employee find their work meaningful enough (to the organization and to society) to warrant them engaging their full self?

- *Safety.* Does the employee feel safe bringing their full self to work without risk of negative consequences?

- *Availability.* Does the employee feel mentally and physically able to harness their full self at this particular moment?[9]

His findings separate engagement from everyday hard work. A diligent employee who is able to harness their full self will display loyalty and ownership. For example, an engaged employee will tackle tasks without being asked because they want to and because they believe that their extra effort will benefit their organization.

Kahn also found that engagement isn't static—an employee's experiences of the workplace in different moments can cause fluctuations in engagement. This is good news for employers, as they have the opportunity to create an environment where engagement can flourish.

Kahn writes, "[P]eople occupy roles at work; they are the occupants of the houses that roles provide and constantly bring in and leave out various depths of their selves during the course of their workdays."[10]

Kahn would claim, "Engagement is both very delicate and fragile, and quite resilient. People have a desire to engage. They have an instinctive drive to express who they are, and who they wish to be, and given a chance at work, they will do so."

Kahn's research was qualitative and, therefore, did not provide a quantitative scale by which engagement could be measured. This may be why Schaufeli wanted to assess if engagement could be measured by simply reverse coding for burnout. Researchers continue to suggest that engagement, rather than being at the opposite end of a continuum from burnout, is in fact a distinct construct in its own right and has cast doubt on the possibility of measuring engagement by reverse scoring burnout scales.

As a result, the UWES has now become the most widely used measure of engagement in the academic world. This scale and the MBI can bolster each other, but neither one would really be considered a replacement survey for the other.

Leon wants to emphasize that there are some dangers to making people think that if they are engaged, they aren't burned out. This is the dialectical theory that he poses in his article. He argues that by putting burnout and engagement on opposing sides, we run the risk of engagement being the thing responsible for our burnout.

"We used to think of engagement, it's just the opposite of burnout," said Leon in our interview. "We would take a burnout measure and then reverse code it and say, 'Well, you're engaged' or take an engagement measure and reverse code it and say, 'Well, you're burned out.' I feel like in the real world, we're talking about two different things here."

Leon finds that the people who have chosen to work in research and academia and stay in these fields do so out of purpose: "It's something they identify with at a personal level, it's something that's fulfilling for them—they're absorbed, they're dedicated—but in too many instances, they're wildly, wildly burned out. It may be in some ways that the engagement actually drives that burnout."

We all require ways for us to recharge, whether that's being outside, having healthy family time, finding hobbies that we choose to master, or just having time to relax and be bored. But engagement may be preventing us from finding those outlets because we feel fulfilled by work and lack the awareness to know when feeling charged has become feeling drained.

When we identify so strongly with our work, we stop seeing the whole person, the human that has a life outside the context of work. We become branded by our job title. "Really, anything where there is a high risk of failure that requires a lot of training, it becomes a part of people's identity," said Leon. "I've noticed it with other people in my field, in academia, where if I meet someone who has a PhD, and you ask who they are and they say, 'I'm a doctor,' I want to say, 'No, that's your job; that's not who you are.' But I think when you commit that much time and effort and energy and resources into something, and you are that engaged with it . . . those two things are the same. People don't tell you, 'Well, I'm Matt from South Alabama, and I have a young child and a wife I love, and I like to travel, and instead I am Dr. Leon' . . . and that's not a sustainable way to live."

Going back to my conversation with Maslach and the analogy of a canary in a coal mine as it relates to burnout. When we put the canary down into the coal mine and the canary starts having problems with breathing and living and functioning, we don't say, "Oh shoot, how do we make that canary more resilient? How can we make it healthier so it can go back down into the mine?" It doesn't matter that there are fumes down there; canaries are tough, they're resilient. No, the canary is the sign that it's a dangerous environment, there is something toxic in there, and we don't want other people going in until we fix it.

Maslach said, "Burnout in some sense ought to be looked at more as that kind of warning signal, that thing that says, 'If you're beginning to see this problem and people are complaining about these same issues, that is your red flag.'"

I'll say it again. We don't send people back into burning buildings.

When people are complaining, we shouldn't assume they're being ungrateful or whiny and dismiss them. We need to say, "How can we help?" And instead of asking, "What do I do about burnout?" we need to ask, "How do we create a better, healthier workplace for people, so they don't burn out?" It's all about intervening upstream.

The Huddle

Maslach described one of these upstream interventions. In a group of health-care professionals, mostly physicians and nurses in a hospital setting, the first thing they did every morning was look at their charts and identify where there might be problems or backlogs, and then ask how people are feeling. They were clear about each other's mental health and personal situations that might impact their actions that day. Some reported they had a sick child at home, they didn't have enough childcare and they're cobbling together a solution, they're working on getting their mother into a home—the issues ran the gamut. But each team member who could would raise a hand to carry a portion of the burden: "I'll take these two cases. I can jump in here."

And mornings when people were feeling good and didn't have issues to share, they'd talk about a cool new film or celebrate a birthday. They affectionately named this meeting the Cuddle Huddle, and it's generated countless benefits, one of them being an increased comfort with speaking up and communicating hard conversations. In health care, there has historically been a solid hierarchical line between specific roles, but since this group has invested in connecting on a personal level, it's changed the interpersonal dynamics in a healthy and productive way.

Maslach said, "They've discovered all these extra benefits that they didn't think about at the time, which is that you get to know who you can trust, who you can talk to when you have a problem. It's a safe place. A safe person."

Why Do "Happiness Interventions" Seem Hokey?

Some of you may have tuned out as soon as I referred to this morning meeting as a Cuddle Huddle. We tend to have a visceral reaction to well-being interventions that feel too simplistic or saccharine. Happiness has a bad brand for some. It conjures a Pollyanna approach to a serious problem. I get it. I'm a well-being expert and I face these validity questions frequently.

I spoke with Shawn Achor, author of *Big Potential*, *The Happiness Advantage*, and *Before Happiness*. His TED Talk is one of the most popular, with over 11 million views. He shared with me why he believes there is an emotional barrier to doing positive psychology interventions: "Often they seem important but not urgent. I think most leaders, even well-intentioned optimistic ones, think that if they can get their work done, then everyone will be happy naturally. They follow the formula that if you work harder, your success will rise and you will accomplish your goals, and then you will be happy. But they have the formula backwards. We now know that the greatest competitive advantage in the modern economy is a positive and engaged brain, so if you're trying to create higher success, you need to start by helping your team create the best brains possible to create that change."

He shared that the leaders he and his team work with also worry, particularly during a global pandemic, that trying to emphasize positivity and happiness will make them tone-deaf. But Achor believes that it's still critical for organizations to engage in positive interventions, and by measuring, you can prove that it works.

Acting on the Insights

The next step in the measuring process is to act on the insights you've gleaned. After we know where the stressors are and how people are feeling, we act. We test interventions to see if we can decrease stress and increase well-being. That doesn't mean we stop measuring. Actually, when acting on the insights, gathering feedback in as many ways as possible will determine whether we were successful.

Here's an example of insights in action.

Achor and his partner, Michelle Gielan, former CBS News anchor and author of *Broadcasting Happiness*, joined with the Genesis Health

System, a group of five hospitals and a regional health center, at a time when they were not profitable. Jordan Voigt, president of the largest medical centers in the group, wanted to instill more positivity into the culture but was just about to lay off staff and cut costs. It was going to be challenging, but Voigt saw the value in the investment.

Achor and Gielan worked with the medical center to roll out a series of positive psychology interventions, department by department, to test the effectiveness compared to groups that had not been exposed to the interventions. Each department designed positive changes tailored to its subculture, spanning from gratitude exercises to increased praise and recognition from managers to team-based conscious acts of kindness.

Despite the significant organizational changes, the percentage of respondents who reported that they were happy at work went from 43 percent to 62 percent. Individuals feeling burned out dropped from 11 percent to 6 percent, while those reporting "high stress at work" dropped by 30 percent. The number of respondents who said, "I feel connected at work," went from 68 percent to 85 percent. In the parts of the hospital that had not participated in the intervention, only 37 percent of respondents claimed Genesis was going in the right direction, compared to 63 percent in the groups who went through the intervention.

Achor and Gielan shared the success of their research in a *Harvard Business Review* article, "What Leading with Optimism Really Looks Like." The pair suggested the following key takeaways for leaders who want to know how to start the conversation.

Role-model from the top

Often leaders give lip service to the value of a positive mindset and people as their greatest asset, but then they don't bother to attend their own internal positive leadership workshops because they are too busy. This signals to the rest of the organization that a positive culture is in fact a much lower priority than they claimed. As president of the medical center, Voigt personally kicked off every workshop. He made sure to follow each round of data-collection findings to determine what was working and whether to continue. He affirmed happiness as a priority, which made the topic more salient in the minds of his staff. This is the first step for leaders who want to create a positive mindset in the midst of setback: show up and model that mindset yourself.

Help employees connect before asking them to change

People don't typically make positive changes alone or in isolation. A positive mindset at work is often a collective exercise, because the behaviors and attitudes are reinforced when a group does it together. At Genesis, the emphasis in the workshops was on developing positive habits, brainstorming new work routines, and discussing culture together in groups. This allowed participants to take ownership over the new mindsets, routines, and ways of working. They were creating new social scripts in real time and connecting these changes to purpose, verbalizing the significant impact their happiness and positivity can have on their patients. It's imperative that leaders help people feel connected first and then deputize them to make positive change.

Make changes part of the routine way of doing work

As a leader, don't just tell people "be happy"; work with them to create patterns that reinforce the positive. It's too hard in the midst of stress to try to invent new ways to be positive, so creating regular patterns as a department can help sustain the positive without having to call on new brain resources. It can be as simple as habituating celebration. For example, the endoscopy department, which was known to be toxic, with a 35 percent vacancy rate, now has regularly scheduled potluck lunches—and a zero percent vacancy rate over six months. Some departments' leaders set the routine of starting all their staff meetings with each person saying one thing they're grateful for. Some have areas where people can post thank-yous or pictures of successes so that any staff or patient walking into that department is given a dose of visual positivity.

All of these changes weren't just good for the hospital staff; they benefited patients, too. Patient experience rates nearly doubled within a twelve-month period. Following the intervention, Genesis Medical Center–Davenport achieved profitability again and exceeded its operating budget by 35 percent during the first part of 2019, going from an operating loss of $2 million to a profit of $8 million. The medical center was recognized in 2019 by Press Ganey Associates as one of the nation's most improved medical centers for performance; six months into the fiscal year, the center increased total operating revenue by $15 million, or 8.7 percent, while expenses increased only $1.9 million, or 1.1 percent. And in October 2019, it achieved a record in its history for gross revenue, $114 million. All of this was happening when so much of the medical industry was financially contracting.[11]

Achor and Gielan proved that when we measure our interventions, we can track if they work. WorkWell analyzes the success of its interventions through survey data and qualitative feedback, but also cross-references it with eNPS and other metrics provided by each company to track what is working and what isn't. There are multiple wins in this scenario. Evidence supports that a solidly executed well-being campaign can improve community and decrease stress; it also positively impacts the bottom line.

Achor and Gielan's final takeaway from their research project reinforces my earlier points. They underscore:

> If there was no perceived change, or if there was no data justifying the approach, the culture change would not take root as readily. If we don't test what works, we lack the motivation to keep that change permanent or top of mind. Positive interventions in particular get thrown by the wayside in challenging times unless you have a clearly established connection between the energy required to continue the positive change and the desired outcomes. In the end, by doing a rolled-out, staggered approach, other teams heard about the intervention and the

results and were actually demanding the positive intervention for their teams.[12]

This example does more than just emphasize the benefits of well-being interventions for revenue and shareholder value. It shows how making data-based decisions drives that impact. We know where to shift our investments. We create efficiencies by learning what works and what doesn't and investing more in what does.

We also achieve more buy-in. When we have evidence to show that "nice-to-haves" are actually "must-haves," it requires less effort trying to convince decision makers of ideas about which they may be wary or feel biased.

And, if we're ever going to clearly define burnout, we need to know what causes and prevents it. Not only does that require measuring, but testing and iterating solutions to see what sticks. We can't get hung up on what those solutions might be; we just need to explore all the possibilities. We also can't get stuck on the perfect way to measure for it; it's all about taking one step forward.

That one step forward can start small and then grow over time. If you haven't yet implemented a measure in your organization, how about starting simple?

Just you and me and five bucks.

PART THREE

Leadership

5

Leading with Curiosity

Curiosity is defined as having a strong desire to learn or know about something. The desire comes from a deeply imbedded genetic need to survive. Curiosity teaches us about threats, but it also helps us develop emotionally, mentally, intellectually, and even physically, through knowledge attainment. When we quash that process, we stop growing. Our imagination atrophies. Our learning dies.

If we don't help our employees to pursue their curiosity, we are essentially telling them to stop growing, which seems counter to what our organizations require to be successful. If we want the companies we lead to flourish, our employees much flourish first.

Sparking curiosity and celebrating discovery inside our cultures will help drive that goal forward. That said, it appears that as adults, our hunger for questioning dissipates.

When we were children, we asked the people in our lives, "Why?" ad nauseum. Most of *us* have experienced a child asking *us* why, over and over again. Mildly irritating at times perhaps, but what a shame that a by-product of aging is losing that desire to investigate further. To care just a little bit more about the answers.

Is this a long-standing part of our evolution, or perhaps has it worsened, a symptom of the times? Do we feel full? Is our information craving satisfied after we get our dose of social media or a rotation of the twenty-four-hour cable news that is now the background music of our lives? Has our need to seek out answers from others been dulled because we can always just Google it?

What if we could reduce burnout by being more curious about others and seek out new learning to benefit ourselves? Wouldn't that be fun?

"The Business Case for Curiosity"

Francesca Gino, behavioral scientist and the Tandon Family Professor of Business Administration at Harvard Business School, wrote the wildly popular *Harvard Business Review* article, "The Business Case for Curiosity."

She challenges business leaders to consider the value of curiosity for all the reasons you'd expect—innovation, creative thinking, competition. "Most of the breakthrough discoveries and remarkable inventions throughout history, from flints for starting a fire to self-driving cars, have something in common: They are the result of curiosity," writes Gino.[1]

But the article also reflects on the other benefits to a culture of curiosity, like nurturing trust, fostering psychological safety, making questions easier to ask, and fostering friendships. Most critically, curiosity, according to Gino's research, increases empathy—a leadership skill recognized for reducing burnout.

"My research found that curiosity encourages members of a group to put themselves in one another's shoes and take an interest in one another's ideas rather than focus only on their own perspective," said Gino.[2]

The results of Gino's work also determined that curiosity helped employees listen more openly and effectively and, when faced with challenges, tend to maintain fortitude and seek out creative solutions.

The case for a curious culture is strong. We just need to practice curiosity in the right way.

And, yes, there is a right and wrong way. You'd be surprised.

The Science of Curiosity

According to Mario Livio, internationally known astrophysicist who has published more than four hundred scientific articles, "By being curious about new kinds of food, about creating new tools, and about the use of fire for cooking, humans probably enhanced their own ability to be curious." But in the brain, the way we process curiosity isn't treated the same every time. "Curiosity may actually encompass a family of different psychological states that are powered by distinct circuits in the brain," said Livio in his *Psychology Today* article, "Why Ask Why?[3]

Let's first take, for example, curiosity that stems from feeling deprived of information—something that we can all relate to from our experience throughout the pandemic. Unknowns became more typical than knowns, and that triggered our perceptual curiosity. That happens when we feel that there is a "gap created by uncertainty so we are driven to seek new insights that will reduce the unpleasant sensation."[4]

Epistemic curiosity—the kind that explores arts and sciences, that connects humanity through discovery and innovation—conjures a "pleasurable state, one in which we anticipate reward."[5]

Perceptual curiosity is primarily associated with an unpleasant feeling, or as Livio suggests, it's like "scratching an intellectual itch." Think news on in the background all day in those first few months of the epidemic and even before Covid-19. Our media consumption has exponentially increased since the 2016 election, with unfortunate results. It's caused so many "unpleasant" feelings that therapists came up with a specific term explaining the resulting symptoms: "headline stress disorder," also known as "breaking news disorder."

Celeste Kidd and Benjamin Hayden, researchers from the Department of Brain and Cognitive Sciences at the University of Rochester, claim that our insatiable demand for information drives much of the global economy. They suggest that on a microscale, our information craving "even drives patterns of foraging in animals."[6]

We know this rabbit hole all too well. We dive in seeking information that soothes, only to find ourselves stuck in a dark, depressing pit we can't seem to wriggle out of.

If he were here, Oscar Wilde would be reminding us that "[t]he public have an insatiable curiosity to know everything, except what is worth knowing." But what if he's wrong.

We just need to focus our attention on epistemic curiosity, the kind of curiosity that follows the pathways that transmit dopamine to trigger our brain's reward systems. When we are curious in this learning-for-fun kind of way, we get to enjoy "intrinsic motivation, an activity undertaken for its own sake, that is also pleasurable."[7]

And since epistemic curiosity makes us feel so damn good, you can imagine there would be some mental health benefits, right? That would be accurate. Actually, our survival depends on it.

1. *Curiosity helped humans to evolve.* We might still be living in caves without fire if we weren't committed to being curious. The urge to explore and the impulse to seek novelty play an important role in our evolution, and we've been hardwired for it. We are rewarded for curiosity by dopamine and opioids (feel-good chemicals in the brain), which are stimulated in the face of something new. The flip side of novelty is boredom—a predictor of burnout. We need to keep moving forward, and we do this by leveraging curious behaviors.

2. *Curiosity increases workplace success.* In the study "Field Investigation of the Relationship Among Adult Curiosity, Workplace Learning, and Job Performance," the authors found that adult-state and trait epistemic (knowledge-seeking) curiosity would influence workplace learning and job performance.[8]

3. *Curiosity can expand our empathy.* Highly empathic people have an insatiable curiosity about strangers. They find other people more interesting than themselves but are not out to interrogate them. Roman Krznaric, founding faculty member of the School

of Life in London, writes in the article "Six Habits of Highly Empathic People" that "[c]uriosity expands our empathy when we talk to people outside our usual social circle, encountering lives and worldviews very different from our own."[9] Curiosity is good for us, too: happiness researcher Martin Seligman identifies it as a key character strength that can enhance life satisfaction.

4. *Our curiosity makes others healthier.* Jodi Halpern, a bioethicist at the University of California, Berkeley, indicates in "Empathy and Patient-Physician Conflicts" that when doctors are genuinely curious about their patients' perspectives, both doctors and patients report less anger and frustration and make better decisions, ultimately increasing the effectiveness of treatment.[10]

5. *Curiosity reduces stress.* Todd Kashdan, in "Curiosity and Exploration: Facilitating Positive Subjective Experiences and Personal Growth Opportunities," found that curiosity displaces stress, anxiety, and depression—all of which can limit cognitive potential and the ability to access high cognitive skills such as advanced communication and negotiation.[11]

Scientists, researchers, and experts alike would argue that we need to keep that authentic, epistemic curiosity alive. Many assert that curiosity can prevent burnout.

Rebecca A. Palacios, senior curriculum adviser at Age of Learning, shared in our conversation that "children are born with a natural inquisitiveness. They want to know about the world around them and constantly ask 'why?' questions." Palacios claimed that as adults, we should continue to be open to asking why and seeking answers: "In this way, we can find out about the world around us, the people in the world and how they feel and how we can support them. When we stop asking why, then we become stagnant and less responsive to the world around us. Or even, we stop asking as many questions."

To nurture cultures of discovery and innovation, we have to be authentically curious. We need to look inward for the answers. We have to be inquisitive of the people we are collaborating with and ensuring that they are healthy and happy. And when they are not, we ask why, and stop the practices and policies based on those learnings. This is what makes prioritizing a culture of curiosity essential to our well-being strategies. Not only do they bring numerous benefits to our mental health, they are consequential to preventing burnout.

Building a culture of curiosity may be simpler than you think.

Becoming a Professional Eavesdropper

Martha Bird, chief anthropologist for ADP, has an atypical role. It is quite progressive for a company to have an anthropologist in the C-suite. Perhaps more organizations should. It seems to be paying off.

In 2019, ADP ranked third on Comparably's "Top 50 Best Large Company Cultures." I'm not normally a fan of "best places to work lists" because they lack employee input, but these rankings are based on anonymous employee sentiment. According to background on the survey methodology, "the final data set was compiled from nearly 10 million ratings across 50,000 US companies on Comparably.com. Winners were determined based on a series of 50+ structured and comprehensive workplace questions in core culture categories, including: Compensation, Leadership, Professional Development, Work-Life Balance, Perks & Benefits, among others."[12]

The reason for ranking third may have something to do with Bird and her role as chief anthropologist. In a profile on women in STEM on ADP's website, you can see why she's leading a big part of its culture strategy.

In her former role at eBay, a multinational e-commerce company based in San Jose, Bird spent her days immersing herself in the culture of the sellers: "She was hanging out with collectors of dolls and magic toys to understand what mattered to them and how technology could be improved to make the site more engaging to them. Martha realized that, in many ways, [eBay] was an online museum and the users were curators trying to figure out what they needed and wanted."[13]

I asked her why immersing yourself in a culture of something—whether it be the language, the customs, or the rituals of a country—when launching a product or company there changes the user experience. She told me that if you are an anthropologist, you "have a very deep respect for the liberality of other people, and that requires moving beyond the reduced to something a little bit more nuanced." She believes it's like being a "professional eavesdropper."

Of course, I love that definition because it's a tenet of empathic leadership, which is essentially "active listening." It is one of the ways that I suggest we can scale good culture by listening to the small data and engaging with it to create a network effect—a contagion—of healthy behaviors.

But something she said really stuck with me. It demonstrated her deep understanding of what makes an exceptional culture—the special sauce you feel in the physical and virtual walls of your workplace—that effortless state-of-belonging vibe that can be uncovered in every single workplace. She said, "People are messy, and the messiness is what tells us the most. We humans attempt to make the mess meaningful. And that meaning is reflected in what we do. So, data has a culture. Technology is cultural. Anthropologists deconstruct the mess to help illuminate patterns and new ways of thinking about old challenges."

When we got into the topic of burnout, I was keen to consider how to address it from an anthropologist's perspective.

Organizational anthropologists analyze the business through storytelling sessions, culture probes, and observational research that help leaders understand what people are really doing. They observe the organization through nuanced filters. They also dig into historical context and the popular lexicon to help bring new understandings to old behaviors.

Anthropologists force us to look deeper into the meanings through visuals, artifacts, symbols, and words to come up with better answers to questions that plague us.

And the magic of discovery is often found in the stories that get shared and passed down. They are found in the random stories about everyday life—the strange things that make people laugh, the art they appreciate, the books they read, their childhood dreams, their memories, and their reality. You can learn more about what motivates a person from a cause button they favor or a picture taped to their desk than you can by measuring productivity and engagement alone. Those big measures—the macro analyses are still important—they tell you how your employees are operating. The small data tells you how your employees are feeling.

Digging Deeper

So, by now you should know I'm going to suggest we measure. But here is another way we can do that. It's a lesson in becoming a professional eavesdropper.

Regardless of organization size, there is always a reason and a mechanism to connect with our people. The idea that the CEO of a twenty-thousand-plus-person company can't engage with every single employee in the organization is a false narrative that has permeated leadership for far too long. Perhaps this was more challenging before conference calling became cheaper and more accessible in the mid-eighties, but since then, there has really been no excuse for leaders at the highest levels to be disconnected from their employees.

How can you actually scale that kind of accessibility? It's easier than you think.

I am a firm believer in the way that organizations like Google build their teams. And, as you might expect from Google, it didn't come to this decision without data. Code name Project Aristotle, a team of researchers, spent years analyzing its top one hundred or so best-performing teams to figure out their culture recipe. After years of analyzing what makes a high-performing team at Google, some were surprised by the answers. (I wasn't.) Here is what the researchers learned.

First, members of the top teams spoke proportionately in meetings—they all had equal time to share ideas, solutions, thoughts, plans, and so on. The Project Aristotle lead researcher, Anita Williams Woolley of

Carnegie Mellon University, described this as "equality in distribution of conversational turn-taking." She shared that "as long as everyone got a chance to talk, the team did well. But if only one person or a small group spoke all the time, the collective intelligence declined."[14]

Second, the best teams all had high "average social sensitivity"—an academic way of saying they were really good at discerning how others felt based on their body language, semiotics, tone of voice, facial expressions, and other nonverbal cues. They used this cool technique to gauge social sensitivity by showing someone photos of people's eyes and asking them to describe what the people were thinking or feeling—an exam known as the "Reading the Mind in the Eyes" test. As you can guess, the high-performing teams scored high on this test; they seemed to be able to better read when someone was upset or stressed or isolated from their teammates. Lower-performing teams scored below average on this test, demonstrating less sensitivity for their coworkers.

Both research and anecdotal evidence confirm that reduced empathy among coworkers and from leadership can increase burnout. So, the evidence should be a clear sign to leaders that building teams with higher average social sensitivity and anchoring equity in thought sharing is good for both preventing burnout and the bottom line.

In "What Google Learned from Its Quest to Build the Perfect Team," Charles Duhigg, author of *The Power of Habit*, writes, "Project Aristotle is a reminder that when companies try to optimize everything, it's sometimes easy to forget that success is often built on experiences—like emotional interactions and complicated conversations and discussions of who we want to be and how our teammates make us feel—that can't really be optimized."[15]

If I asked you, "What is the emotional driver for your highest-performing teams?" would you be able to answer?

Although psychological safety should be broadly accepted across all organizations, it may show up in different forms and leadership styles. This is what Google proved to be true for itself, but every culture is ultimately unique, and that requires each organization to deploy its own version of Project Aristotle.

Cool fact: from the data, Google realized that if it slowed down the lunch lineup by a fraction, it yielded more "collisions." It deduced that when people spent slightly more time waiting in line, they started talking. This led to more people eating lunch together and solving some of their biggest problems.

Based on data gathered from Project Aristotle, Google went on to learn that team size can also have an impact on improving performance. Plenty of research agrees that performance is strengthened with smaller teams, but what about preventing burnout? Evidence continues to support smaller teams in enhancing feedback and improving communication, both highly correlated to reducing burnout if working effectively.

Having a large group of people working together on interdependent tasks unfortunately leads to unexpected problems. Researchers have come to realize that the more people working together, the greater the overhead of communication. And the less opportunity to be curious.

Staying Connected Means Smaller Teams

Alistair Cockburn oversees Scrumplog.org—a site with a mission to build a body of pattern literature for mostly software engineers and developers around a "scrum," which scrum.org defines as "a framework within which people can address complex adaptive problems, while productively and creatively delivering products of the highest possible value."[16]

Some may see the word *scrum* (short form for *scrummage*) and think of rugby. Well, your instincts are right—the term was borrowed from rugby, where a scrum is a formation of players. The term *scrum* was first used in a software development context in a 1986 *Harvard Business Review* article by Hirotaka Takeuchi and Ikujiro Nonaka.[17] The paper's authors chose the term *scrum* because it emphasizes teamwork.

According to "Scrum Guides," scrum has been used to develop software, hardware, embedded software, networks of interacting function, autonomous vehicles, schools, government, marketing, managing the operation of organizations, and almost everything we use in our daily lives, as individuals and societies.[18]

Contributors to the Published Patterns blog are software developers and share tips or advice on leadership in this area. One contributor writes in a post titled "Small Teams" that good communication is essential for effective teamwork, obviously, but as team sizes grow, "there is proportionally less information transferred within the group, yet there needs to be more information transferred with the increased number of people. Taken to extreme, communication and coordination overhead consumes nearly all the resources of the group, leaving almost no time to do productive work. This is like the problem in computers called 'thrashing' where a lot of energy is expended without actually accomplishing anything."[19]

The contributor, in line with other research on the same topic, suggests that with larger groups of people, the relative contribution of everyone diminishes—sort of like getting lost in the crowd, where people can hide in the nonwork and remain less accountable. Scientist Alan Ingham came up with the concept of "social loafing" in the seventies, which helps us understand why the individual effort decreases as the team size increases.

Social loafing can sometimes be explained as an individual's reduction in effort in order to avoid pulling the weight of another member. Ingham reasoned that for every person added beyond five to six people, individual contributions to the group became smaller. What he is emphasizing here is that larger groups might have higher rates of overall productivity than smaller teams, but the individual members of the larger team have lower rates of productivity than those in the smaller team.

In "'It's Not Fair!' Cultural Attitudes to Social Loafing in Ethnically Diverse Groups," coauthors Jill Clark and Trish Baker write, "A major factor in reducing social loafing is keeping the size of the group small and providing reliable performance evaluation mechanisms and clear standards. Providing individuals with feedback about their own performance, or the performance of the group, was also reported as reducing social loafing and enhancing members' personal involvement with the task reduced the effect. Researchers concluded that people tend to exert more effort on challenging, meaningful tasks. On the flip side, individuals who believe that they are better than others are more likely to reduce their contribution to group tasks."[20]

Wharton management professor Katherine J. Klein, in "Team Mental Models and Team Performance," coauthored with Beng-Chong Lim, a professor at Nanyang Technological University, suggests that the widely accepted ideal size for a working team is five people: "If you go beyond five people the team starts to lose individual performance, while teams smaller than five people can experience awkward team dynamics and skills gaps."[21]

Additionally, people working in small teams have a greater sense of attachment to each other and their shared goals and have better communication within the team. They receive more opportunities to be heard and are generally more productive.

But experts suggest that cutting people from an existing team—despite the size—isn't the answer. When a group of individuals is closely knit in the workplace, severing those relationships without a valid reason can negatively impact their experiences of work en masse. And since healthy relationships play a big role in preventing burnout, it's best to look for the right openings to move people out of the group, such as attrition, promotion, or a team member's interest in seeking new internal opportunities.

Building Community through Curiosity

Lack of community is one of the biggest threats to burnout because healthy relationships are foundational to well-being. According to Martin Seligman, a happiness researcher and pioneer in the field of positive psychology, there are five important building blocks of well-being and happiness, or PERMA:

- Positive emotions—feeling good

- Engagement—being completely absorbed in activities

- Relationships—being authentically connected to others

- Meaning—purposeful existence

- Achievement—a sense of accomplishment and success[22]

What we've come to better understand since Seligman theorized PERMA is that the "R" might be the most important contributor to our happiness and well-being. And if we spend ninety thousand hours at work in a lifetime, wouldn't it make sense to focus some time on fostering strong friendships there too?[23] One way to do that is through checking in—being curious about other people's lives.

In "The Surprising Power of Simply Asking Coworkers How They're Doing," author Karyn Twaronite, EY global diversity and inclusiveness officer, suggests that "when people feel like they belong at work, they are more productive, motivated, engaged and 3.5 times more likely to contribute to their fullest potential."[24]

In her research, she found that 39 percent of respondents feel the greatest sense of belonging when their colleagues check in with them, both personally and professionally. On the flip side, she found out which tactics didn't yield the same results; for example, face-to-face with senior leadership that wasn't personal, being invited to big or external events or presentations by senior leaders, and/or being copied on their emails didn't make anyone feel any more connected.[25]

So how should you check in?

According to Twaronite, there is an art to the check-in.

Be considerate

To be authentic, you need to know how someone likes to communicate. In an era when people are suffering from Zoom burnout more than ever, asking someone to jump on another video conferencing meeting may seem tone-deaf. Some people don't like staring face-to-face at someone for an undefined amount of time, particularly someone they don't know that well. Perhaps instead, jump on a phone call or arrange an in-person walk-and-talk, or maybe send an email or a message on Chat. Whatever it is—figure it out first—then set up an appropriate channel of communication.

Be authentic

Try to establish authentic connections with your friends and peers. Don't just ask how they are doing and accept it when they say they're fine—be specific. Dig deeper. Instead of just checking in generally, ask them about a project they're working on. Learn about what they're interested in and reflect that with your curiosity. Maybe you heard they were presenting on a specific topic; ask them to expand on it. Authentic relationships start with genuine, shared interests. This means you have to pay attention. Analyze and assimilate what the people around you are doing. Don't take their actions and behaviors for granted. It may be the key to unlocking a connection.

Remove bias

Take the time to listen to people's perspectives. This is important, particularly in a time of increased polarization. A confirmation bias is a type of cognitive bias that involves favoring information that confirms your previously existing beliefs or biases. When developing relationships, it causes us to narrow our circle, which stops diverse thinking and approaches to solving problems.

For example, imagine that a person holds a belief that left-handed people are more creative than right-handed people. Whenever this person encounters a person who is both left-handed and creative, they place greater importance on this "evidence" that supports what they already believe. The individual might even seek proof that further backs up this belief, while discounting examples that don't support the idea.

Catherine A. Sanderson, author of *Social Psychology*, claims that confirmation bias reaffirms the existing stereotypes we have about people. In her book, she writes, "We are more likely to remember (and repeat) stereotype-consistent information and to forget or ignore stereotype-inconsistent information, which is one way stereotypes are maintained even in the face of disconfirming evidence."[26]

She shares the following example: "If you learn that your new Canadian friend hates hockey and loves sailing, and that your new Mexican friend hates spicy foods and loves sushi, you are less likely to remember this new stereotype-inconsistent information."

According to Francesca Gino, "When our curiosity is triggered, we are less likely to fall prey to confirmation bias and to stereotyping people (making broad judgments, such as that women or minorities don't make good leaders). Curiosity has these positive effects because it leads us to generate alternatives."[27]

This is why we need to come to a conversation with an open mind. We also need to be prepared to actively listen so we can assimilate the new information without attaching bias to it. This will help us to remember those details in future discussions.

Assume the best

Start your conversations with people assuming the best. Believe that they mean well, especially when it comes to difficult issues. When we are in conversations that may be hard to have—say, if we're grieving—someone trying to comfort us might fumble and feel awkward. But assuming positive intent will help to take the good with the discomfort. On the flip side, if you are there to offer a shoulder, don't try to fix the problem or relate with stories of your own. We should only really chime in if we can authentically relate. If you don't know what to say, you should stick with, "Thank you for sharing this with me. I don't have any advice. I just want to listen and learn."

Stay humble

Having the capacity to show humility as a leader and just generally in how we communicate with others is a major asset. The most successful people—particularly in the workplace—rely on a variety of voices to dictate the strategy. It's why we have cross-diagonal meetings and re-verse mentorships; it offers more people a seat at the table.

Fostering positive relationships in the workplace is a critical compo-nent of healthy, well cultures that avoid burnout. Having a best friend at work, according to Gallup, is one of the biggest drivers of retention and engagement.[28] Nurturing inclusive and diverse relationships also plays a role in creative and innovative thinking. We can accomplish most of these goals by practicing the art of the check-in.

But the investment in creating a culture of curiosity has to be authen-tic and protected. Reflect on the image of the dusty pool table here. If you want people to be curious, you have to give them protected time to explore and react. If we're offering "10 percent time," we need to adjust expectations accordingly. No one is going to swap out hitting a deadline for white space.

If you want to authentically create a culture of curiosity, hire for it. Ruma Batheja, the head of organizational development and HR strat-egy at Knowledgetics, a research consulting firm, recommends several strategies for hiring curious people:[29]

1. *During the interview, give candidates a problem to solve.* Assign a real, challenging task that needs immediate attention. Curious people will be confident in their knowledge and will likely try to modify a process or method for creating something better. It isn't about the solution; it's more about how they got there.

2. *Check their interest in learning new things.* Batheja offers a couple of examples: "Tell me something new you have learned in the last six months" or "What recent skill have you acquired, and how have you implemented it in your current role?"

3. *Ask candidates about their outside interests, but be specific.* Suggest they teach you about their hobby. What has their outside interest taught them about life? How can they apply it to their career or the role they are applying for? Or, ask them what books they've read or movies they've watched. Then have them share why they're interested in specific genres of films or literature.

4. *Curious people ask better questions.* The interviewer can try using scenario-based questions to give candidates the opportunity to show if they are naturally driven to ask questions or care to understand how a particular process works.

To amplify a curious culture, try putting curiosity into practice. Alison Horstmeyer, in an article published in the *Graziadio Business Review*, lists the following two exercises we can use to develop curiosity.[30]

Exercise 1: Reflection

At the end of each day, write down how you used your curiosity in ways that contributed to a positive or productive outcome. After two weeks, review what you wrote each day.

- What patterns do you see?

- What insights about your use of curiosity surfaced for you?

- How can these insights help you in the future to connect your curiosity to professional growth and/or to higher satisfaction in your work?

Create a curiosity action plan in which you identify three actions you will continue to practice to encourage your curious mindset.
Alternately, contemplate the following questions:

1. How does your curiosity show up in your work?

2. In what ways can you employ a curious mindset to foster more meaningful connection to others?

3. In what ways can you reframe a challenge into a learning opportunity?

4. What blocks or interferes with your curiosity? What could you do to remove these obstacles?

Identify one "stop" behavior that prevents or interferes with your curiosity, and one "start" behavior that encourages you to remain curious.

For one month, keep a journal tracking your progress of consistently discontinuing your stop and implementing your start behavior. If, at the end of the month, you feel satisfied with your progress, identify a new stop behavior and a new start behavior and track your progress for another month. Each month, you can select new start and stop behaviors or return to previous behaviors.

Exercise 2: Reframing

Select a perceived business issue or problem and organize a meeting to briefly present it to your team or cross-functional group. Then instruct the group that they have four minutes to collaboratively generate fifteen different questions reframing the problem.

The aim of this step is not to solve the problem but to uncover, through different ways of wording it, whether an alternative problem exists whose resolution would be even more organizationally valuable.

After the initial four minutes, take another twenty minutes to identify any additional questions missing from the fifteen-question set created. Then, using the entire question set, select which questions specifically identified new pathways in viewing the problem, and highlight why each pathway seems important or meaningful. Setting aside what might be the most comfortable route to pursue, commit to investigating at least one of the pathways and create an action plan for doing so.

· · ·

By developing curious behaviors, we learn. We learn about each other and we learn about ourselves. What motivates us. What excites us. What drives engagement in others and what detracts from their happiness.

By developing curious behaviors, we increase our cognitive empathy, which enhances not just our leadership skills but makes us better global citizens. When we practice curiosity, overcoming obstacles is reframed as stimulating. Change is thrilling instead of terrifying. Curiosity is a "superskill" to lean on during times of massive, uncertain shift.

Individuals may more readily mobilize to access the resources they need to help them deal with change—building up self-efficacy and hopefulness. When people perceive situations in these ways, it helps to reduce stress and, notably, burnout.

Perhaps most important of all, we are born to be curious. The people we lead are eager to learn and explore novel experiences. By creating a culture of curiosity, we embrace empathy, restore calm, enhance creativity, and cultivate an innovative mindset.

Start today by asking just one person, "Why?"

6

Becoming an Empathetic Leader

When we talk about empathy in leadership, people can feel uncomfortable. Not because they don't have any empathy; they've just been taught that leadership is displayed in behaviors that exhibit authority, emotional discipline, stoicism. And this doesn't jibe with how an empathic leader might behave.

Some people are quick to say empathy is too sentimental, too emotional for the workplace. But in reality, it is challenging to develop, particularly if there isn't a strong genetic predisposition. And empathy can be tough to sustain.

Here's some straight talk. It's annoying when people suggest that empathy is a soft skill. Despite the desire to change the way we think about the term *soft*, that word has almost as much baggage and bias attached to it as burnout. Some terms just need to be changed; soft skills is one of them.

In the dictionary, soft is defined as: easy to mold, cut, compress, or fold; not hard or firm to the touch. "Soft margarine." I'm sorry, but soft margarine as a leadership skill feels totally wrong to me.

Emotional intelligence, or psychological fitness—that is how I think about empathy as a leadership skill. Who doesn't want to be more brain fit or have a higher EQ (emotional quotient)? Deemed a necessary skill for competent leadership in the *US Army Leadership Field Manual*, it's a skill worth having.

Here is how the army wants us to think about empathy, pulled from sections 4.1 and 4.4 in the manual:

> **4.1.** Character, a person's moral and ethical qualities, helps determine what is right and gives a leader motivation to do what is appropriate, regardless of the circumstances or the consequences. An informed ethical conscience consistent with the Army Values strengthens leaders to make the right choices when faced with tough issues. Since Army leaders seek to do what is right and inspire others to do the same, they must embody these values.

> **4-4.** Character is essential to successful leadership. It determines who people are and how they act. It helps determine right from wrong and choose what is right. The factors, internal and central to a leader, which make up the leader's core are:
>
> 1. Army Values.
>
> 2. Empathy.
>
> 3. Warrior Ethos.[1]

And how might empathy be described by one of the world's most popular leaders?

Jacinda Ardern was elected the prime minister of New Zealand in October 2017. She is the country's youngest leader since 1856 and became the world's youngest female head of government when she took office at the age of thirty-seven.

For Ardern, empathy looks like a pledge to increase the minimum wage, write child poverty reduction targets into law, and build affordable homes. During her time as prime minister, Ardern had her first child while leading New Zealand through the aftermath of the Christchurch mosque shootings and the pandemic. She was celebrated for radically changing the gun laws in her country, as well as expertly containing the spread of Covid-19 in her country.

Quoted in the *New York Times*, Adern said, "One of the criticisms I've faced over the years is that I'm not aggressive enough or assertive enough, or maybe somehow, because I'm empathetic, it means I'm weak. I totally rebel against that. I refuse to believe that you cannot be both compassionate and strong."[2]

Making Your Workplace Safe for Grief

Many of us have faced grief in our lifetime, but in 2020, the collective grief was unparalleled. Not since the world wars and the 1918 flu pandemic has the world gone through so much loss at one moment in time.

What is interesting about grief is that we don't just feel it from loss of life. We experience it in myriad ways. We can mourn the loss of marriage in a divorce. We can mourn the loss of a job or an identity. We can mourn the loss of a culture. We can mourn the loss of our old lives, as many did just weeks after the lockdown on March 15, 2020.

In the workplace, grief can cause people to be more disorganized, withdrawn, or anxious. Unfortunately, if leaders lack empathy, they miscalculate these behaviors as performance problems instead of analyzing what is going on behind the late arrivals or less-than-perfect work.

In most cases, leaders forget to change workloads during times of grief or crisis. We saw this during the pandemic, when few managers reassessed workload despite the increasing grief that employees were feeling.

In my article "Making Your Workplace Safe for Grief," for *Harvard Business Review*, I write that many companies lack norms or policies for dealing with grief—or "bereavement," in HR speak. Those that do have policies often find they're insufficient.[3]

There are strict rules around what type of grief makes one eligible for leave. Only New Zealand offers paid bereavement leave after a miscarriage or stillbirth. And there are few organizations globally where the loss of a best friend, a favorite aunt, or a beloved nephew warrants bereavement leave. Most current bereavement policies suggest that an employee should absorb their shock, plan and execute a funeral, cope in a healthy way with their loss, all while working at expected levels of performance.

If we're developing a bereavement leave policy with empathy at the root, we don't need to know what is causing our employees' grief—we just allow them the space to mourn. There should be protected time for someone to deal with all types of loss.

Far too many of our workplace policies assume the worst of our employees. But evidence continues to reinforce that trust in leadership and a healthy respect for norms is a better approach to adherence. We shouldn't be driving policies for the 20 percent of disengaged employees; we need to focus on motivating the other 80 percent of our workforce who haven't done anything to lose our trust.

The term *compliance* is used widely in corporate speak. Essentially, it means the act of following the standard that can be a regulatory requirement (law, or legal standard) or a normative requirement, that is, based on contractual, social, or cultural standards.

Integrity can be described as the honesty and morals exhibited by an individual or collective group. And when we have empathy and compassion, we build policies that support honesty.

Louise Manning studies the impact of compliance-versus-integrity motivated cultures in the food production industry and found that "food supply chain standards that focus on compliance with prescribed product and process requirements alone will not assure food integrity, as compliance alone does not assure that other aspects of integrity such as accountability, trust, and honesty are also addressed."

Manning's work has been leveraged across other industries to understand how to move from a compliance-focused culture to an integrity-focused culture. "Integrity is an active, conscious approach by an organization to define what it is to be moral rather than simply accepting the values and often prescriptive standards," Manning explained to me.

Manning suggests that we engage all employees, irrespective of job title, and inspire and empower staff to understand the bigger role they play in the greater goals of the organization and "drive a sense of personal responsibility, agency, ownership."

In "Managing for Organizational Integrity," in *Harvard Business Review*, Lynn S. Paine references her research on compliance-versus-integrity-based systems of leadership. Table 6-1 shows the differences between the two leadership styles.

The NASA example discussed in chapter 1 fits perfectly here. An integrity-focused mindset would have allowed for more voices to be heard and their counsel actioned, potentially preventing the tragic outcome of the Columbia disaster.

In our interview, Manning provided another example of how compliance-based cultures make bravery a bad thing. One story in particular highlights the stark differences between the two concepts.

Yasmine Motarjemi has an MSc degree in food science and technology from the University of Languedoc and a PhD in food engineering from the University of Lund. Despite her credentials and long-standing career as a corporate food safety manager and assistant vice president from 2000 until 2010 at Nestlé, she was terminated.

Over the course of her tenure, she had found multiple examples of dangers associated with certain products, and yet when she spoke up, she was harassed and bullied by senior leadership and eventually let go. It took eight years to finally receive the court's decision. A declaration written by Motarjemi's lawyer reads in part, "On the 7th January 2020, the Civil Court of Appeal of the canton of Vaud in Lausanne, Switzerland, condemned Nestlé Group for violating Swiss labour law." The judges concluded that "Nestlé's management violated its internal whistleblowing policy."[4] Motarjemi was vindicated.

However, this was a short-lived victory. In early 2021, Nestlé had to recall nearly 762,000 pounds of frozen food for possible glass and plastic contamination, perhaps because no one felt safe to speak up. If speaking up means the potential for ongoing harassment, the loss of your job, and nearly a decade of litigation to protect your professional reputation, it's no wonder people continue to stay silent. Motarjemi is an outlier—a brave, strong, powerful outlier.

This case may be an extreme example, but it's an important one. It says loud and clear that there needs to be more accountability. And, I'm not here to sugarcoat the realities of burnout. I'm here to help fix it.

TABLE 6-1

Compliance versus integrity-based cultures

Elements	Compliance-based systems	Integrity-based systems
Company commitments	Mission statement and company policy drives compliance	Code of conduct that highlights guiding values and commitments that make sense and are clearly communicated
Ethos	Conformity with externally imposed standards	Self-governance according to chosen organizational standards
Objective	Prevent criminal misconduct and reduce organizational risk through compliance with legal and market standards	Ensure responsible conduct through the development of company values and aspirations, and social obligations including legal compliance
Methods	Prescriptivism, organizational systems and decision processes, auditing and control, sanctions, training	Leadership, accountability, organizational systems and decision-making processes, auditing and control, sanctions, training
Company leaders	Committed to ensuring compliance with internal and external standards	Personally committed, credible, and willing to take action on the values they espouse
Organization's systems and procedures	Support and reinforce the need for compliance with requirements	Support and reinforce the organization's values

Reporting and investigation	Mechanisms are in place for reporting and investigating noncompliance	Mechanisms are in place for reporting and investigating noncompliance
Verification activities	Implemented to ensure compliance; for example, audits	Implemented to ensure compliance; for example, audits
Decision making	Managers have the decision-making skills, knowledge, and competencies to make compliance-oriented decisions on a day-to-day basis	Espoused values are integrated into management channels for decision making and are reflected in the organization's critical activities. Managers have the decision-making skills, knowledge, and competencies to make ethically sound decisions on a day-to-day basis.

Source: Adapted from Lynn S. Paine, "Managing for Organizational Integrity," *Harvard Business Review*, March–April 1994, 106–117.

There is an urgency. Burnout is a serious problem. When organizations are not behaving with accountability, it should be called out by other leaders, other organizations, the media, or experts. It is too hard for employees—especially individual employees—to do it alone.

Jill Lepore, professor of American history at Harvard University, famously questioned whether progress at all cost is necessary. What about growth and revenue? In an integrity-based culture, would success be less likely to happen?

Manning gave me an answer to this question: "In some countries, you've got the idea of product liability, and as a result, legal liability is what drives businesses. . . . So, they develop their culture and even the climate within the business around lawful/unlawful. But human beings don't necessarily operate in that sphere. Moral liability is different to legal liability. I think one of the challenges with businesses is we're driving standards and prescriptions, rules-based businesses, and human beings really just want to believe that what they are doing is good and what they believe to be right, and justice is different to law."

In a compliance-based workplace, we also see more values mismatch, a predictor for burnout.

"Burnout happens when you're constantly a square peg trying to fit in a round hole," said Manning. "The rules that are put around you are not rules that you are happy to work in. That has an impact on you as an individual and can cause self-defeating behavior. We want instead for people to practice constructive deviance. So, for example, those people who are looking for innovation, entrepreneurship within the business. To do that we have to encourage people not to be compliant."

"I'm Sorry"

Apology laws in the United States may be another example of compliant-versus integrity-based cultures. Early evidence showed that when a physician apologized for a medical error, it reduced the frequency of malpractice lawsuits. As a result, states initiated a law that protected physicians if they apologized and that couldn't be used against them if the lawsuit went to court.[5]

According to the authors of "Efficacy of a Physician's Words of Empathy: An Overview of State Apology Laws," "the correlation between apologies and lower payouts in malpractice cases was confirmed by a 6-year study at the Lexington Veterans Affairs Medical Center in Kentucky. This study also showed that the medical center, after implementing an apology program, paid less per claim than those hospitals without apology policies."[6]

However, the authors cite research that criticizes these findings, stating that there are major differences to be considered when comparing Veterans Affairs hospitals to nongovernment hospitals.[7] The debate continues as to whether apologizing decreases malpractice lawsuits.

What I see as most damaging here is the lack of trust increasing between patients and physicians. Not only is this dangerous for patient safety, but it also makes saying sorry a compliance-based decision versus an integrity-based one.

It would be valuable to review whether the laws have actually undermined the authenticity of the apology. Does it change its sincerity? Do patients see the apology as lacking empathy or meaningful? Do physicians feel as if they have to apologize to reduce the chances of their hospital getting sued even if they don't believe they made an error?

Unless there are pure motives, our good intentions are destined to fail.

Active Listening

Active listening is a key attribute of empathy. It means having the ability to focus completely on a speaker, understand their message, comprehend the information, and respond thoughtfully. As leaders, this requires us to scale our listening, and it becomes even more necessary during a crisis because there is so much more noise to filter.

Leaders need to be able to set priorities and determine what information to channel and how. When empathy is at the root of that listening, it helps shape how your workforce will weather the changes.

The Workforce Institute at Kronos Incorporated found "only a fraction of employees (20%) felt their organization met their needs during the initial months of the Covid-19 pandemic." Chris Mullen, executive director of the Workforce Institute, stressed to me, "As organizations around the world operated through an unprecedented global pandemic, they needed to double down on their employee experience strategy. However, instead of looking for trendy perks, they needed to get back to the foundational needs every employee requires: physical safety, psychological security, job stability, and flexibility."

Mullen claimed that among employees who trust their organization more now than before the pandemic, 70 percent say the company went above and beyond in their Covid-19 response. "By truly putting the employee first," Mullen said, "a mutual trust will begin to take hold that will propel employee engagement—and the success of the business—to new levels."

Active listening also reduces stress and increases calm. It makes people feel heard, and that diminishes uncertainty. Here's an example of how one of the largest companies in the world was able to scale active listening and empathy to weather one of the most challenging moments in workforce history.

I spoke with Alan May at Hewlett Packard Enterprise (HPE) during the second surge of the pandemic, around mid-October 2020. At the time, nearly all of his sixty thousand employees were remote. May had always put mental health and well-being as a main strategic priority at HPE, but he knew immediately that the pandemic would add more urgency to this need.

"Crises tend to really just accelerate underlying trends," explained May. "So, we have been very active in, for lack of better phrase, wellness, writ large, and mental health benefits for our workforce for many years. We have about 60,000 people, two-thirds of them are outside the United States, not all of them, by the way, in Western type of economies, many of them in places like India, Singapore, China, other countries, so we've got some degree of familiarity of how we can support our team members through this."

May also emphasized how it is necessary to "never lose sight of the importance of the frontline manager." He constantly reinforces to his team that they need to call their direct reports for nothing to do about work and just say, "Hey, how's it going? What's going on? Anything I could help with?" May said that he's not expecting his frontline managers to be mental health experts, but he shared that "in a number of cases where, as a result of some of those interactions, we've detected some concerns, we've been able to escalate those and get more professional help."

When it comes to burnout, although HPE calls it "excessive workload," it tries to be attentive to areas that may see higher stress than typical. May acknowledges that in 2020, there were demands on everyone, but he gave an example of his employees in supply chain who were under incredible stress because of the need to fulfill their product, the difficulties in procuring components around the world, managing the outsource manufacturers, logistic issues that were, as one could imagine, incredible.

May and his team reached out personally and said a simple thank-you. They also asked for feedback about what they could do to help limit or balance the load.

One of the reasons he believes that his employees have withstood the crisis better than those in some other organizations is a long-standing commitment to well-being. He wasn't setting up programs only in response to Covid-19; the campaign that HPE started was already two years old before the pandemic hit. Named "Real Life," the effort hoped to ensure that employees had the kind of workplace terms and conditions, and supervisory treatment, that is wellness friendly. May said, "The goal was to telegraph to our team members that we actually do want to fit their life as opposed to the other way around."

So, what did that mean?

On top of their forward approach regarding parental leave, May and his team also kick-started "Wellness Fridays." It may sound pretty standard, but the intention was more than just a day off to support employees' well-being. For at least a half-day each month, leaders encouraged employees to focus on something wellness-related, like using health benefits (massages, physical therapy, or time with a psychologist), spending time with family, working in the community, going to church, and/or volunteering.

May heard stories of parents with young kids participating in school, and people carving out time for physical activities. About one-third of the stories focused on volunteering and acts of altruism. He cited other activities shared on the social collaboration platform where coworkers described participating in "small group workouts, enjoying an outside lunch with a nice view and calming music, baking with kids, spending time with pets, hiking in the mountains, mom/daughter pedicure, afternoon bike ride, followed by yoga and then an outdoor BBQ dinner at sunset," to name a few.

And to support all of the above, "meeting-less Fridays" were invented to create "white space" for employees to work on ideating or reflecting.

When Covid-19 hit, May realized that although he hadn't planned for his staff to be resiliency-tested, he was thankful his employees had built up some reserves. Employees were more ready for the shift because most of them already knew how to access and lever those supports. This became evident through their feedback.

He sent me the HPE "Employee Work Experience Data" from July 2020:

- Ninety-one percent agree that employee health and well-being is a top priority for HPE.

- Ninety-two percent agree that their direct leader has shown genuine concern for their well-being.

- Ninety-one percent agree that their direct leader has shown flexibility by allowing them to balance personal and professional life.

Employee experience scores like these tell an important story: "Leaders, this is good. Keep it up."

The big "aha" here should be this: to replicate these workplace experience scores during a crisis, don't wait for the crisis to happen before you prioritize well-being.

Less Monologue. More Dialogue.

What we also learned from HPE and its reaction strategy was a focus on communication as paramount and immediately triggering a corporate response plan. This is critical, according to the Workforce Institute survey in which nearly a third (32 percent) claimed they yearned for more communication—both sooner and more transparently—which is a primary regret for more than a third (35 percent) of C-level leaders.

Fran Katsoudas, executive vice president and chief people, policy, and purpose officer at Cisco, agrees that empathy is at the root of strong leadership and healthy cultures.

"We're a big believer that empathy is a superpower," Fran shared in April 2021, after a long and stressful year of leading through the pandemic. "From a workplace perspective, we're going to work so hard to help our leaders and teams get proximate to people that are different from themselves and walk alongside them and understand them. We believe that if we do this, we'll be so much better as a company."

Cisco led with empathy first during the pandemic by:

- Increasing transparency in communication

- Augmenting employee check-ins at all leadership levels

- Having more open conversations about challenging topics including mental health, social justice, and Covid health and safety

- Enhancing existing flexible work options

- Providing more access to health experts

- Creating a bigger focus on campaigns that promote well-being, such as:

  - "Day for Me," which gave all employees and contractors a day off in May to focus on employee mental health and well-being

  - #safetalk, a previously well-established program that offers mental health resources

> – #safespace, which connects like-minded employees to network
> and support one another. Topics include mental health, sub-
> stance abuse, employees who are neurodiverse, employees who
> are gender transitioning, and parents who have lost children.

With a keen awareness that these unique times require unique solutions, the leadership team at Cisco acknowledges there is more work
to be done. In response, they continue to analyze novel approaches to
support the mental and physical health of a workforce under chronic
stress from a pandemic.

Here are some additional suggestions to put empathy into practice
during a crisis:

- Share communication instantly about the company's plan, its un-
  certainties, and how it is going to protect its people.

- Ensure all staff know where to get information related to the
  crisis.

- Ensure employees can immediately access mental health
  supports.

- Reduce hours or offer flexible hours, or even paid time off,
  automatically.

- Develop a peer-to-peer outreach program before the event, training in mental health 101, and select leaders who've already been
  trained become activated as supports for staff.

- Notify frontline direct managers to start checking in on remote
  employees.

- Create a resource page before the crisis that shows available, lo-
  cally based outreach programs and mental health practitioners
  during catastrophic events.

When we have empathy, we try to mitigate uncertainty. Actively listening and communicating with empathy during a crisis helps reduce

underlying fears. Our actions say, "I've heard your messages, I am working hard to understand your needs, and I am doing my best to respond thoughtfully."

Prioritizing Physical and Psychological Safety

Eugenie Fanning, vice president of people at SquareFoot, a tech-enabled commercial real estate company based in Manhattan, shared in our interview that during the pandemic, reinforcing trust has helped to mitigate burnout. She said, "You spend a lot of time and money recruiting and training, you've hired the top 5 to 10 percent of people in their fields, so you have to be able to trust that they are doing a good job. We want results-driven work rather than argue online at 4:59 p.m. on a Wednesday about whether you're achieving your goals and doing what you're supposed to do."

This is why Fanning and her staff let go of the nine-to-five standard workday expectations. She said, "It's important that we're all being super understanding and supportive of how people are balancing work and life so we can take the pressure off of each other. We are engaging in more one-on-ones to check in and make sure that this is all still working for our staff."

SquareFoot had always been pro-office, and the leadership team still believed that being together in a physical space works for their culture. When they were forced to deal with all the anxiety and uncertainty about gathering inside during the pandemic, it was important to be sensitive to those stressors. First, they opened up their offices to anyone who just missed being together in a space with others or who wasn't flourishing at home. To make everyone feel safe, they incorporated symptom checkers, video training to prepare staff for the changes, and other measures to assuage any fears. "We just need to keep listening and responding," said Fanning.

Danny Groner, a marketing director at SquareFoot, shared that it was good to have that choice when it came to returning to a physical office. "People in the office are engaging with one another like old times," Groner said. "So, I've seen the power again of those serendipitous interactions."

These are examples of empathy in leadership, where active listening is core to success and flexibility is the rule not the exception.

Ensuring that staff feel a sense of agency doesn't mean you have to give up your goals or the company's goals. Provide tangible timelines that are open to reassessment if needed. It does mean, however, taking extra steps to demonstrate that both physical and psychological safety is a priority.

If our building was on fire, we would be evacuating. It's important that we don't force anyone to enter a place they don't feel safe both physically and mentally. Chronic stress can be just as harmful to our bodies as inhaling fumes from a fire, causing respiratory diseases, strokes, and heart attacks.[8]

In 2020, we were expeditious in how we adopted safety measures so our workplaces were safe from Covid-19. Why have we not prioritized the same measures to protect our psychological safety? It's not as if chronic stress and burnout aren't similarly dangerous.

Amy Edmondson, professor at Harvard Business School and expert in psychological safety in the workplace, writes, "Psychological safety refers to a climate in which people are comfortable being (and expressing) themselves."[9] To nurture a psychologically safe culture, we need to keep focused on the bigger picture.

Someone messes up, we feel angry. Yes, we all have a right to be frustrated, but who does it serve? Instead, the bigger goal is to get back on track. Edmondson shares that a productive response is: "Thank you for that clear line of sight. What help do you need? What can we do to get this back on track? Which is after all what we both really care about."[10]

If this kind of communication is pervasively accepted, employees will feel safer generally, and more comfortable opening up about topics like mental health.

I will repeat. *Both* physical safety and mental safety need to be a priority in the workplace.

Empathy Builds Trust

Giving people a sense of control over their mental health makes preventing burnout collaborative, not siloed. We don't want to suggest that we know everything about what an employee needs to deal with stress. This is a critical understanding for leaders. We need to pull back on our need to control or micromanage any situation, but even more so during a crisis. As leaders, we want our employees to have agency to navigate their emotional and mental experiences at work too.

What is agency?

Albert Bandura, a Canadian American psychologist and professor emeritus at Stanford University, suggests in "Toward Psychology of Human Agency" that people act as agents who intentionally regulate their behavior and life circumstances. They are self-organizing, proactive, self-regulating, and self-reflecting. "They are producers of their life circumstances and not just the products of them."[11]

In the workplace, these are important behaviors that we want to promote. Bandura believes that today's society is undergoing dramatic social, informational, and technological changes. And arguably, these "revolutionary advances in technology and globalization are transforming the nature, reach, speed, and the loci of human influence. These new realities present vastly greater opportunities for people to exercise control over how they live their lives."[12]

Some may claim the opposite—that technological advancement is shaping us more than we're shaping it. Bandura would argue that with a strongly developed sense of agency, we hold all the power. As our employees struggle with job insecurity and obsolescence, increased agency reduces those fears.

Some leaders have a hard time letting go of that control. Micromanaging plays a serious role in employee burnout. And studies reflect that increased employee autonomy leads to more trust and purpose, which increases intrinsic motivation.

So, now, we have a motivated workforce that runs on individual and collective passion, not compliance or fear. This is a good thing.

During times of stress, make sure a sense of agency is felt organizationwide. Not only does it support our employees' well-being in general, but it helps everyone to remain aligned and connected to corporate mission and goals.

Another benefit of a workforce that has agency over the decisions at work is increased psychological flexibility and emotional regulation—pro-social behaviors that reduce workplace conflict and volatility, all beneficial to workplace mental health and reducing burnout.

I saw this in action in the example of Jamie Coakley at Electric. During the pandemic, Coakley was assessing the in-person versus remote model and decided that it had to be up to each employee. Forcing anyone to come in if it caused them stress seemed counter to her goals of leading a human-centered organization.

Coakley realized that there were other barriers to consider, like the fact that travel to and from the office would generate more fear than being in the office. She responded by providing 100 percent daily reimbursement for Ubers, which led to an increase of five times the number of people in the office.

This also steered her to rethink how it served them to have one office in the center of Manhattan. She said, "We're exploring for 2021—maybe we have three hubs in Brooklyn, New Jersey, in northern New York, in the Bronx area, where we can sort of give people the ability to walk to work or bike to work and have flexibility, because I think our team is very social, especially being a service business, and we want to talk to our customers and our team members."

Coakley's main goal is to give her staff options—agency to choose.

Emotionally flexible workforces

Ensuring people have a strong sense of individual agency will add to our well-being. But leading and helping employees to be open to change is also a critical psychological skill to help them deal with stress.

According to Todd Kashdan and Jonathan Rottenberg, psychological or emotional flexibility spans a wide range of human abilities to:

- Recognize and adapt to various situational demands

- Shift mindsets or behaviors when the original strategy isn't working (think abandoning plan A for plan B)

- Maintain balance among important life domains (knowing when to turn off work and rejoin family, friends, hobbies, and life in general)

- Be aware, open, and committed to behaviors that are congruent with deeply held values (e.g., do not stay in a role that isn't a values match)[13]

In a crisis, psychological flexibility is of enormous value.

Research by Danielle Lamb, from University College London, "Examining Psychological Flexibility at the Individual, Team, and Leadership Levels in Crisis Resolution Teams," showed that psychological flexibility predicts better well-being at the individual level in CRT staff. Lamb also discovered that increased manager psychological flexibility was also found to be positively associated with better staff well-being.[14] The spillover effect of emotional flexibility is noteworthy here. It appears to generate a positive network effect that promotes well-being across all team members.

According to clinical psychologist Rob Archer, emotional flexibility can help "minimise experiential avoidance which occurs when someone tries to avoid unpleasant thoughts and feelings by avoiding the behaviors that give rise to them. A large body of research shows that higher experiential avoidance is associated with lower well-being, work performance and quality of life."[15]

Stress may be an emotional by-product of a crisis, but so is learning. And, whenever we have to work through challenging experiences, we also develop the skills to handle change more effectively. You might say that we've had a few crash courses in emotional flexibility over recent years.

From repeating recessions, political and social uprisings, and a global pandemic, most of us look at change differently now. For the people we lead, their response will be similar and will help our organizations to navigate change with less fear.

Our brains don't like unknowns. Therefore, after something is known, we can lean on that to predict how we'll deal with the future. These disruptions in our past have taught us that despite the discomfort, we persevere. As leaders, that must be our message. We need to consistently ask, "What have we learned?"

Here's an example of an intervention that can help build emotionally flexible teams:

- Ask employees to write down a high-stress, challenging moment in their life. It should not be so personal that they aren't comfortable discussing or could cause emotional harm by retelling it.

- Have them describe why it was challenging, why this particular moment in time sticks out to them.

- Now, ask everyone to write down or discuss how this could have been a highlight in their life. They have to force themselves to put on the opposition hat and explain as many positives as they can from the experience.

The stories we tell and retell change shape. Since our memories configure new realities every time we reflect on them, we can consider other ways to interpret the same set of events. Which ways of seeing things may serve us better?

Now ask individuals to practice challenging every negative thought within their story. Instead of seeing things the way they always have, they start to adopt thoughts that fit the situation that reflect a more positive outlook.

It doesn't mean that bad things never happen. That is the myth about reframing. We aren't asking anyone (including ourselves) to put on rose-colored glasses. It is about looking at an event from two polarizing sides and eventually ending up somewhere near the truth.

I will use an example: the pandemic.

First, we need to notice our thoughts. How are we describing this experience? Are we making permanent statements like "I hated every minute of it." Or "I never want to think about the lockdown again." Or "I didn't grow professionally at all—it was a waste of a year for my career."

Now, challenge those thoughts. An effective part of reframing involves examining the truth and accuracy (or lack thereof) of our stories. So, we need to ask, Are the things we're telling ourselves the absolute truth?

What if we never actually thought about 2020 again—what would we miss? Perhaps it would be the birth of a new baby in the family. A new opportunity that came up at work. A friend who came to help when you were in need. An increase in compassion, empathy, resilience—all beneficial to our personal and professional life. That we slowed down and had more time with family around the dinner table.

It is highly improbable, perhaps even impossible, that there was not a single minute of good in an entire year. As soon as we call it out, these statements are no longer valid, and our brains can accept new realities.

We need to help our people adjust the filter for themselves. It is not up to us to sugarcoat or try to Pollyanna our way to well-being. However, it's vital to give our people the tools to see that they have more control over their future than they realize.

If we can get to a point where someone hard hit by a major stress event can say, "It felt like hell and I'm still working through it, but there was one good that came out of it, and that was . . ." At that point, we're making strides as leaders. And our people will be healthier and happier for it.

Connecting Each Other through Stories

Storytelling has been around for thousands of years. It's deeply imbedded in our nature. It's how we entertain and communicate and pass on our history. It's how we evolved and innovated to extend our life span. It's also how we formed long-lasting relationships and create attachment to our loved ones. Storytelling is the tie that binds.

When we are leading organizations and looking to make transformational change, these stories create the bonds between us and the people we lead. Researchers have found that "storytelling can leverage the knowledge of an organization, particularly its tacit knowledge, to build core capabilities."[16] Stories have the ability to build trust, which is needed in times of uncertainty and when a transformation is necessary.

Since everyone in the organization is able to take part in storytelling processes, this, according to researchers Karl E. Weick and Larry D. Browning, "fosters equality compared to other styles of leadership. Leaders and followers are able to feel that they share the same organizational reality rather than being trapped behind barriers arising from hierarchical levels and differences of power in the organization."[17]

In "Constructing Leadership by Storytelling—the Meaning of Trust and Narratives," the authors claim that storytelling can be a valuable source of trust by creating a shared context and sense of meaning among leaders and the workforce they oversee.[18]

In early 2021, I had the chance to speak to staff members at Royal LePage, one of the world's leading real estate companies. Headquartered in Canada, Royal LePage participated in $81 billion in transactional dollar volume nationally.

In preparation for the event, I spoke to several employees about the standard logistical things—part of the job of a public speaker. They mentioned that Phil Soper, the CEO, would be speaking first, so I would have to wait while he spoke. I guess no one is ever certain of the length of his talks; they could be thirty minutes, they could be an hour. No one found that to be a problem because he was so beloved and they appreciated his updates.

Alicia Omand, one of Soper's employees, described Soper as a charismatic and fearless leader, someone who is also approachable and relatable, which is important when you're going through a tumultuous year.

While I was standing by waiting to go on after Soper's warm-up speech, I was in agreement. Who knew EBITA could be that exciting? It all made sense why folks loved Soper.

Good storytelling makes you feel included. Suddenly, I felt like just another employee celebrating our successes.

In general, good communication is critical to a healthy culture. But there's a fine line between too much and too little. It's the Goldilocks zone that requires constant tweaking to find. During times of stress, it's even more challenging.

For example, in the early days of the 2020 crisis, leaders were figuring out how to communicate effectively. What would be enough? Is this too little? Too much? Too scary? Too cheery? Just right?

Soper said they moved from sending out a communication once or twice per month to daily. Sometimes they would broadcast eight times a week. He said it was probably "huge overkill," but he just didn't want anyone on his team to feel like they didn't know what was going on, or that they were desperate for information that he wasn't providing them.

Yet, he also wanted to connect people with his communication, so he came up with an idea. Let's tell the stories of our people and how they are handling this experience.

One example was the story of a middle manager who was a mom of two young kids and married to an essential worker. There was constant worry that the kids were sick or getting sick. "I could tell that she was struggling when I was talking with her," Soper said. "As a perfectionist who likes to have control of her situation, this was the opposite of that. She was really stressed out. So, I convinced her to do a small piece on the struggles she was facing, essentially being a single parent of young children. Why she kept feeling that she was letting people down. It was a way for her to say that I'm not just doing a job counting widgets, this is hard."

She agreed and what came out of that personal sharing across the company was transformative.

Soper continued, "The biggest cathartic moment or realization was knowing that we had her back, everyone had her back—her friends, her family, her coworkers. That we'll get through this. And that she had to be OK with doing the best she could. And, you know, as a perfectionist, that is hard to accept. It was clear that she felt she wasn't living up to her personal standards. But after she shared this, it sure helped to know that there were hundreds of other people in the company who were feeling this exact same way, and that had to be OK for them too. And that this too shall pass. It was really, really critical that we continually pointed to the light at the end of that tunnel."

Phil-osophy Friday was also established during the same time frame. Soper seemed to get a kick out of it playing on his name Phil, which was funny and charming. When leaders don't take themselves too seriously, I always enjoy our conversations much more. In any event, he kicked off this weekly chat in a light talk format that got really great engagement from staff.

One of the first installments of Phil-osophy Friday was an on-site interview with a member of his senior staff, John, and his partner, who were both living and working in a five-hundred-square-foot condo. Soper wanted to learn and share with others what it's like to work side by side in such a confined space.

"It was all about communication," Soper explained. "It was quite entertaining actually, to eventually have them talk about how John is quite loud, so loud that his partner could barely think, she told us. We did touch back with them later, and they said it really helped, like a group therapy session. And it helped everyone else who was in the same situation. You know, these stories are shared for the same reason we read, why we watch movies, why we relate someone's situations to our lives or our imagination. It's getting into someone else's shoes."

I was nodding and thinking to myself—once again—good leadership tying back to empathy.

Soper added, "Oh, another happy ending to this story is that they moved . . . to an 1,800-square-foot space."

Flashback to me waiting for Soper to wrap up. He's just gone through the exciting highlights of a year full of challenges. The lows of spring and the highs of summer, then fall, and even, atypically, winter. Soper says that 2020 in real estate will go down as the year of the three Ps: Puppies. Peloton. Property.

Being funny helps, too.

.   .   .

Any great leader knows that empathy drives great leadership. If that tenet is at the root of our decision making, we are more likely to prevent burnout because the pro-social payoffs are plenty.

Empathetic leaders build trusted relationships with and among their teams; have an integrity-based workforce connected to shared goals; make people feel psychologically safe during times of uncertainty; create a healing space for grief and mourning; spark inclusive discussions by making people part of the organizational story; and are more likely to listen actively as a means to prevent future harm.

What empathy isn't? Soft margarine.

7

Take Care
of Yourself, Too

We've spent almost the entirety of the book with strategies and tactics for supporting our people. But the last time I checked, I was still a human being. And so are you.

Leaders tend to pull the motivation and fuel from leading their teams, but they can also get depleted from that passion. We've discussed passion-driven burnout already, but we haven't analyzed what kind of interventions are required to defend against it. If we can maintain harmonious passion in our work, that is the ideal. The data reinforced how meaning and purpose in work can be a prophylaxis to burnout.

In addition to empathy, resilience is a valuable psychological fitness skill to develop. Resilient leaders have high emotional flexibility and can pivot quickly. They remain calm under duress and find the benefits of a crisis. They move on. They rebound. They bounce back.

This is what resilient leaders do.

And to reiterate. Resiliency doesn't mean we stop systemic burnout. We don't battle overwork or poor organizational hygiene with resilience. Lack of fairness and values mismatch aren't resolved with resilience either. That requires a different strategy.

Self-care won't fix broken organizational systems, but it's the part we can control in a world full of the uncontrollable.

Feeling Meaning

To prevent leadership burnout, it's essential to find the meaning in our work. That feeling can ebb and flow, which is natural throughout our careers. But if it feels permanently lost, our well-being can suffer.

So, how can we connect meaning to our roles as leaders, which will in turn inspire the people we lead? First, we need to find what it is about our job that we love. And what about being a leader makes it our calling?

Connect the Impact

I was a guest on a radio call-in show, and the host was asking her listeners to share how they were finding joy as we went into the fall season of the pandemic. For obvious reasons, 2020 for most had been challenging, so this was an opportunity for people to say what they'd been doing to get out of their rut.

One listener, Jennifer, described how it was her work that had seen her through the last few months. She worked for the Canadian government overseeing a large park in a major city. Among other responsibilities, her job duties included getting rid of dead brush, picking up garbage, sweeping, and so on. For some, this wouldn't sound like a dream job. But for Jennifer, she deeply connected her maintenance work with the pride she felt for the park. Her manager reminded her of how essential she was to giving people a place to meet, since they couldn't connect inside.

On the call, she shared that the pandemic had encouraged people in her community to explore places they hadn't ventured to before. Some of her day consisted of welcoming new people and chatting with the regulars. It was important that the park—her park—looked its best.

When we can attach the daily routines of our job to something greater, it makes those tasks so much more meaningful.

You're leading employees in manufacturing; perhaps they are on the line. What are they creating every day?

Are you making brakes for a vehicle? Or are you building in the difference between an expectant mother making it to the hospital safely or getting into an accident on the way?

Are you building a wheelchair? Or are you finally giving a newly paralyzed father mobility so he can go back to work?

Are you selling real estate? Or are you providing people a place where they feel safe, where they can start out their lives, and where they can grow old?

We need to see the bigger picture in our work every day to keep focused on the mission.

To that end, try this exercise every few months to ensure you're still on track. Keep adding to your responses and assess how meaning morphs and fluctuates over time. Analyze and write down:

- What features of your work give it meaning?

- In what ways do you push through feelings of demotivation?

- What do you love about being a leader?

- How do you choose to inspire purpose in your teams?

- How should your staff feel about the meaning of their work?

To increase our well-being at work, it's easier if that is a focus from the top, once again, modeling behaviors we want to see in our employees. We can do that by making happiness at work a values-based strategy.

I belong to a think tank of politicians and researchers intended to promote happiness and subjective well-being through the identification of public policy for policy makers worldwide and the standardization of happiness as a measure to guide governments. The Global Happiness Council meets annually in Dubai as part of the World Government Summit to discuss the newest research, evidence, and data reinforcing the values of well-being across all areas of life. I sit on the global workplace well-being committee within the council and contribute to the workplace chapter of the annual *Global Happiness Policy Report*.

The key strategy in forming the council was to ensure there were scholars, practitioners, economists, scientists, politicians, experts, and more around the table, looking at both well-being and its impact on the world.

We all understand that when there is evidence to support win-win scenarios, it assists policy makers and leaders with the adoption of well-being strategies. In other words, my people *and* my shareholders are happy.

Chairs of the council include Richard Layard of the London School of Economics; Jan-Emmanuel De Neve, economics professor at Oxford University; Martine Durand, chief statistician and director of statistics directorate of the Organisation for Economic Co-operation and Development; and Jeffrey Sachs, well-known American economist and director of the Center for Sustainable Development and professor at Columbia University.

The chair of my committee is Jan-Emmanuel De Neve, who over the years has been able to prove that well-being has a causal impact on business outcomes. The 2018 report also shared that purpose increases motivation significantly over pay. And, before that, the 2017 workplace chapter of the report identified that employees will take a 37 percent reduction in pay to feel increased purpose in their work.[1]

Even more eye-opening, LinkedIn's latest workplace culture report claims that nearly nine out of ten, or 86 percent, of millennials (those born between 1981 and 1996) would consider taking a pay cut to work at a company whose mission and values align with their own. By comparison, only 9 percent of baby boomers (those born between 1946 and 1964) would.

But what if I shared that well-being and profitability go hand in hand? Recently, as of 2019, several researchers were able to put a stake in the ground and announce that happiness is causal to profitability. Nonacademics may be thinking, so what? Academics are probably already checking out the peer reviews.

In the world of research, being able to claim that something is causal versus correlated is a big deal. That means that enough research, modeling, measuring, dissection from peers, reproving, and showing your work has happened, likely for years until this point.

I say all this because it isn't just warm and fuzzy to make happiness a strategic priority; it is an upstream effort that impacts mental health and well-being (including yours). It also prevents burnout.

Here's the evidence.

In 2019, Jan-Emmanuel De Neve in collaboration with George Ward, associate of the well-being program at Centre of Economic Performance, and Clément S. Bellet, assistant professor at Erasmus School of Economics, Rotterdam, presented evidence of a causal effect of workers' week-to-week happiness on their productivity at one of the UK's largest private employers—British Telecom (BT), a global telecommunications company.

Prior research of worker well-being and performance has been forced to rely on subjective outcomes such as managerial performance evaluations. De Neve and his team saw the benefits of studying a call-center population with a range of objective, quantitative performance metrics that the firm measures routinely.

They analyzed eighteen hundred sales workers distributed across eleven call centers. The researchers observed the happiness of these workers on a weekly basis over a six-month period. They matched the self-reported happiness data to detailed administrative data on a number of workplace behaviors and performance outcomes. The team also wanted to factor in the weather to determine if local adverse weather conditions impacted sales performance.

Their main outcome measure focused on the number of weekly sales made by each employee. To access productivity, they measured minutes per call, the percentage of calls converted to sales, and the extent to which employees adhered to their scheduled work.

First, they found that happiness had a causal impact on productivity and subsequently increased sales. Being in the happiest state (compared to a neutral emotional state) is associated with around a 6 percent rise in weekly sales. Being in a negative emotional state (compared to the neutral) is associated with around a 7 percent decrease in weekly sales.

Comparing weeks when workers report being very unhappy with weeks when they are very happy, the difference in sales is around 13 percent.

Another, second measurement using a different model also determined a strong causal effect of happiness on sales performance. A one-point increase in the one-to-five happiness measure led to a 24 percent increase in weekly sales.

Even a 13 percent difference between unhappy and very happy employees is significant. Scale that across any organization, and you'll find those margins are beneficial. De Neve and his team also found that employees who were higher in happiness were better able to multitask compared to their less happy peers. Happiness also increased the speed and efficiency of workers; they made more calls, and those calls were more productive.[2]

When it comes to weather, the team found that poor weather in the geographic region of the call center had a negative effect on sales performance. Their findings reinforce the well-documented evidence of the negative impact of bad weather on well-being. For example, based on the findings from 207,000 court cases, temperature showed a significant effect on the decision making of judges in high-stakes court cases.[3] Equally, behavior in stock markets is affected by sunshine and daylight hours, even national soccer results.[4]

De Neve and his team also found further evidence to support prior research that suggests induced happiness has a positive effect on processes like motivation, cognitive flexibility, negotiation, and problem-solving skills. Plus, they were able to confirm that allowing call-center employees to work from home improves their productivity, while also enhancing happiness and satisfaction—good news for the thousands of call-center employees who moved to remote work in 2020.

In our interview, De Neve shared why it's important for more people to feel meaning and engagement in their work: "Your employment gives you a sense of identity, gives you social connections, and gives you a routine and a structure throughout the day, and these things matter very much indeed."

De Neve worked with an extraordinarily large data set—the Gallup World Poll—and based on that data and on research from 18 million employee engagement surveys, he came up with these evidence-backed suggestions for how leaders can adopt a more powerful well-being strategy:

- Prioritize an organizational focus on improving managerial skills, specifically empathy.

- Emphasize positive contribution. This can be achieved by increasing peer-recognition programs—De Neve names Bravo as an example, used currently by LinkedIn. The company has been celebrating this system as an excellent use case within its culture. This specific software incentivizes people to reward and recognize efforts of people who have gone beyond the call of duty within the firm to help their peers.

- Make compensation packages that are more participatory. De Neve offered this example: "If a part of your compensation package consists of profit sharing, group bonuses rather than individual bonuses, and share purchase plans, it's a way of bringing people together, especially in the case of group bonuses, and also we're getting people engaged with the company if there's aspects of profit sharing involved."

- Prioritize life over work. This means offering flextime, autonomy, possibly a four-day workweek. De Neve shares case studies where this is going really well, including most recently Microsoft Japan.

In our call, De Neve's enthusiasm was palpable. For someone who has dedicated their career to studying the economics of happiness, this is encouraging. He said, "So, as we look and delve into the data in a more detailed fashion, we find that it reveals more and more interesting insights about the power of happiness in terms of driving productivity. This is quite exciting, I would argue, and probably the best, most robust field evidence out there today."

How Leaders Can Be Happy, Healthy, and High-Performing

Research demonstrates that well-being is not only valuable because it feels good, but also because it has beneficial real-world consequences. Compared to people with low well-being, individuals with higher levels of well-being:

- Perform better at work

- Experience more satisfying relationships

- Are more cooperative

- Have stronger immune systems

- Are in better physical health

- Enjoy an increased life span

- Have reduced cardiovascular mortality

- Deal with fewer sleep problems

- Are less likely to burn out

- Have greater self-control

- Are more self-regulated and cope better

- Are more prosocial

- Suffer less depression and anxiety

Obviously, this list highlights the many positive benefits of a well workforce. Perhaps more interesting is how a healthy workplace can increase employee well-being. It can be a powerful symbiotic relationship if harmonious. It was why I shifted the focus of my research away from general life happiness to workplace well-being. If we spend 50 percent of our waking hours at work and our work makes us miserable, how can we expect to be truly happy?

The science of flourishing was the basis of my earlier consulting efforts. It grounded so much of the research and subsequent steps. But, it lacked in that it felt more like a destination to me and less like a journey. Although Martin Seligman and his team at the University of Pennsylvania are the pioneers of this work and remain the leaders in this space, as a practitioner in the field, I wanted to see how we could create more buy-in from leadership to adopt well-being as a strategy. This meant proving, with data, that well-being matters.

Our team of researchers, data scientists, and workplace experts zoomed in on culture and the importance of a happy one. We started by measuring traits consistent with Seligman's first building block, positive emotion, but added a few more. These skills, which can be developed through short but intentionally daily acts, were identified as HERO traits: hope, efficacy, resilience, optimism, gratitude, empathy, and mindfulness. After years of research and testing, we found that people high in these clustered traits were also the healthiest, happiest, and highest-performing people in work and life.

There are thousands of examples of interventions that can improve these cognitive skills. But, it would be our connection to neuroplasticity—the ability of the brain to form new connections and pathways and change how its circuits are wired—that made engaging these traits in the workplace even more possible for organizations to adopt.

Rick Hanson explains in *Hardwiring for Happiness* that the brain has this unique ability to rewire itself for positivity. This requires time and intention, but can be a way that we reduce our negativity bias and decrease our body's threat responses.

We took components from several scientists and researchers and combined them to start our former company Plasticity Labs. It was the foundation of our learning. I've listed some of my favorite interventions for anyone—leaders and employees—to leverage: think "Grandma's Rules" backed by science.

Hope

Charles Robert Snyder was a psychologist and professor of clinical psychology at the University of Kansas. He also put forth the concept of cognitive hope theory. Snyder defines hope as the belief in oneself to create the pathways (plans) to meet desired goals and to self-motivate using agency thinking to stick to those plans. He suggests that hope theory can be compared to theories of learned optimism, optimism, self-efficacy, and self-esteem. His research has shown that "higher hope consistently is related to better outcomes in academics, athletics, physical health, psychological adjustment, and psychotherapy."[5]

So what if we want to build cognitive hope? Science suggests we make our bed. Sounds silly, right? I usually ask how many people make their bed when I'm speaking in front of a large audience and everyone tends to raise their hands. Actually, seven out of ten people make their bed every day, so most of them are being truthful.

In a commencement speech at the University of Texas, William McRaven, who authored *Make Your Bed: Little Things Can Change Your Life . . . and Maybe the World*, told students that the importance of making your bed every day was one of the most powerful lessons he learned during his time as a Navy SEAL.

"If you make your bed every morning, you will have accomplished the first task of the day," he said. "It will give you a small sense of pride, and it will encourage you to do another task, and another, and another. And by the end of the day that one task completed will have turned into many tasks completed."[6]

He added that making your bed helps to reinforce the importance of life's finer details. He emphasized that "if by chance you have a miserable day, you will come home to a bed that is made—that you made."

However, the bed is just one example. Any goal accomplished tells your brain, "Good job! Now you're up for a bigger challenge! Keep going!"

Hope can be found in the small goals. In times of crisis, that is extremely important. At work, starting off your day by accomplishing a small task is important. Perhaps it's tidying your desk. Or writing a checklist of the three big priorities you need to focus on. Maybe it's clearing time in your schedule to take a break or sending out a quick thank-you to a colleague. It's mostly about checking off one thing—and then patting yourself on the back for it.

Efficacy

According to Albert Bandura, psychologist and professor emeritus at Stanford University, self-efficacy is essentially a person's belief in their ability to succeed in a particular situation.[7]

Our self-efficacy was hard hit in 2020. So many of us had to pivot quickly, we stopped being as effective in our jobs. It took more time to reach our goals, and most of us were just trying to learn how to video-conference and lead teams while working from home. Many of us (me) sucked at homeschooling. It was embarrassing to be so bad at it.

To increase self-efficacy, we need to go back to a time when we learned how to be masters of a new concept or learned something new. I can definitely say that 2020 showed me how to work through a challenge and come out the other side. I may not be a videoconferencing master, but I am better at it than I was. As a public speaker going virtual, I had to jump in and test plenty of new tools, even one where I had to be an avatar. (That was weird.)

To develop your self-efficacy (self-esteem), write down one thing you didn't think you'd ever do or know before 2020 and now you may actually be quite good at it. This tells your brain: "I did it before. I can do it again."

Resilience

We've discussed resilience at length in this chapter, but here is one way to develop it. Try your own version of benefit finding, also called re-framing. Think of a really challenging time in your life. Now list all the positives you can think of that came as a result of that experience. It may seem impossible—seeing the good in a bad situation—but try. What did you learn? What did you gain?

Optimism

We are considered to be optimistic when we have hopefulness and confidence about the future or the successful outcome of something. We tend to believe that everything is going to turn out all right. At work, this is consequential because optimistic leaders tend to have more support for their ideas. They are more comfortable taking risks and allowing others to take risks as well.

We can practice optimism through the language we use. For the next week, try saying "I get to" versus "I have to" about even the most tedious work. It helps us to feel that we have choice and that what we do has value. We aren't slaves to these tasks, but they are part of a bigger set of goals.

Gratitude

The gateway drug to happiness, gratitude gives us the quickest return on our investment. When we practice gratitude for any length of time, it begins to rewire our brain to focus on what we have versus what we don't have. A study by Robert Emmons, professor at UC Davis, found that just by writing down the positives from our week, once every Friday for ten weeks, we could improve our immune systems, get better sleep, feel less lonely, become more compassionate, and enrich our relationships.[8]

If you look at it from a neurosciences perspective, what is happening here is that when we tell our brain we have to report something, it listens. We tell it you have a task now; every Friday you have to write down what you're grateful for. OK, well, I guess I better start paying more attention to those moments in the day that make me feel grateful.

Let's imagine a child is learning French. At first, they are constantly translating from their first language into French. But, after immersing themselves in it each day, little by little they stop translating, but start thinking in this new language, until one day, they are fluent. That is how gratitude works. You go from translating gratitude into being grateful.

Try this exercise. Set a stopwatch for sixty seconds. Hit start and write down all the things you're grateful for until the minute is up. How many items did you list? Try this for a week and see if you get faster. The faster you can access these items, the better your fluency.

Another exercise I like is to set a recurring meeting on my work calendar for 2:49 p.m. on Friday, the time that researchers claim is when we mentally check out of work each week. So, make that recurring meeting a thank-you meeting and send out a one- or two-sentence email, text, Slack message—whatever communication tool you want to use—and thank someone for a specific thing they did to improve your life this week.

Gratitude is a social contagion. It doesn't just impact our experience at work; it can positively impact someone else's.

Empathy

I have put out the rallying cry, "More empathy in our policies and practices." I believe it to be paramount to the success of the future workforce. As you already know, I've dedicated an entire chapter to being an empathetic leader, but if you're looking for one more skill set to develop, look to the celebrated Brené Brown.

Brown is a research professor who has spent the past two decades studying courage, vulnerability, shame, and empathy. She implores us to stop saying "at least." Brown says that no empathetic response should start with "at least."

Next time someone is struggling and needs you to listen, just do that—listen. No one wants a silver lining to their story. We just need to say, "I hear you and thanks for sharing how you felt with me. That must have been hard."

Mindfulness

The practice of paying attention to the present moment is not only an essential life skill, but it is hugely valuable in the workplace because when we practice mindfulness, the stress region in the brain where our fight-or-flight response lives is calmed. When we engage in present mindfulness, our primal responses to stress are superseded by more thoughtful ones.

So imagine an angry, emotional, or stressed-out employee comes to your door to talk with you about how they're feeling. How do you want to meet them? With chaos? Or calm? If we practice mindfulness, we don't have to meet people in their heightened state. This allows us to control the emotion in the room and cool it down if it feels too hot.

And, when it comes to managing tasks, practicing mindfulness improves attention, awareness, and concentration. According to a study of high-level athletes, even pain can be managed better by practicing mindfulness.[9]

To develop present mindfulness isn't hard. We can do that by savoring more. Take your next meal and slow down when you eat it. Focus on what you're eating. How it smells and tastes. Slowing down in general is really key here. Another exercise I suggest is the "Three Things Activity." At some point in your day, stop and look around. Name three things:

- You can *see*

- You can *hear*

- You can *feel*

Just by stopping and checking in with your brain and your senses, you can gain all the cognitive benefits I've mentioned.

Again, all of these activities are simple. But they yield so many complex benefits. Like I said, Grandma's Rules backed by science. Combined, they make you a healthier, happier, and high-performing leader.

Post-Traumatic Growth

As leaders, we need to care for and empathize with others, all while handling our own responsibilities and emotions. It can be overwhelming, especially when we're leading during a crisis or difficult time—for ourselves, our employees, or our organizations.

These situations aren't ideal. They're stressful. At times they're intolerable. But they're also unavoidable. Tragedies. Pandemics. Downturns. They're going to happen. And it's up to us to learn and grow from these experiences as much as we can.

I connected with Tracy Brower, a sociologist who has spent the last thirty years exploring perspectives on work-life and fulfillment. She is the author of *Bring Work to Life by Bringing Life to Work: A Guide for Leaders and Organizations*. She believes that after any major crisis or trauma, we can experience a post-traumatic growth moment.

What does that mean?

Post-traumatic growth is a theory that explains this kind of transformation following trauma. Richard Tedeschi and Lawrence Calhoun coined the term "post-traumatic growth" to capture this phenomenon, defining it as the positive psychological change that is experienced as a result of the struggle with highly challenging life circumstances.

They found that many who experience trauma not only show incredible resilience but actually thrive in the aftermath of the traumatic event. Studies show that the majority of trauma survivors do not develop post-traumatic stress disorder, and a large number even report growth from their experience.

Considering that, before the pandemic, approximately 61 percent of men and 51 percent of women in the United States reported at least one traumatic event in their lifetime, the human capacity for resilience is quite remarkable.[10]

According Tedeschi and Calhoun, these seven areas of growth have been reported to spring from adversity:

- Greater appreciation of life

- Greater appreciation and strengthening of close relationships

- Increased compassion and altruism

- The identification of new possibilities or a purpose in life

- Greater awareness and utilization of personal strengths

- Enhanced spiritual development

- Creative growth[11]

Granted, we don't want to have to experience trauma to experience growth. However, since the majority of us will face big moments of stress in our lives, I'd rather come out of it stronger than completely derailed. Reframing also helps us to make sense of an incomprehensible event.

This was the case for Lucy Hone, a world-renowned researcher who started studying resilience over a decade ago at the University of Pennsylvania. She was part of the research team that trained 1.1 million American soldiers to be as mentally fit as they always have been physically fit.

Hone had returned home to Christchurch in New Zealand to start her doctoral research when in 2014, on a long weekend holiday, she and two other families had decided to go to a lake. At the last minute, her twelve-year-old daughter, Abigail (Abi) decided to hop in the car with her best friend, Ella, also twelve, and Ella's mom, Sally, one of Lucy's best friends. As they traveled toward the lake, a car sped through a stop sign, crashing into them and killing all three of them instantly.

In a moment, Hone went from being the resilience expert to a grieving mother. As she told me, "Suddenly, I'm the one on the end of all this expert advice. And I can tell you, I didn't like what I heard one little bit."

She found that the leaflets and the grief counselors, although well intentioned, only made her feel worse. She said, "But in all of that advice, they left us feeling like victims. Totally overwhelmed by the journey ahead, and powerless to exert any influence over our grieving whatsoever. I didn't need to be told how bad things were. Believe me, I already knew things were truly terrible. What I needed most was hope. I needed a journey through all that anguish, pain, and longing. Most of all, I wanted to be an active participant in my grief process."

So Hone, determined to take a different route for her healing, found new strategies to handle her grief. Five years later, she found three that worked. Three strategies to overcome massive trauma and adversity that we can all access if we try:

- "Resilient people get that shit happens," Hone said. Highly resilient people know that suffering is part of life. This doesn't mean they actually welcome it in; they're not actually delusional. It's just that when the tough times come, they seem to know that suffering is part of every human existence. "And knowing this stops you from feeling discriminated against when the tough times come. Never once did I find myself thinking, 'Why me?' In fact, I remember thinking, 'Why not me? Terrible things happen to you, just like they do everybody else. That's your life now, time to sink or swim.'"

- Resilient people are really good at choosing carefully where they select their attention. They have a habit of realistically appraising situations, and typically, managing to focus on the things that they can change, and somehow accepting the things that they can't.

  Hone explains how our evolutionary hangovers are at play here. "Since we have such a deeply wired threat response, we tend to ignore the good news and take in all the bad. It may have served us well when we needed to protect ourselves from danger like saber-tooth cats, but today, we're just getting bombarded with threats so we're "permanently dialed up." Hone underlines that resilient people don't diminish the negative, but they also have worked out a way of tuning in to the good.

  In her now-famous TED talk, "3 Secrets of Resilient People," Hone shares, "One day, when doubts were threatening to overwhelm me, I distinctly remember thinking, 'No, you do not get to get swallowed up by this. You have to survive. You've got so much to live for. Choose life, not death. Don't lose what you have to what you have lost.' In psychology, we call this benefit finding. In my brave new world, it involved trying to find things to be grateful for. At least our wee girl hadn't died of some terrible, long, drawn-out illness. She died suddenly, instantly, sparing us and her that pain. We had a huge amount of social support from family and friends to help us through. And most of all, we still had two beautiful boys to live for, who needed us now, and deserved to have as normal a life as we could possibly give them. Being able to switch the focus of your attention to also include the good has been shown by science to be a really powerful strategy."[12]

- Resilient people ask themselves, "Is what I'm doing helping or harming me?" Hone talked about how she had to make a lot of decisions in those early days after Abi died, and she had to keep asking herself, Is this helping or harming me? When she was poring over old photos of Abi, getting more and more upset, she'd ask, "Is this helping you or is it harming you? Put away the photos, go to bed for the night, be kind to yourself."

Ask yourself right now if there is anything you are doing that is harming you? Are you ruminating or worrying or holding on to anger or forgiveness? Are you withholding love from someone or from yourself? Are you feeling ashamed or guilty for something that requires self-compassion instead? Is it serving you or is it harming you?

Lucy Hone offers us these three simple yet brilliant strategies for post-traumatic growth—all accessible and at our disposal.

I shared with Hone in our interview that her story simultaneously shatters our hearts and then stitches it back together. Her message is so tangible. Resilience is possible. She said, "If you ever find yourselves in a situation where you think there's no way I'm coming back from this, I urge you to lean into these strategies and think again. I won't pretend that thinking this way is easy. And it doesn't remove all the pain. But if I've learned anything over the last five years, it is that thinking this way really does help."

When we consider what we've gone through recently as a collective, Tracy Brower said that we need to dig deep and find the benefits. "Burnout is on the rise, and mental health issues are rife," Brower told me. "It's a rare week that there isn't some new study on the extent of our mental health issues. But burnout isn't evidence of how we won't come back; it's actually fodder for our growth. These are really hard times, and we are learning so much and building resilience. The greatest innovations come from the most significant barriers and challenges—so these times are causing us to reset, rethink, and find new ways of doing everything from raising children to working and living."

Unfortunately, leaders feel isolated in their roles—this is the expectation of the job. Yet, according to Brower, "those with a greater sense of purpose—people who cope most effectively—are those with strong community connections and those who have weathered other storms before."

And in times of trauma and stress, it can catalyze a post-traumatic growth opportunity. "Nothing is more significant in creating bonds than a common enemy, and crises like the coronavirus struggle are a perfect example of what will strengthen relationships," Brower clarified. "We can go through very tough times and when we come out on the other side—having gone through it together—we will have new levels of connection with our colleagues and the people we lead."

In "Leadership and Loneliness," Ami Rokach writes that "leaders (educational, state, business, and organizational) endure stress, alienation, loneliness, and emotional turmoil. These may lead to health problems and negatively affect social and familial relationships as well."[13]

Leadership can become isolating because the role tends to separate leaders from former peers who are now reporting to them. This can result in feeling less connection and support. Rokach said that "loneliness of command" has been used frequently in the context of leadership: "The inability to test one's perceptions, the tendency to lose touch with reality because one occupies a top position, is a danger anyone can fall victim to when in a leadership position."

In our conversation, he shared some key differences in how we need to define loneliness so we can identify if we're facing an acute or a chronic experience of isolation.

"Acute loneliness commonly should be situational, due to a loss in one's life. A chronic loneliness may stem from two sources," explained Rokach. "Essential loneliness is a chronic loneliness that is intertwined into a person's soul or personality, usually as a result of their connection with parents or significant others, based on which they understood that the world is an uncaring place that will disregard their needs and may not even notice them. That loneliness, in my opinion, can be dealt with only in long-term psychotherapy," he said.

Rokach described "a situational, or transient, bout of loneliness, which the person is unable to exit—a significant loss that resulted in loneliness and possibly depression, which the person may feel unable to cope with, develops learned helplessness, and thus it drags on and on."

Rokach mentioned learned helplessness—an important term for all leaders and their employees to understand. Learned helplessness is "a condition in which a person suffers from a sense of powerlessness, arising from a traumatic event or persistent failure to succeed. It is thought to be one of the underlying causes of depression."

This occurs when someone continuously faces a negative, uncontrollable situation and stops trying to change their circumstances, even when they have the ability to do so. For example, a smoker may repeatedly try and fail to quit and then just accept that they will be a lifelong smoker.

For leaders, "It's lonely at the top" can sound like a joke, but it's often not the case. Choosing narratives like "Being on my own is just part of the job" or "I have to handle this alone—there's no one else who can help me" supports a defeatist mentality, an attitude that becomes pervasive and can lead to burnout.

What was interesting throughout my research and the conversations I had with leaders, particularly throughout the coronavirus pandemic, is that they aren't actually alone. I kept hearing how letting go of that stoicism enhanced their relationships and flattened the notion of hierarchy during the crisis. In one of my leadership workshops, one executive said that she realized they all may be in different boats, but they were navigating the same storm.

Perhaps I occupy a dissimilar role in the organization, but I am still juggling the same familial demands, feeling chronically worried about getting sick, worrying about other family members. This bonding helped leaders to realize that they don't have to be on an island. Just because someone reports to us doesn't mean that we have to remain disconnected. We can give them a window into our lives, and our culture will be better off for it.

In another workshop I led that analyzed perspectives from the crisis, instead of "I never want to think about 2020 again," I heard, "Our team became so close. We were really connected in a shared goal and I felt like we were all in this together."

"This period, which none of us may have ever experienced, was a wake-up call to us all," said Rokach. "We, in the Western world, have lived in a rat race pushing for material possessions, advancements on the job, and taking care of number one. We were reminded of how much we longed for a hug, for real human contact, for warmth and support—which requires mostly face-to-face interaction. We learned to relate more meaningfully to others, to appreciate them, and to realize how much we need them in our lives."

· · ·

So, how does all of this connect to burnout? I imagine it's self-explanatory, but just to wrap it up, these are the upstream impacts that will help us manage our part of the burnout equation. We need to combine our efforts, and this is how we participate. This is how we show up to lead.

By coming to work with high levels of psychological fitness, the little stuff won't wear on us as much. It helps us to give others grace when they need it and self-compassion when we need it, particularly as we deal with major stress events like the pandemic, or the eight economic crashes, or the sweeping fires, or before the next crisis hits. We will be able to take on whatever comes at us.

Going forward in all instances, we need to give ourselves a break when we don't have all the answers.

Giving and receiving grace in turbulent times can only happen if we've built up our mental capacity. We do that by practicing emotional intelligence skills, building up our HERO traits, and working on our psychological fitness.

It requires a joint effort to increase well-being and happiness through personal and individualized efforts and the promise for healthy corporate hygiene, better systems and policies that support mental health, and a commitment to solving this problem for good.

Leaders, I believe in us. I'm feeling optimistic—perhaps for the first time—that together we may just be able to battle burnout and win.

Notes

Introduction

1. "More Than 2.6 Billion Worldwide Told to Observe Lockdowns," *MedicalXpress*, March 24, 2020, https://medicalxpress.com/news/2020-03-billion -worldwide-told-lockdowns.html; "Coronavirus: Four Out of Five People's Jobs Hit by the Pandemic," *BBC News*, April 7, 2020, https://www.bbc.com/news /business-52199888.

2. Reuters, "Zoom's Daily Participants Jumped from 10 Million to Over 200 Million in 3 Months (Updated)," April 2, 2020, *VentureBeat*, https://venturebeat .com/2020/04/02/zooms-daily-active-users-jumped-from-10-million-to-over-200 -million-in-3-months/.

3. "Burn-out an 'Occupational Phenomenon': International Classification of Diseases," World Health Organization, May 28, 2019, https://www.who.int /news/item/28-05-2019-burn-out-an-occupational-phenomenon-international -classification-of-diseases.

4. "A Message from the Maslach Burnout Inventory Authors," *Mind Garden Blog*, March 19, 2019, https://www.mindgarden.com/blog/post/44-a-message -from-the-maslach-burnout-inventory-authors.

5. Jim Clifton, "The World's Broken Workplace," *Gallup Chairman's Blog*, June 13, 2017, https://news.gallup.com/opinion/chairman/212045/world -broken-workplace.aspx.

6. "One-Third of Your Life Is Spent at Work" Gettysburg College, n.d., https://www.gettysburg.edu/news/stories?id=79db7b34-630c-4f49-ad32 -4ab9ea48e72b&pageTitle=1%2F3+of+your+life+is+spent+at+work; Karl Thompson, "What Percentage of Your Life Will You Spend at Work?" ReviseSociology, August 16, 2016, https://revisesociology.com/2016/08/16 /percentage-life-work/.

7. Jeffrey Blitz, dir., *The Office*, season 5, episode 13, "Stress Relief," aired February 1, 2009, on NBC.

8. Kristine D. Olson, "Physician Burnout—A Leading Indicator of Health System Performance?," *Mayo Clinic Proceedings* 92, no. 11 (November 1, 2017), https://www.mayoclinicproceedings.org/article/S0025-6196(17)30690-0/fulltext.

9. Dirk Enzmann and Dieter Kleiber, *Helfer-Leiden: Streß und Burnout in Psychosozialen Berufen* (Heidelberg: Asanger, 1989), 18.

Chapter 1

1. Frederick Herzberg, "The Hygiene Motivation Theory," *Thinker 001*, Chartered Management Institute, n.d., https://www.managers.org.uk/~/media /Campus Resources/Frederick Herzberg - The hygiene motivation theory.ashx.

2. "Maslow's Hierarchy of Needs," *Encyclopedia of Child Behavior and Development*, 2011, https://link.springer.com/referenceworkentry/10.1007 %2F978-0-387-79061-9_1720.

3. Ibid.

4. Kathleen Stassen Berger, *The Developing Person through the Life Span* (New York: Worth, 1983), 44.

5. Ben Wigert, "Employee Burnout: The Biggest Myth," Gallup, March 13, 2020, https://www.gallup.com/workplace/288539/employee-burnout-biggest -myth.aspx.

6. Rob Edwards, "Pyramids Broke the Backs of Workers," *New Scientist*, January 20, 1996, https://www.newscientist.com/article/mg14920131-100 -pyramids-broke-the-backs-of-workers/.

7. Joel Goh, Jeffrey Pfeffer, and Stefanos A. Zenios, "The Relationship between Workplace Stressors and Mortality and Health Costs in the United States," *Management Science* 62, no. 2 (2016): iv–vii.

8. "World Day for Safety and Health at Work," International Labour Organization, April 28, 2019, https://www.ilo.org/global/topics/safety-and -health-at-work/events-training/events-meetings/world-day-for-safety /lang--en/index.htm.

9. "Three Out of Five Employees Are Highly Stressed, According to ComPsych Survey," press release, ComPsych, October 30, 2017, https://www .compsych.com/press-room/press-article?nodeId=37b20f13-6b88-400e -9852-0f1028bd1ec1.

10. Michelle Davis and Jeff Green, "Three Hours Longer, the Pandemic Work-Day Has Obliterated Work-Life Balance," *BNN Bloomberg*, April 27, 2020, https://www.bnnbloomberg.ca/three-hours-longer-the-pandemic-workday ˋ-has-obliterated-work-life-balance-1.1425827.

11. Oracle, "Global Study: 82% of People Believe Robots Can Support Their Mental Health Better Than Humans," press release, October 7, 2020, https://www.theglobeandmail.com/investing/markets/stocks/ORCL-N /pressreleases/389382/.

12. Durairaj Rajan "Negative Impacts of Heavy Workload: A Comparative Study among Sanitary Workers," *Sociology International Journal* 2, no. 6 (2018): 465–474.

13. Anna Dahlgren, Göran Kecklund, and Torbjörn Åkerstedt, "Different Levels of Work-Related Stress and the Effects on Sleep, Fatigue, and Cortisol," *Scandinavian Journal of Environmental Health* 31, no. 4 (2005): 277–285.

14. John Ross, "Only the Overworked Die Young," *Harvard Health Blog*, Harvard Health Publishing, Harvard Medical School, December 14, 2015, https://www.health.harvard.edu/blog/only-the-overworked-die-young -201512148815.

15. Gonzalo Shoobridge, "Dealing with Chronically Overworked Employees," *LinkedIn Pulse*, February 18, 2016, https://www.linkedin.com/pulse/chronic -overwork-gonzalo-shoobridge/.

16. Evan DeFilippis et al., "Collaborations during Coronavirus: The Impact of COVID-19 on the Nature of Work," National Bureau of Economic Research, working paper 27612, July 2020, https://www.nber.org/papers/w27612.

17. Davis and Green, "Three Hours Longer, the Pandemic Work-Day Has Obliterated Work-Life Balance."

18. "Four-Day Week Pays Off for UK Business," Henley Business School, July 3, 2019, https://www.henley.ac.uk/news/2019/four-day-week-pays-off-for -uk-business.

19. "Looking After Our Mental Health," #Healthy at Home, World Health Organization, n.d., https://www.who.int/campaigns/connecting-the-world -to-combat-coronavirus/healthyathome/healthyathome---mental-health.

20. "Mental Health—Having Courageous Conversations," Canadian Centre for Occupational Health and Safety, n.d., https://www.ccohs.ca/oshanswers /psychosocial/mentalhealth_conversations.html.

21. Palena Neale, "'Serious' Leaders Need Self-Care, Too," hbr.org, October 22, 2020, https://hbr.org/2020/10/serious-leaders-need-self-care-too.

22. Ibid.

23. Ibid.

24. "Breaking Boredom: What's Really Driving Job Seekers in 2018," Korn Ferry, https://www.kornferry.com/insights/this-week-in-leadership/job -hunting-2018-boredom.

25. Elizabeth Grace Saunders, "6 Causes of Burnout, and How to Avoid Them," hbr.org, July 5, 2019, https://hbr.org/2019/07/6-causes-of-burnout -and-how-to-avoid-them.

26. Susan K. Collins and Kevin S. Collins, "Micromanagement—a Costly Management Style, *Radiology Management* 24, no. 6 (2002): 32–35.

27. Robert Karasek, "Lower Health Risk with Increased Job Control among White Collar Workers," *Journal of Organizational Behavior* 11, no. 3 (1990): 171–185.

28. Collins and Collins, "Micromanagement."

29. Timothy A. Judge et al., "Do Nice Guys and Gals Really Finish Last? The Joint Effects of Sex and Agreeableness on Income," *Journal of Personality and Social Psychology* 102, no. 2 (2011): 390–407.

30. Michael Cabbage, "Still Haunted by Columbia's End," *Baltimore Sun*, February 1, 2004, https://www.baltimoresun.com/news/bs-xpm -2004-02-01-0402010042-story.html.

31. Shahram Heshmat, "Eight Reasons Why We Get Bored," *Psychology Today*, June 16, 2017, https://www.psychologytoday.com/ca/blog/science-choice/201706/eight-reasons-why-we-get-bored.

32. "How We Form Habits, Change Existing Ones," *Science Daily*, August 8, 2014, https://www.sciencedaily.com/releases/2014/08/140808111931.htm.

33. Jane E. Dutton et al., "Being Valued and Devalued at Work: A Social Valuing Perspective," *Qualitative Organizational Research: Best Papers from the Davis Conference on Organizational Research*, vol. 3 (Charlotte, NC: Information Age Publishing, 2012).

34. Ibid.

35. J. M. Violanti et al., "Effort–Reward Imbalance and Overcommitment at Work: Associations with Police Burnout," *Police Quarterly* 21, no. 4 (2018): 440–460.

36. A. B. Bakker et al., "Effort-Reward Imbalance and Burnout among Nurses," *Journal of Advanced Nursing* 31, no. 4 (2000): 884–891.

37. Beata Basinska and Ewa Wilczek-Rużyczka, "The Role of Rewards and Demands in Burnout among Surgical Nurses," *International Journal of Occupational Medicine and Environmental Health* 26 (2013): 593–604.

38. Wale Aliyu, "25 Investigates: Overworked Police Departments Paying Big Money in Overtime," *Boston 25 News*, November 21, 2019, https://www.boston25news.com/news/25-investigates-overworked-police-departments-paying-big-money-in-overtime/1010669867/.

39. A. M. Williamson and Anne-Marie Feyer, "Moderate Sleep Deprivation Produces Impairments in Cognitive and Motor Performance Equivalent to Legally Prescribed Levels of Alcohol Intoxication," *Occupational and Environmental Medicine* 57 (2000): 649–655.

40. Alison Duquette, "Fact Sheet—Pilot Fatigue Rule Comparison," Federal Aviation Administration, December 21, 2011, https://www.faa.gov/news/fact_sheets/news_story.cfm?newsKey=12445.

41. Michael J. Gaynor, "43 Percent of Internships at For-Profit Companies Don't Pay. This Man Is Helping to Change That," *Washington Post*, January 15, 2015, https://www.washingtonpost.com/lifestyle/magazine/his-quest-to-get-interns-paid-is-paying-off/2019/01/11/93df2b2a-ff2a-11e8-83c0-b06139e540e5_story.html.

42. Nicolas A. Pologeorgis, "Unpaid Internship Impact on the Labor Market," Investopedia, June 25, 2019, https://www.investopedia.com/articles/economics/12/impact-of-unpaid-internships.asp#:~:text=Unpaid%20internships%20take%20labor%20away,employees%2C%20thus%20contributing%20to%20unemployment.

43. 2020 Branch Report, https://www.branchapp.com/resources/the-2020-branch-report.

44. Sabrina Son, "The Most Embarrassing Employment Stories We've Heard," *TinyPulse*, February 25, 2015, https://www.tinypulse.com/blog/the-most-embarrassing-employee-recognition-stories-weve-heard.

45. S. Alexander Haslam et al., "Social Identity, Health and Well–being: An Emerging Agenda for Applied Psychology," *Applied Psychology* 58, no. 1 (2009): 1–23.

46. Mary McCarthy, Grace Pretty, and Vic Catano, "Psychological Sense of Community and Burnout," *Journal of College Student Development* 31 (May 1990): 211–216.

47. Karl Thompson, "What Percentage of Your Life Will You Spend at Work?" ReviseSociology, August 16, 2016, https://revisesociology.com/2016/08/16/percentage-life-work/.

48. Deloitte Insights, "The Social Enterprise at Work: Paradox as a Path Forward: 2020 Deloitte Global Human Capital Trends," Deloitte Insights, n.d., deloitte-cn-hc-trend-2020-en-200519.pdf.

49. "The Value of Belong at Work: New Frontiers for Inclusion in 2021 and Beyond," BetterUp, https://www.betterup.com/en-us/resources/reports/the-value-of-belonging-at-work-the-business-case-for-investing-in-workplace-inclusion.

50. "WorkWell: Living Your Best Life, At Work," YMCA, n.d., https://www.thisisy.ca/workwell/#lp-pom-block-8.

51. "Item 10: I Have a Best Friend at Work," Gallup, Workplace, May 26, 1999, https://www.gallup.com/workplace/237530/item-best-friend-work.aspx.

52. Ibid.

53. Ibid.

54. Tom Rath and Jim Harter, "Your Friends and Your Social Well-Being," *Gallup Business Journal*, August 19, 2010, https://news.gallup.com/businessjournal/127043/friends-social-wellbeing.aspx.

55. Arie Shirom et al., "Work-Based Predictors of Mortality: A 20-Year Follow-up of Healthy Employees," *Health Psychology* 30, no. 3 (2011).

56. Dan Schawbel, *Back to Human: How Great Leaders Create Connection in the Age of Isolation* (Cambridge, MA: Da Capo Press, 2018).

57. Jaime Ballard, "During COVID, Many Millennials Still Feel Lonely," YouGov, May 1, 2020, https://today.yougov.com/topics/relationships/articles-reports/2020/05/01/loneliness-mental-health-coronavirus-poll-data.

58. Emmy Kenny, "Why Workplace Friendships Are Worth the Effort," Milkround, January 22, 2021, https://www.milkround.com/advice/why-workplace-friendships-are-worth-the-effort.

59. "Creative Thinking and the Brain," *Harvard Health Letter*, December 2010, https://www.health.harvard.edu/newsletter_article/creative-thinking-and-the-brain.

60. Gavin Kilduff et al., "The Psychology of Rivalry: A Relationally Dependent Analysis of Competition," *Academy of Management Journal* 53, no. 5 (2010): 943–969.

61. John T. Cacioppo and Louise C. Hawley, "Perceived Social Isolation and Cognition," *Trends in Cognitive Science* 13, no. 10 (2009): 447–454.

62. "Item 10," Gallup.

63. Constanze Leineweber et al., "Interactional Justice at Work Is Related to Sickness Absence: A Study Using Repeated Measures in the Swedish Working Population," *BMC Public Health* 17, no. 1 (2017).

64. Ibid.

65. "Resolving Human Rights Issues in the Workplace," Ontario Human Rights Commission, 2008, http://www.ohrc.on.ca/en/iv-human-rights-issues -all-stages-employment/12-resolving-human-rights-issues-workplace.

66. Adia Harvey Wingfield, "The Disproportionate Impact of Covid-19 on Black Health Care Workers in the U.S.," hbr.org, May 14, 2020, https://hbr.org/2020/05/the-disproportionate-impact-of-covid-19-on -black-health-care-workers-in-the-u-s.

67. Tiana Clark, "This Is What Black Burnout Feels Like," *BuzzFeed News*, January 11, 2019, https://www.buzzfeednews.com/article/tianaclarkpoet /millennial-burnout-black-women-self-care-anxiety-depression.

68. Brianna Holt, "Beyond Burnout," *The Cut*, August 13, 2020, https://www .thecut.com/article/black-women-on-burnout.html.

69. Ibid.

70. Saunders, "6 Causes of Burnout, and How to Avoid Them."

71. Arne L. Kalleberg, "The Mismatched Worker: When People Don't Fit Their Jobs," *Academy of Management Perspectives* 22, no. 1 (2008): 24–40.

72. "Millennials: The Overqualified Workforce," Deloitte Insights, January 2019, https://www2.deloitte.com/us/en/insights/economy/spotlight /economics-insights-analysis-01-2019.html.

73. Camilla Turner and Olivia Rudgard, "Almost One in Three Graduates Are Overqualified for Their Job, Major Report Finds," *Telegraph*, September 12, 2018, https://www.telegraph.co.uk/education/2018/09/11/almost-one-three -graduates-overqualified-job-major-report-finds/.

74. "Millennials: The Overqualified Workforce," Deloitte Insights.

75. Ibid.

76. Richard Fry, "Share of Young Adults Not Working or in School Is at a 30-Year Low in U.S.," Pew Research Center, October 29, 2019, https://www .pewresearch.org/fact-tank/2019/10/29/share-of-young-adults-not-working -or-in-school-is-at-a-30-year-low-in-u-s/.

77. "Tuition Costs of Colleges and Universities," National Center for Education Statistics, n.d., https://nces.ed.gov/fastfacts/display.asp?id=76.

78. Michael Harari, Archana Manapragada, and Chockalingam Viswesvaran, "Who Thinks They're a Big Fish in a Small Pond and Why Does It Matter? A Meta-analysis of Perceived Overqualification," *Journal of Vocational Behavior* 102 (October 2017): 28–47.

79. Ibid.

80. Ibid.

81. Terrence Jermyn Porter, "Employees' Responses to the Mismatch between Organizations' Espoused Values and Basic Assumptions about Organizational Culture," PhD dissertation, University of St. Thomas, St. Paul, MN, 2013, https://ir.stthomas.edu/cgi/viewcontent.cgi?article=1025&context=caps_ed_orgdev_docdiss.

82. Sue Shellenbarger, "The Dangers of Hiring for Cultural Fit," *Wall Street Journal*, September 23, 2019, https://www.wsj.com/articles/the-dangers-of-hiring-for-cultural-fit-11569231000.

Chapter 2

1. Herbert J. Freudenberger, "Staff Burn-Out," *Journal of Social Issues* 30, no. 1 (Winter 1974): 1–7.

2. E. R. Thompson, "Development and Validation of an International English Big-Five Mini-Markers,"*Personality and Individual Differences* 45, no. 6 (2008): 542–548.

3. Sharon Maylor, "The Relationship Between Big Five Personality Traits and Burnout: A Study among Correctional Personnel," PhD dissertation, Walden University, Minneapolis, MN, 2018, https://scholarworks.waldenu.edu/cgi/viewcontent.cgi?article=6214&context=dissertations.

4. Gloria Mark et al., "Neurotics Can't Focus: An In Situ Study of Online Multitasking in the Workplace," *Proceedings of the 2016 CHI Conference on Human Factors in Computing Systems*, May 2016, 1739–1744.

5. Jason M. Fletcher, "The Effects of Personality Traits on Adult Labor Market Outcomes," *Journal of Economic Behavior and Organization* 89 (2013): 122–135.

6. Turhan Canli, "Functional Brain Mapping of Extraversion and Neuroticism: Learning from Individual Differences in Emotion Processing," *Journal of Personality* 72 (2005): 1105–1132.

7. Susan Cain, *Quiet: The Power of Introverts in a World That Can't Stop Talking* (New York: Crown, 2013).

8. Molly Owens, "Personality Type and Career Achievement," Typefinder, February 2015, https://www.truity.com/sites/default/files/PersonalityType-CareerAchievementStudy.pdf.

9. Elizabeth Layman and Janet A. Guyden, "Reducing Your Risk of Burnout," *Health Care Supervisor* 15, no. 3 (1997): 57–69.

10. Joachim Stoeber and Kathleen Otto, "Positive Conceptions of Perfectionism: Approaches, Evidence, Challenges," *Personality and Social Psychology Review* 10 (2006): 259–319.

11. Andrew P. Hill and Thomas Curran, "Multidimensional Perfectionism and Burnout: A Meta-Analysis," *Personality and Social Psychology Review* 20, no. 3 (2016): 269–288.

12. David Burns, *Feeling Good: The New Mood Therapy* (New York: Quill, 2000).

13. David Burns, "Secrets of Self-Esteem #2," *Feeling Good* (blog), https://feelinggood.com/2014/01/06/secrets-of-self-esteem-2-negative-and -positive-distortions/.

14. Mick Oreskovich and James Anderson, "Physician Personalities and Burnout," *Bulletin of the American College of Surgeons*, June 1, 2013, https://bulletin .facs.org/2013/06/personalities-and-burnout/.

15. Scott Gottlieb, "Patients Are at Risk Because of Nurses' Long Hours, Says Report," *British Medical Journal* 327, no. 7424 (November 15, 2003): 1128.

16. Amy Witkoski Stimpfel, Douglas M. Sloane, and Linda H. Aiken, "The Longer the Shifts for Hospital Nurses, the Higher the Levels of Burnout and Patient Dissatisfaction," *Health Affairs* 31, no. 11 (November 2012): 2501–2509.

17. Jane Ball et al., "The 12-Hour Shift: Friend or Foe?" *Nursing Times* 111, no. 6 (2015): 12–14.

18. Peter Donald Griffiths et al., "Nurses' Shift Length and Overtime Working in 12 European Countries," *Medical Care*, September 2014, https://www .researchgate.net/publication/265692122_Nurses'_Shift_Length_and_Over- time_Working_in_12_European_Countries_The_Association_With_Perceived_ Quality_of_Care_and_Patient_Safety.

19. Jin Wen et al., "Workload, Burnout, and Medical Mistakes among Physicians in China: A Cross-Sectional Study," *BioScience Trends 2016* 10, no. 1 (2016): 27–33.

20. Charles M. Balch et al., "Personal Consequences of Malpractice Lawsuits on American Surgeons," *Journal of the American College of Surgeons* 213, no. 5 (November 2011): 657–667.

21. Edward R. Melnick et al., "The Association between Perceived Electronic Health Record Usability and Professional Burnout among US Physicians," *Mayo Clinic Proceedings* 95, no. 3 (2020): 476–487.

22. Ibid.

23. Yale University, "Obama Administration Pumped $27 Billion into Electronic Health Records—Doctors Give an 'F,'" *SciTech Daily*, November 17, 2019, https://scitechdaily.com/obama-administration-pumped-27-billion -into-electronic-health-records-doctors-give-an-f/.

24. Ibid.

25. Tait D. Shanafelt et al., "Changes in Burnout and Satisfaction with Work-Life Integration in Physicians and the General US Working Population between 2011 and 2017," *Mayo Clinic Proceedings* 94, no. 9 (September 1, 2019): 1681–1694.

26. American Academy of Family Physicians, "COVID-19 Is Increasing Physician Burnout," *Quick Tip*s (blog), September 18, 2020, https://www.aafp.org/journals/fpm/blogs/inpractice/entry/covid_burnout_survey.html.

27. Edward M. Ellison, "Beyond the Economics of Burnout," *Annals of Internal Medicine*, June 4, 2019, video, https://www.acpjournals.org/doi/10.7326/M19-1191.

28. Margo M. C. van Mol et al., "The Prevalence of Compassion Fatigue and Burnout among Healthcare Professional in Intensive Care Units: A Systematic Review," *PLOS ONE* 10, no. 8 (August 31, 2015), https://journals.plos.org/plosone/article?id=10.1371/journal.pone.0136955.

29. Dr. Lorna Breen Heroes' Foundation, https://drlornabreen.org/.

30. Maureen O'Connor, "A Doctor's Emergency," *Vanity Fair*, September 17, 2020, https://www.vanityfair.com/style/2020/09/will-lorna-breens-death-change-doctors-mental-health.

31. Emma Garcia and Elaine Weiss, "The Teacher Shortage Is Real, Large and Growing, and Worse Than We Thought," Economic Policy Institute, March 26, 2019, https://www.epi.org/publication/the-teacher-shortage-is-real-large-and-growing-and-worse-than-we-thought-the-first-report-in-the-perfect-storm-in-the-teacher-labor-market-series/.

32. Keith Lambert, "Why Our Teachers Are Leaving," *Education World*, n.d., https://www.educationworld.com/why-our-teachers-are-leaving.

33. "The World Needs Almost 69 Million New Teachers to Reach the 2030 Education Goals," UNESCO Institute for Statistics, October 2016, https://unesdoc.unesco.org/images/0024/002461/246124E.pdf.

34. Dian Schaffhauser, "Educators Feeling Stress, Anxious, Overwhelmed and Capable," *Journal*, June 2, 2020, https://thejournal.com/articles/2020/06/02/survey-teachers-feeling-stressed-anxious-overwhelmed-and-capable.aspx.

35. Rachel Krantz-Kent, "Teachers' Work Patterns: When, Where, and How Much Do U.S. Teachers Work?" *Monthly Labor Review* (March 2008): 52–59.

36. Sylvia Allegretto and Lawrence Mishel, "The Teacher Pay Penalty Has Reached a New High," Economic Policy Institute, September 5, 2018, https://www.epi.org/publication/teacher-pay-gap-2018/; National Center for Education Statistics, "Table 211.10: Average Total Income, Base Salary, and Other Sources of School and Nonschool Income for Full-Time Teachers in Public and Private Elementary and Secondary Schools, by Selected Characteristics: 2017–18," Digest of Education Statistics, https://nces.ed.gov/programs/digest/d19/tables/dt19_211.10.asp?current=yes.

37. Katie Reilly, "'I Work 3 Jobs and Donate Plasma to Pay the Bills.' This Is What It's Like to Be a Teacher in America," *Time*, September 24, 2018, https://time .com/magazine/us/5394910/september-24th-2018-vol-192-no-12-u-s/.

38. David Cooper and Teresa Kroeger, "Employers Steal Billions from Workers' Paychecks Each Year," Economic Policy Institute, May 10, 2017, https://www.epi.org/publication/employers-steal-billions-from-workers -paychecks-each-year/.

39. National Education Association, "Teacher Compensation: Fact vs. Fiction," September 1, 2018, https://www.nea.org/resource-library/teacher -compensation-fact-vs-fiction.

40. Christian Krekel, George Ward, and Jan-Emmanuel de Neve, "Employee Well-being, Productivity, and Firm Performance: Evidence and Case Studies," Global Happiness Council, *Global Happiness and Well-Being Policy Report 2019*, presented at World Government Summit, Dubai, February 10, 2019, 39–42.

41. James H. Fowler and Nicholas A. Christakis, "Dynamic Spread of Happiness in a Large Social Network: Longitudinal Analysis over 20 Years in the Framingham Heart Study," *British Medical Journal* (2008), https://www.bmj.com /content/337/bmj.a2338.

42. Ezra Golberstein et al., "Social Contagion of Mental Health: Evidence from College Roommates," *Health Economics* 22, no. 8 (2013): 965–986.

43. Jodi Kantor and David Streitfeld, "Inside Amazon: Wrestling Big Ideas in a Bruising Workplace," *New York Times*, August 15, 2015, https://www.nytimes .com/2015/08/16/technology/inside-amazon-wrestling-big-ideas-in-a-bruising -workplace.html.

44. Parul Koul and Chewy Shaw, "We Built Google. This Is Not the Company We Want to Work For," *New York Times*, January 4, 2021, https://www .nytimes.com/2021/01/04/opinion/google-union.html.

45. Jennifer Moss, "Disrupting the Tech Profession's Gender Gap," Society of Human Resource Management, May 19, 2019, https://www.shrm.org/hr-today /news/all-things-work/pages/disrupting-the-tech-profession-gender-gap.aspx.

46. Rich Kleiman, "Jack Dorsey," *Out of the Office* podcast, n.d., https://podcasts .apple.com/us/podcast/episode-1-jack-dorsey/id1526198958?i=1000487879010.

47. Jennifer Moss, "When Passion Leads to Burnout," hbr.org, July 1, 2019, https://hbr.org/2019/07/when-passion-leads-to-burnout.

48. Robert J. Vallerand et al., "On the Role of Passion for Work in Burnout: A Process Model," *Journal of Personality* 78, no. 1 (February 2010): 289–312.

Chapter 3

1. Kathryn Walton et al., "Exploring the Role of Family Functioning in the Association between Frequency of Family Dinners and Dietary Intake among Adolescents and Young Adults," *JAMA Network Open*, November 21, 2018, https://jamanetwork.com/journals/jamanetworkopen/fullarticle/2715616.

2. Michelle J. Saksena et al., "American's Eating Habits: Food Away from Home," *Economic Information Bulletin* 196 (September 2018), https://www.ers.usda.gov/webdocs/publications/90228/eib-196.pdf.

3. "Want to Eat Better and Live Longer? Learn to Cook," Blue Zones, April 2018, https://www.bluezones.com/2018/04/want-to-eat-better-and-live-longer-learn-to-cook/.

4. Sandra L. Hofferth and John F. Sandberg, "How American Children Spend Their Time," *Journal of Marriage and Family* 63, no. 2 (2001): 295–308.

5. Jennifer Elias, "Google Is Accelerating Partial Reopening of Offices and Putting Limits on Future of Remote Work," CNBC, March 31, 2021, https://www.cnbc.com/2021/03/31/google-speeds-partial-office-reopening-and-puts-limits-on-remote-work.html.

6. Haley Messenger, "Google Delays Return to Office, Announces Plan to Test 'Flexible Work Week,'" NBC News, December 14, 2020, https://www.nbcnews.com/business/business-news/google-delays-return-office-announces-plan-test-flexible-work-week-n1251194.

7. Laura M. Giurge and Vanessa K. Bohns, "3 Tips to Avoid WFH Burnout," hbr.org, April 3, 2020, https://hbr.org/2020/04/3-tips-to-avoid-wfh-burnout.

8. Andrew J. Oswald et al., "Happiness and Productivity," *Journal of Labor Economics* 33, no. 4 (2015): 789–822.

9. David Wyld, "Do Happier Employees Really Stay Longer?" *Academy of Management Perspectives* 28, no. 1 (2014): 1–3; Claudia M. Haase, Michael J. Poulin, and Jutta Heckhausen, "Happiness as a Motivator: Positive Affect Predicts Primary Control Striving for Career and Educational Goals," *Personality and Social Psychology Bulletin* 38, no. 8 (May 8, 2012): 1093–1104.

10. Shung J. Shin et al., "Cognitive Team Diversity and Individual Team Member Creativity: A Cross-Level Interaction," *Academy of Management Journal* 55, no. 1 (2013), https://journals.aom.org/doi/abs/10.5465/amj.2010.0270; Julian Barling et al., "Effects of Transformational Leadership Training on Attitudinal and Financial Outcomes: A Field Experiment," *Journal of Applied Psychology* 81, no. 6 (1996): 827–832; Hui Wang et al., "Leader-Member Exchange as a Mediator of the Relationship between Transformational Leadership and Followers' Performance and Organizational Citizenship Behavior," *Academy of Management Journal* 48, no. 3 (2005), https://journals.aom.org/doi/abs/10.5465/amj.2005.17407908.

11. Julia K. Boehm and Sonja Lyubomirsky, "Does Happiness Promote Career Success?," *Journal of Career Assessment* 26, no. 2 (2018), http://sonjalyubomirsky.com/wp-content/themes/sonjalyubomirsky/papers/BLinpressb.pdf.

12. Namely, "HR Mythbusters: The Reality of Work at Mid-Market Companies Worldwide," 2017, https://cdn2.hubspot.net/hubfs/228948/Namely%20HR%20Mythbusters%20Report.pdf.

13. Sabine Sonnentag, "Psychological Detachment from Work during Leisure Time: The Benefits of Mentally Disengaging from Work," *Current Directions in Psychological Science* 21, no. 2 (March 2012): 114–118.

14. William J. Zukel et al., "The Multiple Risk Factor Intervention Trial (MRFIT): I. Historical Perspectives," *Preventive Medicine* 10, no. 4 (1981): 387–401.

15. Justin McCarthy, "Taking Regular Vacations May Help Boost Americans' Well-Being," *Gallup Wellbeing*, December 30, 2014, https://news.gallup.com /poll/180335/taking-regular-vacations-may-help-boost-americans.aspx.

16. John La Place, "The EY Better You Survey Uncovers Benefits Preferences of Employed Adults and College Students," press release, EY, February 25, 2020, https://www.ey.com/en_us/news/2020/02/ey-better-you-survey-uncovers -benefits-preferences-of-employed-adults-and-students.

17. Gerhard Strauss-Blasche et al., "Does Vacation Enable Recuperation? Changes in Well-Being Associated with Time Away from Work," *Occupational Medicine* 50, no. 3 (2000): 167–172.

18. Vatsal Chikani et al., "Vacations Improve Mental Health among Rural Women: The Wisconsin Rural Women's Health Study," *Wisconsin Medical Journal* 104, no. 6 (2005): 20–23.

19. Laura M. Giurge and Kaitlin Woolley, "Don't Work on Vacation. Seriously," hbr.org, July 22, 2020, https://hbr.org/2020/07/dont-work-on-vacation -seriously.

20. John Pencavel, "The Productivity of Working Hours," working paper, Stanford University, Palo Alto, CA, April 2014, http://ftp.iza.org/dp8129.pdf.

21. Ibid.

22. Global Wellness Institute, *2018 Global Wellness Economy Monitor*, https:// globalwellnessinstitute.org/industry-research/2018-global-wellness-economy -monitor/.

23. Statista, "Health and Fitness App Downloads Worldwide from 1st Quarter 2019 to 2nd Quarter 2020," n.d., https://www.statista.com/statistics /1127248/health-fitness-apps-downloads-worldwide/.

24. "Wearable Fitness Trackers Market to Reach $48.2 Billion," GlobeNewswire, March 28, 2018, https://www.globenewswire.com/news-release /2018/03/28/1454453/0/en/Wearable-Fitness-Trackers-Market-to-Reach-48-2 -Billion-by-2023-P-S-Market-Research.html.

25. "How Fitness Trackers Can Improve Your Health," *Harvard Women's Health Watch*, December 2015, https://www.health.harvard.edu/staying -healthy/how-fitness-trackers-can-improve-your-health.

26. Robert A. Sloane et al., "Effectiveness of Activity Trackers with and without Incentives to Increase Physical Activity (TRIPPA): A Randomised Controlled Trial," *Lancet Diabetes and Endocrinology* 4, no. 12 (December 1, 2016): 983–995.

27. Rui Wang, "Mental Health Sensing Using Mobile Phones," PhD thesis, Dartmouth College, Hanover, NH, September 28, 2018, https://www.cs.dart mouth.edu/~campbell/dr_rui_wang_thesis-2018.pdf.

28. Daniel B. Kline, "Be Merry (But Not That Merry): A Guide to Office Holiday Parties," Yahoo, November 4, 2018, https://www.yahoo.com/news /merry-not-merry-guide-office-114600017.html.

29. Randstad USA, "What Do American Employees Really Want for the Holidays? Hint: Not a Cookie Swap," press release, November 16, 2017, https://rlc.randstadusa.com/press-room/press-releases/what-do-american -employees-really-want-for-the-holidays-hint-not-a-cookie-swap.

30. Jennifer Moss, "Holidays Can Be Stressful. They Don't Have to Stress Out Your Team," hbr.org, December 18, 2018, https://hbr.org/2018/12/holidays -can-be-stressful-they-dont-have-to-stress-out-your-team.

31. Zoya Gervis, "A Lot of People Have Office Holiday Party Regrets," *New York Post*, November 28, 2018, https://nypost.com/2018/11/28/a-lot -of-people-have-office-holiday-party-regrets/.

32. Greenberg Quinlan Rosner, "Holiday Stress," press release, December 12, 2006, https://www.apa.org/news/press/releases/2006/12/holiday-stress.pdf.

33. P. J. Feinstein, "An Office Holiday Party Survival Guide for Introverts and Shy People," Muse, n.d., https://www.themuse.com/advice/office-holiday -party-survival-guide-introvert-shy.

34. Moss, "Holidays Can Be Stressful."

35. Rebecca Mead, "Cold Comfort: Tech Jobs and Egg Freezing," *New Yorker*, October 17, 2014, https://www.newyorker.com/news/daily-comment/facebook -apple-egg-freezing-benefits.

36. Ethics Committee of the American Society for Reproductive Medicine, "Planned Oocyte Cryopreservation for Women Seeking to Preserve Future Reproductive Potential: An Ethics Committee Opinion," *Fertility and Sterility* 110, no. 6 (2018), https://www.asrm.org/globalassets/asrm/asrm -content/news-and-publications/ethics-committee-opinions/planned_oocyte _cryopreservation_for_women_seeking_to_preserve-pdfmembers.pdf.

Chapter 4

1. Morris S. Viteles, *Motivation and Morale in Industry* (New York: Norton, 1953).

2. Linda V. Heinemann and Torsten Heinemann, "Burnout Research: Emergence and Scientific Investigation of a Contested Diagnosis," *SAGE Open*, January–March 2017, 1–12.

3. Michael P. Leiter and Christina Maslach, "Areas of Worklife: A Structured Approach to Organizational Predictors of Job Burnout," *Emotional*

and Physiological Processes and Positive Intervention Strategies, vol. 3, eds. Pamela L. Perrewe and Daniel C. Ganster (Bingeley, UK: Emerald Insight, 2003), 91–134; Jennifer Moss, "Rethinking Burnout," (survey), https://wlu.ca1.qualtrics.com/jfe/preview/SV_3n4KhcTKet5fsMJ?Q_SurveyVersionID=current&Q_CHL=preview.

4. "A Message from the Maslach Burnout Inventory Authors," Mind Garden, March 19, 2019, https://www.mindgarden.com/blog/post/44-a-message-from-the-maslach-burnout-inventory-authors.

5. Ben Stiller (dir.), *Reality Bites*, Universal Pictures, 1994.

6. Wilmar B. Schaufeli et al., "The Measurement of Engagement and Burnout: A Two Sample Confirmatory Factor Analytic Approach," *Journal of Happiness Studies* 3 (2002): 71–92.

7. Toon W. Taris, Jan Fekke Ybema, and Ilona van Beek, "Burnout or Engagement: Identical Twins or Just Close Relatives?" *Burnout Research* 5 (June 2017): 3–11.

8. Leslie A. Baxter and Barbara M. Montgomery, *Relating: Dialogues and Dialectics* (New York: Guilford Press, 1996).

9. William A. Kahn, "Psychological Conditions of Personal Engagement and Disengagement at Work," *Academy of Management Journal* 33, no. 4 (2017), https://journals.aom.org/doi/abs/10.5465/256287.

10. Ibid.

11. Shawn Achor and Michelle Gielan, "What Leading with Optimism Really Looks Like," hbr.org, June 4, 2020, https://hbr.org/2020/06/what-leading-with-optimism-really-looks-like.

12. Ibid.

Chapter 5

1. Francesca Gino, "The Business Case for Curiosity," *Harvard Business Review* (September–October 2018): 48–57.

2. Ibid.

3. Mario Livio, "Why Do We Ask Why?" *Psychology Today*, June 23, 2017, https://www.psychologytoday.com/ca/blog/why/201706/why-do-we-ask-why.

4. Ibid.

5. Ibid.

6. Celeste Kidd and Benjamin Y. Hayden, "The Psychology and Neuroscience of Curiosity," *Neuron* 88, no. 3 (November 4, 2015): 449–460.

7. Stefano I. Di Domenica and Richard M. Ryan, "The Emerging Neuroscience of Intrinsic Motivation: A New Frontier in Self-Determination Research," *Frontiers in Human Neuroscience* 11 (March 24, 2017), https://www.ncbi.nlm.nih.gov/pmc/articles/PMC5364176/.

8. Thomas G. Reio Jr. and Albert Wiswell, "Field Investigation of the Relationship among Adult Curiosity, Workplace Learning, and Job Performance," *Human Resource Development Quarterly* 11, no. 1 (2001): 5–30.

9. Roman Krznaric, "Six Habits of Highly Empathic People," *Greater Good Magazine*, November 27, 2012, https://greatergood.berkeley.edu/article/item /six_habits_of_highly_empathic_people1.

10. Jodi Halpern, "Empathy and Patient-Physician Conflicts," *Journal of General Internal Medicine* 22, no. 5 (2007): 696–700.

11. Todd B. Kashdan et al., "Curiosity and Exploration: Facilitating Positive Subjective Experiences and Personal Growth Opportunities," *Journal of Personality Assessment* 82, no. 3 (2004): 291–305.

12. Yancy Berns, "Best Company Culture 2019," Comparably, December 10, 2019, https://www.comparably.com/news/best-company-culture-2019/.

13. Heather Bussing, "ADP Women in STEM Profile: Martha Bird," ADP Spark, n.d., https://www.adp.com/spark/articles/2018/11/adp-women-in-stem -profile-martha-bird.aspx.

14. Charles Duhigg, "What Google Learned from Its Quest to Build the Perfect Team," *New York Times*, February 25, 2016, https://www.nytimes .com/2016/02/28/magazine/what-google-learned-from-its-quest-to-build-the -perfect-team.html.

15. Ibid.

16. "What Is Scrum?" Scrum.org, n.d., https://www.scrum.org/resources /what-is-scrum.

17. Hirotaka Takeuchi and Ikujiro Nonaka, "The New New Product Development Game," *Harvard Business Review* (January 1986): 137–146.

18. Scrum Guides, https://scrumguides.org/.

19. "Small Teams," Published Patterns, n.d., https://sites.google.com/a /scrumplop.org/published-patterns/product-organization pattern-language /development-team/small-teams.

20. Jill Clark and Trish Baker, "'It's Not Fair!' Cultural Attitudes to Social Loafing in Ethnically Diverse Groups," *Intercultural Communication Studies* 20 (2011): 124–140.

21. Beng-Chong Lim and Katherine J. Klein, "Team Mental Models and Team Performance: A Field Study of the Effects of Team Mental Model Similarity and Accuracy," *Journal of Organizational Behavior* 27, no. 4 (2006): 403–418.

22. Positive Psychology Center, "Perma Theory of Well-Being and Perma Workshops," University of Pennsylvania, 2021, https://ppc.sas.upenn .edu/learn-more/perma-theory-well-being-and-perma-workshops.

23. "One-Third of Your Life Is Spent at Work," Gettysburg College, n.d., https://www.gettysburg.edu/news/stories?id=79db7b34-630c-4f49-ad32 -4ab9ea48e72b&pageTitle=1%2F3+of+your+life+is+spent+at+work.

24. Karyn Twaronite, "The Surprising Power of Simply Asking Coworkers How They're Doing," hbr.org, February 28, 2019, https://hbr.org/2019/02/the -surprising-power-of-simply-asking-coworkers-how-theyre-doing.

25. Ibid.

26. Catherine A. Sanderson, *Social Psychology* (Hoboken, NJ: Wiley, 2009), 344.

27. Gino, "The Business Case for Curiosity."

28. Annamarie Mann, "Why We Need Best Friends at Work," Gallup, January 15, 2018, https://www.gallup.com/workplace/236213/why-need-best -friends-work.aspx.

29. Ruma Betheja, "Here's How You Can Hire Curious Talent," People Matters, October 3, 2019, https://www.peoplemattersglobal.com/article/talent -acquisition/heres-how-you-can-hire-curious-talent-23321.

30. Alison Horstmeyer, "Using Curiosity to Enhance Meaningfulness of Work," *Graziadio Business Review* 22, no. 2 (August 8, 2019), https://gbr.pepper dine.edu/2019/08/using-curiosity-to-enhance-meaningfulness-of-work/.

Chapter 6

1. Center for Army Leadership, *The U.S. Army Leadership Field Manual: Battle-Tested Wisdom for Leaders in Any Organization* (New York: McGraw-Hill, 2004).

2. Maureen Dowd, "Lady of the Rings: Jacinda Rules," *New York Times*, September 8, 2018, https://www.nytimes.com/2018/09/08/opinion/sunday/jacinda -ardern-new-zealand-prime-minister.html.

3. Jennifer Moss, "Making Your Workplace Safe for Grief," hbr.org, June 6, 2017, https://hbr.org/2017/06/making-your-workplace-safe-for-grief.

4. Ms. Yasmine Motarjemi *v.* Société des Produits Nestlé SA (formerly Nestec SA), https://assets.gov.ie/88067/21cee589-2411-4197-a280-7a9b6ef7f5dd.pdf.

5. Benjamin J. McMichael, "The Failure of 'Sorry': An Empirical Evaluation of Apology Laws, Health Care, and Medical Malpractice," *Lewis and Clark Law Review* 22, no. 4 (March 1, 2019): 1199–1281.

6. Nicole Saitta and Samuel D. Hodge Jr., "Efficacy of a Physician's Words of Empathy: An Overview of State Apology Laws," *Journal of the American Osteo-pathic Association* 112 (2012): 302–306.

7. Ibid.

8. Anne Pietrangelo, "The Effects of Stress on Your Body," Healthline, March 29, 2020, https://www.healthline.com/health/stress/effects-on-body#4.

9. Amy Edmondson, "Psychological Safety, Trust, and Learning in Organizations: A Group-Level Lens," ResearchGate, October 2011, https://www .researchgate.net/publication/268328210_Psychological_Safety_Trust_and _Learning_in_Organizations_A_Group-level_Lens.

10. Amy Edmondson, "Creating Psychological Safety in the Workplace," HBR Podcast, January 22, 2019, https://hbr.org/podcast/2019/01/creating -psychological-safety-in-the-workplace.

11. Albert Bandura, "Toward a Psychology of Human Agency," *Perspectives on Psychological Science* 1, no. 2 (2006): 164–180.

12. Ibid.

13. Todd B. Kashdan and Jonathan Rottenberg, "Psychological Flexibility as a Fundamental Aspect of Health," *Clinical Psychology Review* 30, no. 7 (2010): 865–878.

14. Danielle Jessica Lamb, "Examining Psychological Flexibility at the Individual, Team, and Leadership Levels in Crisis Resolution Teams," PhD thesis, University College London, 2018, https://discovery.ucl.ac.uk/id /eprint/10043365/1/DL%20PhD%20thesis%20-%20final%20version.pdf.

15. Brian Thompson, "Experiential Avoidance and Its Relevance to PDST," Portland Psychotherapy, n.d., https://portlandpsychotherapytraining .com/2012/09/22/experiential-avoidance-and-its-relevance-to-ptsd/.

16. Walter Swap et al., "Using Mentoring and Storytelling to Transfer Knowledge in the Workplace," *Journal of Management Information Systems* 18, no. 1 (2001): 95–114.

17. Karl E. Weick and Larry D. Browning, "Argument and Narration in Or- ganizational Communication," *Journal of Management* 12, no. 2 (1986): 243–259.

18. Tommi Auvinen, Iiris Aaltio, and Kirsimarja Blomqvist, "Constructing Leadership by Storytelling—the Meaning of Trust and Narratives," *Leadership and Organization Development Journal* 34, no. 6 (August 23, 2013): 496–514.

Chapter 7

1. Jan-Emmanuel De Neve and George Ward, "Happiness at Work," *World Happiness Report*, 2017, https://s3.amazonaws.com/happiness-report/2017/HR17 -Ch6_wAppendix.pdf.

2. Jan-Emmanuel De Neve, "Equation for Happiness," Global HR Forum, 2019, https://www.youtube.com/watch?v=bZKLvIBJtFc&.

3. Anthony Heyes and Soodeh Saberian, "Temperature and Decisions: Evidence from 207,000 Court Cases," *American Economic Journal: Applied Economics* 11, no. 2 (2019): 238–265.

4. David Hirshleifer and Tyler Shumway, "Good Day Sunshine: Stock Returns and the Weather," *Journal of Finance* 58, no. 3 (2003): 1009–1032; Alex Edmans et al., "Sports Sentiment and Stock Returns," *Journal of Finance* 62, no. 4 (2007): 1967–1998.

5. Charles R. Snyder, " Hope Theory: Rainbows in the Mind," *Psychological Inquiry* 13, no. 4 (2002): 249–275.

6. William H. McRaven, "Commencement Address," University of Texas at Austin, May 19, 2014, https://www.youtube.com/watch?v=pxBQLFLei70.

7. Albert Bandura, "Regulation of Cognitive Processes through Perceived Self-Efficacy," *Developmental Psychology* 25, no. 5 (1989): 729–735.

8. Robert A. Emmons, Michael E. McCollough, and Jo-Ann Tsang, "The Assessment of Gratitude," in S. J. Lopez and C. R. Snyder (eds.), *Positive Psychological Assessment: A Handbook of Models and Measures* (Washington, DC: American Psychological Association, 2003), 327–341.

9. Jui-Ti Nien et al., "Mindfulness Training Enhances Endurance Performance and Executive Functions in Athletes: An Event-Related Potential Study," *Neural Plasticity* (August 28, 2020), https://www.ncbi.nlm.nih.gov/pmc/articles /PMC7474752/.

10. Beatriz Olaya, "Association between Traumatic Events and Post-Traumatic Disorder: Results from the ESEMeD-Spain Study," *Epidemiology and Psychiatric Sciences* 24, no. 2 (April 2015): 172–183.

11. Richard G. Tedeschi and Lawrence G. Calhoun, "Posttraumatic Growth: Conceptual Foundations and Empirical Evidence," *Psychological Inquiry* 15, no. 1 (2004): 1–18.

12. Lucy Hone, "3 Secrets of Resilient People," TEDxChristchurch, August 2019, https://www.ted.com/talks/lucy_hone_3_secrets_of _resilient_people?language=en.

13. Ami Rokach, "Leadership and Loneliness," *International Journal of Leadership and Change* 2, no. 1 (2014): 48–58.

Index

Acknowledgments

Writing a book about burnout during a global pandemic was not easy. It required extraordinary support from the people closest to me and plenty of cheerleading from my personal and professional circle. Most of all, it asked my family to be the calm in the chaos of an upended world. Particularly, my husband Jim. Thank you, Jim, for being my Sweden. Your counsel was unbiased, insightful, persuasive, and kind. You were enthusiastically generous with your time. I didn't feel alone—ever—in this process. You have my gratitude.

Thank you to my children, Wyatt, Olivia, and Lyla, for your respect and patience. I was especially grateful for the moments when you would come into my bedroom/office to kiss me on the forehead and leave just as quietly as you came in. These small gestures were the most meaningful. You are the parts that make me whole.

Since I can remember, my dad would say I was going to change the world. That consistent narrative playing in the background had an incredibly positive impact on me. All dads should tell their daughters they have superpowers. But the way my parents lived their day-to-day lives impacted me perhaps even more. My mom was the first nurse practitioner in our country—a trailblazer and caregiver. My dad's first job at the bank was rolling pennies. He retired as an assistant vice president of that same bank. This instilled in me the work ethic and drive that helped me write a book in lockdown. Thank you, Sally and Doug, for walking the talk. I love you.

I want to thank my siblings, Janice and Allen, my sisters by luck, Patti and Melissa, and Jim's parents (my other mom and dad), Connie and Ron, for being my constant champions. Janice, thank you for loving me without question. Coming over to take the kids, anticipating my needs—you helped get me and this book over the finish line. Allen and Melissa, thank you for being there as a family to listen to my worries and fears and for adding laughter to my life. Our weekly games helped me to escape. Patti, thank you for pushing me intellectually and reminding me why this book matters to the world. There is more to life than metrics. Connie and Ron, I am truly fortunate to have you in my life. Connie (aka Gigi), thank you for showing such pride and appreciation for my work—you encouraged me to stay the course.

I need to thank my friends, especially my soulmate, Lydia Vargo. The psychological safety you bring to my life, the effortless state of belonging I feel when I'm with you, is beyond measure. When I suggest that we all need friends who would bail us out of jail—that's you, Lydia. Thank you, Jen Schneider, Sandra Leelook, Sarah Simpson, and Lindsay Lane, for being my people. The phone calls, the virtual visits, the drive-bys, the car coffees, the tiny windows of social distancing under masks, and the earliest days of freedom as the vaccines arrived. The belly laughs, the tears—you were there through it all, and wow, did I need it! You helped me avoid being the burnout expert who burned out while writing a book about burnout. Thank you.

Katie Lewis, thank you. You have no idea how much you've helped me, both professionally and personally, during the writing of this book. From handling every single logistical aspect of my business to making sure I was still practicing self-care, your support was invaluable. It was a year of survival and you were always there, towing a lifeboat.

Of course, I want to thank my powerhouse team of editors at Harvard Business Review Press. First, Kevin Evers. Thank you for advocating for this book and seeing its early potential. I appreciate how you let me tell the story in the way I needed while giving me that freedom you also teased out the best parts of my work. Thank you for keeping this book on the right trajectory (which wasn't always easy). You are seriously good at what you do. Anne Starr and Jane Gebhart, thank you for perfecting my unpolished prose by making it clean, tidy, organized, and so much more readable! Anne, your guidance through this process was incredibly helpful.

I'd also like to thank the whole HBR team for bringing the book to life. Dana Rousmaniere, you are the reason this book exists. We're here because of your advocacy and passionate interest in the topic. Thank you—I love working with you. Gretchen Gavett, thank you for believing in me and trusting me with "The Big Idea." It was a passion project that has positively impacted my life. Kelsey Gripenstraw, thank you for putting me in touch with business leaders across the HBR globe. I continue to get feedback about how that kick-started conversations about preventing burnout in their workplaces.

Thank you to Barbara Henricks, Jessica Krakoski, and Emily Lavelle, my incredible PR team at Cave Henricks. All of you believed in the change-making power of this book and worked tirelessly on its behalf. Thank you to the marketing and communications team at HBR Press: Julie Devoll, Lindsey Dietrich, Alicyn Zall, Alexandra Kephart, Felicia Sinusas, Erika Heilman, Jon Shipley, Sally Ashworth, Ella Morrish, and Brian Galvin. I am so grateful for your efforts to get *The Burnout Epidemic* into the hands of readers across the world.

Thank you to the scientists, researchers, and experts who have come before me and continue to campaign for more awareness on the topic of burnout. Christina Maslach, Michael Leiter, and Susan Jackson, thank you for authoring the academic scales that have remained the gold standard for measuring burnout for decades. Christina and Michael, thank you for partnering with me, along with David Whiteside, during the pandemic. Our data showed how a crisis can exacerbate an existing problem like burnout to epidemic levels. Sharing that with the world has kick-started change, and for that I am extremely grateful. This group, along with other scientists, from Freudenberger to Herzberg to Schaufeli, have known for years the catastrophic impact that burnout causes. Their effort to find a solution to this rapidly evolving problem is unmatched. I will do my best to honor their work through passionate advocacy and continued research in the field.

And, last but not least, thanks to all of you reading this book and striving for real change. The daily outreach from global companies and their leaders, asking for my help, is a reminder that there's a strong appetite out there for building a well and flourishing workforce—a future of work where burnout lives in the past.

About the Author

JENNIFER MOSS is an award-winning journalist, author, and international public speaker. She is a nationally syndicated radio columnist and regularly contributes to *Harvard Business Review*. She is considered a global workplace expert and speaks frequently to the media, including the BBC, CBS, CNN, NBC, *Forbes, Fortune, Time* magazine, and the *Wall Street Journal,* among others. Moss is a burnout strategist for large global enterprises and workforce research think tanks.

The Burnout Epidemic is Moss's second leadership book focused on workplace culture and wellness. Her last book, *Unlocking Happiness at Work,* was named a business book of the year in the UK. She has been acknowledged as a Canadian Innovator of the Year and International Female Entrepreneur of the Year, and she is the recipient of a Public Service Award from the Office of President Obama. Her best-loved role to date is that of mom to her three kids and wife to her husband of twenty years.